By Motor to the Golden Gate

By Motor to the Golden Gate

Emily Post

Annotated and with an
introduction by Jane Lancaster

McFarland & Company, Inc., Publishers
Jefferson, North Carolina, and London

Frontispiece: Emily Post and her son Ned traveling along the California coastline, sometime around May 31, 1915. The original caption to this illustration, which appeared in the first edition of *By Motor to the Golden Gate,* read, "The Pacific at last!"

LIBRARY OF CONGRESS CATALOGUING-IN-PUBLICATION DATA

Post, Emily (1873–1960).
    By motor to the Golden Gate / Emily Post ;
annotated and with an introduction by Jane Lancaster.
    Originally published: New York : D. Appleton, 1916.
        p.   cm.
    Includes bibliographical references and index.

    ISBN 0-7864-1940-7 (softcover : 50# alkaline paper) ∞

    1. United States—Description and travel.   2. Automobile travel—United States.   3. Post, Emily, 1873–1960—Travel—United States.   I. Lancaster, Jane.   II. Title.
E169.P85   2004
917.304'913—dc22   2004008623

British Library cataloguing data are available

Cover photographs: *foreground:* "A straight, wide road and a speed limit of twenty miles an hour"; *background:* "Paso Robles to Monterey," Monday, June 7, 1915. Both from original 1916 edition.

Manufactured in the United States of America

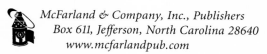
McFarland & Company, Inc., Publishers
Box 611, Jefferson, North Carolina 28640
www.mcfarlandpub.com

To
my younger son,
Bruce
— E.P.

Acknowledgments

I must thank Peter Post, of the Emily Post Institute, for his support. Melissa Bingmann of the University of Indiana read an early draft and gave me many useful suggestions about western history. Laura Prieto and Rich Canedo read a draft of the introduction and provided numerous insightful ideas.

In addition, I wish to thank Karen D. Osburn of the Geneva (NY) Historical Society; Tom Wolf of the Ohio Historical Society; Jamie Kelley of the Wheaton (IL) History Center; Betty A. Barnes of the Flagg Township (IL) Historical Society; Kevin Knoot of the State Historical Society of Iowa; the reference staff at the Cedar Rapids Public Library; the Brainard family; Joan Arnett at the Iowa State House; Carl Hallberg at the Wyoming State Archives; Allan Affeldt, owner of La Posada Hotel, Winslow, Arizona; and John Notz, Jr., of Chicago.—J.L.

Contents

Acknowledgments   vii
Introduction by Jane Lancaster   1
Preface   11

I. It Can't Be Done — But Then, It Is Perfectly Simple   13
II. Albany, First Stop   25
III. A Breakdown   30
IV. Pennsylvania, Ohio and Indiana   36
V. Luggage and Other Luxuries   55
VI. Did Anybody Say "Chicken"?   58
VII. The City of Ambition   61
VIII. A Few Chicagoans   66
IX. Tins   71
X. Mud!!   77
XI. In Rochelle   82
XII. The Weight of Public Opinion   85
XIII. Muddier!   89
XIV. One of the Fogged Impressions   94
XV. A Few Ways of the West   97
XVI. Halfway House   104
XVII. Next Stop, North Platte!   112
XVIII. The City of Recklessness   127

XIX. A Glimpse of the West That Was   141

XX. Our Little Sister of Yesterday   157

XXI. Ignorance with a Capital I   161

XXII. Some Indians and Mr. X.   164

XXIII. With Nowhere to Go but Out   175

XXIV. Into the Desert   178

XXV. Through the City Unpronounceable to
        an Exposition Beautiful   191

XXVI. The Land of Gladness   204

XXVII. The Mettle of a Hero   210

XXVIII. San Francisco   218

XXIX. The Fair   232

XXX. "Unending Sameness" Was What They Said   239

XXXI. To Those Who Think of Following
         in Our Tire Tracks   242

XXXII. On the Subject of Clothes   248

XXXIII. How Far Can You Go in Comfort?   254

Appendix: Emily Post's Journey, April 25–June 8, 1915   257

Index by Jane Lancaster   259

Introduction
by Jane Lancaster

EMILY POST'S GREAT ADVENTURE

It was a warm spring day in late April 1915. Shortly after lunch, a long, low, custom-built automobile, stuffed to the gills with luggage, left a hotel in Gramercy Park, New York, and drove slowly up Fifth Avenue. The driver was a tall, dark-haired young man in a tweed suit; he was smoking a pipe. His passengers, two women in their early forties, were both wearing large and fashionable hats. One of the women, looking decidedly uncomfortable, was wedged in the back seat between a pile of fur coats and a solid silver picnic set. When the car stopped at Forty-second Street to allow the cross-town trolley to pass, some friends in another waiting car called out: "Emily! Ned! Where are you off to?" Waving a big bunch of violets, the woman in the front seat replied, "To San Francisco!"

She later wrote, "But not one of them believed us."

The reason her friends found this incredible lies partly in the difficulty of cross-continental motor travel in 1915 and partly in the identity of the travelers. The tall, elegant woman in the front seat was Emily Post, whose name would soon become synonymous with correct behavior. The driver was her twenty-two-year-old son Edwin, a junior at Harvard, and the woman in the back seat was her cousin Alice Beadleston.

They were off on "Emily Post's Great Adventure."

WHO WAS EMILY POST?

Before she wrote *Etiquette*, the book that made her famous, Emily Post was in turn a sparkling debutante, a wronged wife, a divorcee, and a

1

single mother trying to make a living. And on that Sunday in 1915 she was a journalist, investigating for *Collier's Weekly*, the foremost news magazine of the day, whether it was possible to drive across the continent in comfort.

Emily Price was born in Baltimore in 1872, the only child of Bruce Price, a well-known architect who designed Tuxedo Park, one of America's first gated communities. Her mother, Josephine Lee Price, an astute stock market investor, was daughter of a wealthy Pennsylvania mine owner. Young Emily was educated by governesses and at an exclusive New York girls' school. Had she been born a century later, she might have become an architect like her father, but marriage was the only respectable career for upper class women in America's Gilded Age.

She "came out" as a debutante in 1892; her beauty and charm were the talk of the Season. Shortly afterwards she married businessman Edwin M. Post, and after a lengthy European honeymoon she bore him two sons, Edwin Jr. (1893) and Bruce Price (1895). The couple gradually grew apart, Emily preferring to stay in the country at Tuxedo Park, her husband pursuing his affairs— both business and extramarital — in the city. Like many other "sporting gentlemen," Edwin Post was a target of the blackmailing Colonel William D. Mann, editor of the scandal sheet *Town Topics*. Post refused to pay, and he was one of the witnesses against Mann in a scandalous libel suit in 1905.

Although she supported her husband's decision to testify, the public disgrace was too much for Emily Post, so after packing her boys off to boarding school, she filed for divorce. Because Edwin Post had recently lost money in bad investments Emily received no alimony and had to earn a living. Over the next fifteen years she tried her hand at interior decoration and published six Edith Wharton-style society novels and numerous essays and short stories. *By Motor to the Golden Gate* was her only travel book.

In 1921 an editor asked her to write a book on etiquette. Published the following year as *Etiquette in Society, in Business, and at Home,* it made Emily Post a household name. Her timing was perfect, as the children of the millions of immigrants who had arrived in the United States since the 1880s wanted to know which fork to use, as did upwardly aspiring native-born Americans, and Emily was prepared to tell them. Her advice was so sought after that she soon had a column to answer readers' questions in *McCall's* magazine, and later her advice was syndicated to more than 150 newspapers. In 1946 she set up the Emily Post Institute, which organized her business affairs. *Etiquette* was frequently updated. Ten new editions came out in Emily Post's lifetime, incorporating her reactions to changing times. Her family continues the business of etiquette; the sixteenth edition of *Etiquette* was published in 1997, and the Emily Post Institute sponsors business etiquette seminars and deals with areas of polite behavior undreamt of in 1922.

Why 1915?

Cross-continental motoring was all the rage in 1915. While only twenty automobiles had completed the journey up to 1913, a combination of factors meant that 1915 was a bumper year for travelers. Europe was at war and effectively closed to American tourists, and the scheme to "See America First" was in full swing. California was an exciting destination as both San Francisco and San Diego were hosting major expositions. The Lincoln Highway, a grandiose plan to build a road across America, was "open for business" if not actually built. Newspaper proprietor William Randolph Hearst, no slouch when it came to publicity, was offering a gold medal to the writer of the "Best Story About the Trip" along the Lincoln Highway to San Francisco, and silver medals designed by Louis C. Tiffany for all those who "won their spurs" by reaching the Panama-Pacific International Exposition by automobile. Seventy-nine silver medals were awarded in 1915, five of them to women. The roads were almost crowded!

Meanwhile, American business was entranced by the possibilities of the automobile. Magazines and periodicals advertised cars, tires, batteries, and enterprising editors commissioned articles on heroic journeys which were devoured by a fascinated public. The infrastructure of hotels, gas stations and restaurants was in place across most of the country, and maps and touring guides were available. *Motor Magazine*, one of Hearst's publications, even offered a free pamphlet on the best routes to the west, together with lists of equipment no serious motorist should be without.

Why Collier's Weekly?

Collier's (like many contemporary periodicals) was heavily dependent on automobile advertising, and in January 1915 it published a double issue touting automobile travel. Emily Post wanted to go to the Exposition in San Francisco, but she didn't want to take the train: she wanted an adventure. She knew some of the senior people at *Collier's*, which had published some of her short fiction, and a story on an upper-class woman traveling across country in an automobile was a natural fit for the magazine. She knew *Collier's* ambitious business manager, Condé Nast, and its editor, Mark Sullivan, who commissioned a series of articles from her. The Emily Post series would complement an earlier *Collier's* commission, whereby author Julian Street traveled across America by train. Street's purpose was to see the country at work: he wrote about the grain elevators in Buffalo, the coal docks in Cleveland, and the stock yards in Chicago. He also visited the Ford plant at Highland Park and talked to prostitutes in Cripple Creek.

Emily Post wrote three long articles for *Collier's*; they appeared in the magazine on September 4, 11, and 18, 1915, under the title "By Motor to the Fair." She then reworked them, adding more detail and some amusing dialogue, and the resulting manuscript was published by D. Appleton and Company as *By Motor to the Golden Gate* in 1916.

Emily Post and Motoring in Comfort

Emily Post wanted to see how far she could go in comfort, staying in good hotels, eating in good restaurants, traveling on smooth roads. When her friends told her alarming stories about road conditions in the west she called her editor, but Sullivan cheerfully told her to return to New York as soon as she became uncomfortable. She was sorely tempted to turn back after days of mud and rain in Illinois and when she faced spending a night in the desert sleeping in the car, but she stuck it out, despite the fact the car gave up the ghost in Arizona and had to be rail-freighted to Los Angeles.

Women and Automobiles

Emily Post was a passenger rather than a driver, and was far from the first woman to cross America by automobile. Starting with Louise Hitchcock Davis in 1899 (who traveled with her husband; they were forced to abandon the attempt in Chicago) several women had already made well-publicized cross-country journeys, including Alice Ramsey in 1909, and Blanche Scott in 1910. Automobile companies anxious to prove the reliability of their vehicles sponsored both of these women. The message was both consumerist and gendered. Women in the first decade of the twentieth century were far from equal and had still to win the vote, but the success of Ramsey and Scott signaled to women what daring females could achieve if they owned an automobile, and to men that the car must be easy to drive.

What Kind of Car Was It?

Unlike some of her predecessors, Emily Post was not advertising any particular make of vehicle; indeed, the car she rode in was most unsuited to the task at hand. It had an American engine (of unspecified make), an immensely long wheelbase (one hundred and forty-four inches, to be exact) and a custom-built English chassis with only eight inches' road clearance. It had very narrow tires and experienced great difficulty on muddy roads in the Midwest and on hairpin bends in the mountains.

Post's son Ned did the actual driving. She had informed his professors that he would learn more driving her to California than by completing his junior year at Harvard. And in any case, it would be good for his health. The third traveler was Post's cousin Alice Beadleston, who had begged to come with them; as a last minute addition to the party, she was wedged in the back of the car with the luggage.

What Did They Take with Them?

Emily Post's New York friends deluged her with advice on what to take; their suggestions ranged from a block and tackle to African water bags. Other friends sent gifts, and while a box of hand made chocolates was very welcome, the solid silver picnic set, whose weight made the butler stagger as he brought it into the house, turned out to be just one item too much. The same went for clothes, most of which Emily Post found totally unsuitable — too cold, too hot, or too creased. She must have looked rather strange as she sat in state wrapped in a brown duster coat and wearing an orange veil to avoid sunburn and keep the dust out of her eyes and mouth.

They soon jettisoned much of their original equipment; in Chicago they freighted the silver picnic set back to New York and replaced it with an enamel bread bin, which they proceeded to fill with paper plates, tin spoons and paté de foie gras.

Emily Post the Tourist

Emily Post detailed each day of the journey, describing what she saw, what misadventures befell and what kindnesses were experienced. She was very impressed by Statler hotels where lunch was "very good and beautifully served" and cost a dollar a head. She enjoyed frugality and celebrated an evening in Davenport, Iowa, where she and her traveling companions walked along the riverbank "and spent *nothing.*"

They were good tourists. In Des Moines they hired a jitney driver to take them sightseeing, and at the Grand Canyon Edwin Post hired a mule for $4, while his mother watched moving pictures of a trip down the Colorado River. They took a side trip to Niagara Falls, visited cave dwellings near Santa Fe, and watched a movie being made in Santa Barbara. Before arriving in San Francisco the Posts spent three days at the other California Exposition in San Diego, where they visited the Indian Village and the Panama Canal and hired an "electriquette"— an electric-powered chair — to transport them around. It cost $4 for the whole day "*and held all three of us.*"

She was an enthusiastic traveler, interested in new experiences; rather to her surprise, she enjoyed a night sleeping under the desert stars, though she still preferred a luxury hotel. She was also skeptical, wondering on several occasions whether she was being told a tall tale for the benefit of credulous tourists.

WHAT DID IT COST?

Emily Post was meticulous about listing her expenses. She tabulated the cost of accommodation, meals, tips (which were quite generous), fuel and automobile repairs. The grand total was a little over $1,800, with more than $800 being spent on motoring expenses. A contemporary guided automobile tour cost $650 per person, so the Posts were a little ahead of the game. Gas prices ranged from 8 cents to 22 cents, but the car guzzled gas at the rate of eight and a half miles to the gallon. It also used a lot of oil (some 28 gallons during the trip) and repairs were frequently necessary and very expensive, mainly because it was a custom car with metric wheels.

The car eventually needed more extensive repairs than could be done in Arizona, so the Posts shipped it to Los Angeles (at a cost of $151.20) and the travelers were forced to take a Pullman car.

HOW LONG DID IT TAKE?

Emily Post and her party left New York after lunch on Sunday, April 25, 1915, and arrived in San Francisco forty-five days later, on Tuesday, June 8. Twenty-seven days were actually spent motoring; the other eighteen were taken up with sightseeing, visiting friends, and waiting for the car to be fixed or for the weather to improve.

Themes of the Book:
Patriotism, Race, and Class

Although *By Motor to the Golden Gate* is on the surface a light-hearted travelogue, several important themes emerge. In addition to being a chapter in automotive history, it is also a first-hand account of elite automobile travel before the process was democratized after World War I. The date of the journey is important: although the slogan "See America First" had been promulgated since 1906, it gained momentum as Europe was effectively closed to American tourists. "Seeing America" was intertwined with patriotism, just as visiting the Panama-Pacific Exposition was intertwined with the latest stage of manifest destiny, as American influence spread across the Pacific.

Emily Post's book is also an important document in the history of the southwest, particularly on the invention of the myths that made towns such as Santa Fe an "authentic" tourist destination, and transformed the Native Americans from "savages" to domesticated craftspeople. She was astute enough to see the Native Americans who were selling their rugs and baskets at the Harvey Hotel in Albuquerque as part of an elaborate theatrical performance put on for the benefit of rail travelers.

It is also a document about class and ethnicity; she meets inscrutable (and authoritarian) Chinese servants, unfriendly and suspicious Mennonites, a chatty cowboy, some silent Indians, numerous boosters, polite hotel clerks, perky waitresses, depressed TB patients, as well as society women transformed by living in California. The fire chief in Rochelle, Illinois, becomes a (short-term) friend, while Ned joins a fraternity of garage mechanics.

It is also a document about style. Emily Post casts a caustic eye on pretentiousness, preferring simplicity. She has a keen eye for design and for fashion; her comments on architecture, interior design and clothes can tell us a great deal about elite taste — a taste she was soon to impose on generations of Americans. Her slightly acid comments on the profusion of decoration at the Panama-Pacific Exposition contrast with her delight at the simple friendships she found in part of the Midwest.

What Did Emily Post Learn?

She learned that the roads as far as Pueblo, Colorado, were adequate or good, and that there were excellent hotels across much of the United States, though some of the most-touted were also the most disappointing. She regretted, however, what she saw as an inhospitable gap in the provision of good hotels between Omaha, Nebraska, and Cheyenne, Wyoming, and between Albuquerque, New Mexico, and Winslow, Arizona. She learned that bad experiences—such as a nameless flea-ridden hotel—could be memorable. She learned to respect Chicagoans' enthusiasm for their city, while she positively admired the spirit of small towns like Rochelle, Illinois. She learned to take some of the stories she was told with a pinch of salt. She also realized that traveling by automobile was somehow more "authentic" than traveling by train. She regretted that taking the Pullman insulated her from new experiences, and "carefully preserves for you the attitude you started with!" She said that another time she would take camping equipment, and as she hated camping "this proves the change that can come over you as you go out into the West."

A Note on the Notes

The text of the book is exactly as Emily Post wrote it in *By Motor to the Golden Gate*, though I have indicated where the book version differs from the articles published a year earlier in *Collier's*. It includes the occasional typo, unusual spelling or punctuation. She only included a few footnotes—these have been included, with a note describing them as "Emily Post original footnote." The expense lists were originally between chapters 32 and 33, while the sketch maps were at the end of the book. I have included them close to the relevant text.

The images were originally interspersed (in a somewhat random manner) throughout the book. I have placed them where they seem to belong, with the original caption in quotation marks. In some cases I have added more explanation to the original caption.

I started footnoting references that I did not quite understand, and soon realized that I was writing an annotated edition of *By Motor to the Golden Gate*. My notes and Emily Post's text should be read together as they provide a point-counterpoint, her story and mine.

I used traditional sources, including scholarly works from the Brown University library, and correspondence with a dozen or more local historical societies all over the United States. Historians and archivists responded to my email queries with wonderful detail — the results of their efforts can be found in notes throughout the book. I also used a newer research tool by spending many hours "Googling" on an Internet search engine. When I put in a few keywords (and I soon realized that adding "history" to my key words would yield a better search), Google gave me links to local historical societies as well as such delights as a scholarly essay on the author of the first diet book, a list of the seventy-nine Tiffany Silver Medal winners in 1915, and an article about U.S. Grant's son and his role in building San Diego.

Preface[1]

"Qui s'excuse s'accuse." Which, I suppose, proves this a defense to start with! But having been a few times accused, there are a few explanations I want very much to make.

When this cross-continent story was first suggested, it seemed the simplest sort of thing to undertake. All that was necessary was to put down experiences as they actually occurred. No imagination or plot or characterization—could anything be easier? But when the serial was published and letters began coming in, it became unhappily evident that writing fact must be one of the most unattainably difficult accomplishments in the world.[2]

In the first place, only those who, having lived long in a particular locality and knowing it in all its varying seasons, are qualified truly to pre-

---

1. I have compared Emily Post's original story of her trip, which was published as "By Motor to the Fair," in *Collier's Weekly* on September 4, 11 and 18, 1915, with the book version *By Motor to the Golden Gate*. This preface did not appear in *Collier's*. There were a number of differences, some minor, others quite significant, between the text of the book and the text of the articles upon which it was based. The minor word changes will be ignored, but the major differences will be included in the footnotes. *Collier's Weekly* was published by Robert Collier (d. 1918), son of the founder Peter Fenelon Collier (1849–1909). An Irish immigrant and a devout Roman Catholic, the elder Collier began by selling Catholic books on installment to the urban poor. He went on to produce inexpensive editions of the classics, and by 1880 he had his own printing factory. His firm printed and sold more than 50 million books in his lifetime. *Collier's Weekly* was founded in 1896 and soon became one of the country's major news magazines. P.F. Collier refused advertisements for alcohol and dubious patent medicines, and published new writers. Although *Collier's* editorials disapproved of New York "society" publications, P. F.'s son Robert Collier became a fixture in New York society and spent much of his time hunting and playing polo. See *American National Biography Online* for a full account of the elder Collier.
2. Emily Post had already published five "society" novels. They were *The Flight of a Moth* (New York: Dodd, Mead & Co., 1904); *Purple and Fine Linen* (New York: Appleton & Co., 1906); *Woven in the Tapestry* (New York: Moffat, Yard & Co., 1908); *The Title Market* (New York: Dodd, Mead & Co., 1909); and *The Eagle's Feather* (New York: Dodd, Mead & Co., 1910). She also published non-fiction articles in magazines such as the *Delineator* and *Everybody's*. *By Motor to the Golden Gate* was to be her first non-fiction book.

sent its picture. The observations of a transient tourist are necessarily superficial, as of one whose experiences are merely a series of instantaneous impressions; at one time colored perhaps too vividly, at another fogged; according to the sun or rain at one brief moment of time.[3]

It would be very pleasant to write nothing but eulogies of people and places, but after all if a personal narrative were written like an advertisement, praising everything, there would be no point in praising anything, would there?[4]

Compared with crossing the plains in the fifties, the worst stretch of our most uninhabited country is today the easiest road imaginable. There are no longer any dangers, any insurmountable difficulties. To the rugged sons of the original pioneers, comments upon "poor roads"—that are perfectly defined and traveled-over highways—or "poor hotels"—where you can get not only a room to yourself, but steam heat, electric light, and generally a private bath—must seem an irritatingly squeamish attitude. "Poor soft weaklings" is probably not far from what they think of people with such a point of view.

On the other hand if I, who after all *am* a New Yorker, were to pronounce the Jackson House perfect, the City of Minesburg beautiful, the Trailing Highway splendid, everyone would naturally suppose the Jackson House a Ritz, Minesburg an upper Fifth Avenue, and the Trailing Highway a duplicate of our own state roads, to say the least!

I am more than sorry if I offend anyone—it is the last thing I mean to do—at the same time I think it best to let the story stand as it was written; taking nothing back that seems to me true, but acknowledging very humbly at the outset, that mine is only *one* out of a possible fifty million other American opinions.[5]

---

3. Emily Post was traveling through the Midwest during one of the wettest springs in living memory; the weather necessarily colored her account of the problems of travel.

4. As Earl Pomeroy, the dean of historians of western tourism, has suggested, the democratization of car ownership and improvement of road surfaces after World War I meant books describing automobile adventures became less popular: "Within one short decade, trips that had been worth a book depreciated to the value of a newspaper item, and the dangers of the West with them" (*In Search of the Golden West: The Tourist in Western America* New York: Knopf, 1957, pp. 149, 219–21). Emily Post's book was, thus, part of a dying breed.

5. As the population of the United States in 1915 was approximately 100,546,000, perhaps Emily Post believed that only half of the people might have opinions?

I

It Can't Be Done —
But Then, It Is
Perfectly Simple

"Of course you are sending your servants ahead by train with your luggage and all that sort of thing," said an Englishman.

A New York banker answered for me: "Not at all! The best thing is to put them in another machine directly behind, with a good mechanic. Then if you break down the man in the rear and your own chauffeur can get you to rights in no time. How about your chauffeur? You are sure he is a good one?"[1]

"We are not taking one, nor servants, nor mechanic, either."

"Surely you and your son are not thinking of going alone! Probably he could drive, but who is going to take care of the car?"

"Why, he is!"

At that everyone interrupted at once. One thought we were insane to attempt such a trip; another that it was a "corking" thing to do. The majority looked upon our undertaking with typical New York apathy. "Why do

---

1. Some of the early travelers either were mechanics or took a chauffeur/ mechanic with them. In 1899, the first attempt to drive across country from east to west (an attempt which ended in Chicago after three difficult months) was by John D. Davis, a mechanic, and his journalist wife Louise Hitchcock Davis. Horatio Nelson Jackson, a Vermont doctor, completed the first successful transcontinental journey four years later, accompanied by mechanic Sewell K. Crocker. See Dayton Duncan, *Horatio's Drive: America's First Road Trip* (New York: Alfred A Knopf, 2003) and the Ken Burns documentary film of the same name. On the other hand, twenty-two-year-old Alice Ramsey, who traveled with three female companions in 1909 and became the first woman to drive from coast to coast, changed her own tires and cleaned her own spark plugs, though she occasionally hired garage mechanics along the way. See Curt McConnell, *"A Reliable Car and a Woman Who Knows It": The First Coast-to-Coast Auto Trips by Women, 1899–1916* (Jefferson, North Carolina: McFarland, 2000).

anything so dreary?" If we wanted to see the expositions, then let us take the fastest train, with plenty of books so as to read through as much of the way as possible.[2] Only one, Mr. B., was enthusiastic enough to wish he was going with us. Evidently, though, he thought it a daring adventure, for he suggested an equipment for us that sounded like a relief expedition: a block and tackle, a revolver, a pickaxe and shovel, tinned food — he forgot nothing but the pemmican![3] However, someone else thought of hardtack, after which a chorus of voices proposed that we stay quietly at home![4]

"They'll never get there!" said the banker, with a successful man's finality of tone. "Unless I am mistaken, they'll be on a Pullman inside of ten days!"[5]

"Oh, you *wouldn't* do that, would you?" exclaimed our one enthusiastic friend, B.

I hoped not, but I was not sure; for although I had promised an editor to write the story of our experience, if we had any, we were going solely for pleasure, which to us meant a certain degree of comfort, and not to advertise the endurance of a special make of car or tires. Nor had we any intention of trying to prove that motoring in America was delightful if we should find it was not. As for breaking speed records — that was the last thing we wanted to attempt![6]

"Whatever put it into your head to undertake such a trip?" someone asked in the first pause.

"The advertisements!" I answered promptly. They were all so opti-

2. The original sentence was a little more caustic: Emily Post wrote; "...let us take the fastest train, with plenty of books and bromide powders so as to read and sleep through as much of the way as possible." *Collier's* September 4, 1915.

3. This sentence originally included "an English lunch basket and sleeping bags." Pemmican was made from dried buffalo meat mixed with wild berries; it was highly nutritious, kept indefinitely, and required no cooking.

4. Hardtack was a dry cracker made of flour and water and sometimes salt. Portable and highly nutritious (if not tasty or easy to eat) it was given to sailors and soldiers. Although it was earlier called by various names including sea biscuit, by the 1860s it was known as "hardtack" a nickname supplied by the Army of the Potomac during the Civil War.

5. Tourism was changing by 1915 with the development of the convention business, the efforts by the railroad companies to promote tours, and the emergence of published guides. Upper class travelers such as Emily Post and her friends needed to preserve their social distance from the newer tourists, and luxurious Pullman cars and first–class hotels were one way of achieving this. See Catherine Cocks, *Doing the Town: The Rise of Urban Tourism in the United States, 1850–1915* (Berkeley: University of California Press, 2001). In addition, the roads were still not good. Only about ten percent of the nation's two and a half million roads had been "improved" in any way. Most were dirt tracks. See Drake Hokanson, *The Lincoln Highway: Main Street Across America* (Iowa City: University of Iowa Press, 1988), 7.

6. This, as well as the two preceding paragraphs, was not in the original *Collier's* article. As for proving the worth of certain makes or car or tires, Henry B. Joy, president of the Packard Automobile Company, set off from Detroit on May 27, 1915 to test the new Packard 1–35 touring car. He met similarly muddy conditions.

mistic, that they went to my head. "New York to San Francisco in an X—car for thirty-eight dollars!" We were not going in an X—car, but the thought of any machine's running such a distance at such a price immediately lowered the expenditure allowance for our own.[7] "Cheapest way to go to the coast!' agreed another folder. "Travel luxuriously in your own car from your own front door over the world's greatest highway to the Pacific Shore." Could any motor enthusiasts resist such suggestions? We couldn't.[8]

We had driven across Europe again and again. In fact I had in 1898 gone from the Baltic to the Adriatic in one of the few first motor-cars ever sold to a private individual. We knew European scenery, roads, stopping-places, by heart.[9] We had been to all the resorts that were famous, and a few that were infamous, but our own land, except for the few chapter headings that might be read from the windows of a Pullman train, was an unopened book — one that we also found difficulty in opening. The idea of going occurred to us on Tuesday and on Saturday we were to start, yet we had no information on the most important question of all — which route was the best to take. And we had no idea how to find out![10]

The 1914 Blue Book was out of print, and the new one for this year not issued. I went to various information bureaus — some of those whose

---

7. According to the expenses Emily Post listed in the book, the total cost of this journey was a little over $1,800; $984.72 went for hotels, food and sundries, and $817.32 for gas, oil, repairs and the cost of shipping the car from Winslow to Los Angeles. At $600 for each of the three travelers this compares favorably with prices charged by travel company Raymond and Whitcomb, who organized the first cross-country group tour by automobile in 1912 and charged participants $875 for the thirty-day tour. See Margaret S. Shaffer, *See America First: Tourism and National Identity, 1880–1940* (Washington, D.C.: Smithsonian Institution Press, 2001), 136–7.

8. In addition to a number of minor changes, Emily Post's original *Collier's* piece concluded this paragraph with a rather heartless reference to the war in Europe, writing, "Until it began to seem rather a delight that the good roads in Europe were closed." While Emily Post was driving west thousands of Australians died in the Gallipoli Campaign, tens of thousands of British and French soldiers were killed or maimed by poisonous chlorine gas at the Second Battle of Ypres, and over one thousand lives were lost when the Lusitania sank.

9. The young Emily Price had visited France and Germany with her father, architect Bruce Price, and toured England, France, Switzerland, Italy, Austria and Germany during her honeymoon in 1892. She was in Europe again in 1902, when several of her friends went to London for the Season, which was to coincide with the coronation of Edward VII. (The coronation, however, was postponed from the intended June 26 to August 9, because the king had appendicitis.) Emily skipped London, but joined her friends in a party in a French chateau, then went on to another house party in a German castle. Her visit came to a sudden end when she received a cable from her mother-in-law telling her to return to America, because Emily's husband Edwin was ill. (It seems his illness was not serious). See Edwin Post, *Truly Emily Post*, (New York: Funk & Wagnalls, 1961), 50–62, 90–105. Her son's book does not include any details of the drive from the Baltic to the Adriatic.

10. In spite of their best intentions, they finally set out on Sunday April 25, 1915.

advertisements had sounded so encouraging — but their personal answers were more optimistic than definite.[11] Then a friend telegraphed for me to the Lincoln Highway Commission asking if road conditions and hotel accommodations were such that a lady who did not in any sense want to "rough it" could motor from New York to California comfortably.[12]

We wasted a whole precious thirty-six hours waiting for this answer.[13] When it came, a slim typewritten enclosure informed us that a Mrs. Somebody of Brooklyn had gone over the route fourteen months previously and had written them many glowing letters about it. As even the most optimistic prospectus admitted that in 1914 the road was not yet a road, and hotels along the sparsely settled districts had not been built, it was evident that Mrs. Somebody's idea of a perfect motor trip was independent of roads or stopping-places.[14]

Meanwhile I had been told that the best information was to be had at the touring department of the Automobile Club.[15] So I went there.

A very polite young man was answering questions with a facility altogether fascinating. He told one man about shipping his car — even the hours at which the freight trains departed. To a second he gave advice about a suit for damages; for a third he reduced New York's traffic complications to simplicities in less than a minute; then it was my turn:

"I would like to know the best route to San Francisco."

"Certainly," he said. "Will you take a seat over here for a moment?"

"This is the simplest thing in the world," I thought, and opened my

---

11. Here she wrote in *Collier's*: "I went to the office of the A.A.A. at the wrong hour and found it, naturally, closed." From 1915 the Automobile Blue Book Publishing Company, which issued guides either by state or by region, published Gulf Refining Company road maps and bound them in their books. These maps were also available free from Gulf gas stations, and had been since 1913.

12. The Lincoln Highway was the brainchild of Carl G. Fisher, founder of the Indianapolis Motor Speedway, and later promoter of the huge land boom at Miami Beach, Florida. The Lincoln Highway Association, a group of businessmen and motor manufacturers (with the significant exception of Henry Ford, who believed that roads should be built with tax money) set up its headquarters in Detroit on July 1, 1913. For a biography of Fisher, see Jerry M. Fisher, *The Pacesetter: The Untold Story of Carl G. Fisher, Creator of the Indy 500, Miami Beach & the Lincoln Highway* (Fort Bragg, California: Lost Coast Press, 1998).

13. She originally wrote "forty-eight hours."

14. This was probably Effie Price Gladding, who published *Across the Continent by the Lincoln Highway* (New York; Brentano's, 1915). She and her husband drove from San Francisco to their home in Montclair, New Jersey, in the summer of 1914. She did not come from Brooklyn, but in the original version, "Mrs. Somebody"'s hometown was not mentioned.

15. The American Automobile Club was founded on March 4, 1902, after a meeting attended by members of the New York Automobile Club and others. The AAA aimed to protect the rights of motorists, and encourage enactment of more liberal laws governing speed limits etc; they also pressed for improved highways and cars, and stressed road safety.

notebook to write down a list of towns and hotels and road directions. He returned with a stack of folders. But as I eagerly scanned them, I found they were all familiarly Eastern.

"Unfortunately," he said suavely," we have not all our information yet. And we seem to be out of our Western maps! But I can recommend some very delightful tours through New England and the Berkshires!"

"That is very interesting, but I am going to San Francisco."[16]

His attention was fixed on a map of the "Ideal Tour." "The New England roads are very much better," he said.

"But, you see, San Francisco is where I am going. Do you know which route is, if you prefer it, the least bad?"

"Oh, I see." He looked sorry. "Of course if you *must* cross the continent, there is the Lincoln Highway!"

"Can you tell me how much work has been done on it — how much of it is finished?[17] Might it not be better on account of the early season to take a Southern route? Isn't there a road called the Santa Fé trail?"

"Why, yes, certainly," said the nice young man. "The road goes through Kansas, New Mexico and Arizona. It would be warmer assuredly."

"How about the Arizona desert? Can we get across that?"

"That *is* the question."

"Perhaps we had better just start out and ask the people living along the road which is the best way farther on?"

The young man brightened at once. "That would have been my suggestion from the beginning."

Once outside, however, the feasibility of asking our road as we came to it did not seem very practical, so I went to Brentano's to buy some maps. They showed me a large one of the United States with four routes crossing it, equally black and straight and inviting. I promptly decided upon one through the Allegheny Mountains to Pittsburgh and St. Louis when two women I knew came in, one of them Mrs. O., a conspicuous hostess in the New York social world, and a Californian by birth.[18] "The very person I need," I thought. "She knows the country thoroughly and her idea of comfort and mine would be the same."

"Can you tell me," I asked her," which is the best road to California?"

---

16. In *Collier's* she wrote: "Oh, I wouldn't advise that, madam."

17. In *Collier's*, she had the young man reply: "No, I really couldn't. But it is the best known route."

18. Emily Post may have been referring to Tessie Fair Oelrichs, the fabulously rich heiress to the Comstock silver lode, who came from California. She was a noted New York society woman, as well as one of Newport, Rhode Island's most prominent hostesses. In the original *Collier's* article she is referred to as Mrs. Z.

Without hesitating she answered: "The Union Pacific."

"No, I mean motor road."

Compared with her expression the worst skeptics I had encountered were enthusiasts. "Motor road to California!" She looked at me pityingly. "There isn't any."

"Nonsense! There are four beautiful ones and if you read the accounts of those who have crossed them you will find it impossible to make a choice of the beauties and comforts of each."[19]

She looked steadily into my face as though to force calmness to my poor deluded mind. "You!" she said. "A woman like you to undertake such a trip! Why, you couldn't live through it! I have crossed the continent one hundred and sixty odd times. I know every stick and stone of the way. You don't know what you are undertaking."

"It can't be difficult; the Lincoln Highway goes straight across."

"In an imaginary line like the equator!" She pointed at the map that was opened on the counter. "Once you get beyond the Mississippi the roads are trails of mud and sand. This district along here by the Platte River is wild and dangerous; full of the most terrible people, outlaws and 'bad men' who would think nothing of killing you if they were drunk and felt like it. There isn't any hotel. Tell me, where do you think you are going to stop? These are not towns; they are only names on a map, or at best two shacks and a saloon! This place North Platte why, you *couldn't* stay in a place like that!"[20]

---

19. One such might have been Gertrude Phillips's account of the adventures of Blanche Stuart Scott, the second woman to drive across the United States. It was called *5000 Miles Overland/ Wonderful Performance of a Wonderful Car/ The Story of Miss Scott's Journey Overland* (Toledo, Ohio: Willys-Overland Company, 1910). Alice Ramsey, who, in 1909, was the first woman to complete the journey, did not publish her memoirs until 1961. See Alice Huyler Ramsey, *Veil Duster, and Tire Iron* (Pasadena, Calif., Castle Press, 1961). See also Carey S. Bliss, *Autos Across America: A Bibliography of Transcontinental Automobile Travel: 1903–1940* (Austin, Texas: Jenkins and Reece, 1982).

20. Mrs. O. was correct in her view that it was an imaginary line: Fisher had been intentionally vague as to the exact location, in order to tempt towns along potential routes to support construction of the Lincoln Highway. When the route was finally announced in 1913, it was to start in Times Square, New York, go southwest through Trenton, New Jersey and Philadelphia, then west though Pennsylvania via Pittsburgh, through Ohio, skirting Chicago and crossing Iowa to cross the Missouri at Omaha, Nebraska. It would then follow the Platte River valley, go through Wyoming to Salt Lake City, cross the Sierra Nevada at the Donner Pass, and reach San Francisco via Stockton and Oakland. By the time Emily Post set out only a few miles of the Lincoln Highway had actually been built; the first was a "seedling" mile built in 1914 near De Kalb, Illinois; made out of concrete and paid for by the town and individual donors, it was supposed to inspire other towns to help build the road. Four more miles were built in 1915, two in Nebraska, one in Illinois and one in Indiana. On the other hand, many local groups painted red white and blue Lincoln Highway markers on almost any vertical surface they could find: barns, rocks, fence posts, even trees. See Hokanson, *The Lincoln Highway* 14–19.

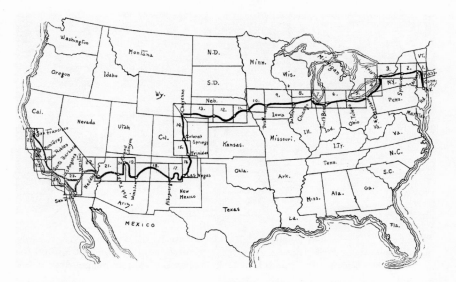

"Map showing the entire route by days' runs." The route Emily Post eventually took crossed thirteen states. The twenty-seven numbered squares refer to detailed maps of each day's drive. The actual journey took from April 25 to June 8, a little over six weeks.

I began to feel uncertain and let down, but I said, "Hundreds of people have motored across."

"Hundreds and thousands of people have done things that it would kill you to do. I have seen immigrants eating hunks of fat pork and raw onions. Could you? Of course people have gone across, men with all sorts of tackle to push their machines over the high places and pull them out of the deep places; men who themselves can sleep on the roadside or on a barroom floor. You may think 'roughing it' has an attractive sound, because you have never in your life has the slightest experience of what it can be. I was born and brought up there and I know." She quietly but firmly folded the map and handed it to the clerk. "I am sorry," she said, "if you really wanted to go! By and by maybe if they ever build macadam roads and put up good hotels—but even then it would be deadly dull."[21]

---

21. A macadam road incorporates a durable layer of asphalt and rocks over a layer of well-drained and compacted subsoil. It wears well and sheds water. Although synthetic asphalt is now available, "true" asphalt came only from a pitch lake in Trinidad in the Caribbean. The system was named after John Loudon McAdam (1736–1836), the general surveyor for the Turnpike Trust in Bristol, England from 1816; he adapted the idea from Roman roads.

"What we finally carried." From the left, Harvard student Edwin "Ned" Post, smoking a pipe and surveying the paraphernalia; Emily Post, hand on hip, and on the porch, cousin Alice Beadleston in a remarkable hat, perhaps saying goodbye to her husband.

For about five minutes I thought I had better give it up, and I called up my editor. "It looks as though we could not get much farther than the Mississippi."

"All right," he said, cheerfully, "go as far as the Mississippi. After all, your object is merely to find out how far you *can* go pleasurably! When you find it is too uncomfortable, come home!"[22]

No sooner had he said that than my path seemed to stretch straight and unencumbered to the Pacific Coast. If we could get no further information, we would start for Philadelphia, Pittsburgh and St. Louis, as we had many friends in these cities, and get new directions from there, but as a last resort I went to the office of a celebrated touring authority and found him at his desk.[23]

"I would like to know whether it will be possible for me to go from here to San Francisco by motor?"

"Sure, it's possible! Why isn't it?"

---

22. *Collier's* editor was Mark Sullivan (1874–1952) a Harvard educated lawyer, who became on of the first "muckraking" journalists when he published "The Ills of Pennsylvania" in the *Atlantic Monthly* in October 1901. He was editor of *Collier's* from 1914–1917. A Progressive Republican, he supported Theodore Roosevelt and later Herbert Hoover.

23. The last part of this sentence originally read: "I went to the office of the A. A. A. This time the celebrated touring authority was at his desk." She is undoubtedly referring to A. L. Westgard who drove across the continent several times to find and map routes for the American Automobile Association, and by 1913 was also vice president and map-making consultant to the National Highways Association.

"Leaving Gramercy Park, New York," after their final briefing with their editor. Emily Post is sitting in state in the front passenger seat. Note right hand drive, the solid wheels, and the low-slung exhaust pipe (or muffler).

"I have been told the roads are dreadful and the accommodations worse."

He surveyed me from head to foot with about the same expression that he might have been expected to use if I had asked if one could travel safely to Brooklyn.

"You won't find Ritz hotels every few miles, and you won't find Central Park roads all of the way. If you can put up with less than that, you can go — easy." Whereupon he reached up over his head without even looking, took down a map, spread it on the table before him, and unhesitatingly raced his blue pencil up the edge of the Hudson River, exactly as the pencil of Tad draws cartoons at the movies.[24]

"You go here — Albany, Utica, Syracuse."

"No, please!" I said. "I want to go by way of Pittsburgh and St. Louis."

"You asked for the best route to San Francisco!" He looked rather annoyed.

"Yes, but I want to go by way of St. Louis."

---

24. Thomas Aloysius "TAD" Dorgan (1877–1929), a cartoonist for the Hearst Newspapers, is popularly credited for coining the phrase "hot dog" in 1906 for his drawing of a dachshund inside a long bun. The road Emily Post's informant was tracing had been established many years before as the simplest way to Chicago. Both the Erie Canal and the New York Central railroad followed this route, which avoided the mountains.

"Why do you want to go to St. Louis?"

"Because we have friends there."

"Well, then, you had better take the train and go and see them!" Indifferently he took down another map and made a few casual blue marks in the mountains of Pennsylvania. "They're rebuilding roads that will be fine later on the season, but at the moment [April, 1915] all of these places are detours.[25] You'll get bad grades and mud over your hubs! Of course, if you're set on going that way, if you want to burn any amount of gasoline, cut your tires to pieces, and strain your engine — go along to St. Louis. It's all the same to me; I don't own the roads! But you said you wanted to take a motor trip."

"Then Chicago is much the best way?"

"It is the *only* way!"

He did not wait for my agreement, but throwing aside the second map and turning again to the first, his pencil swooped down upon Buffalo and raced to Cleveland as though it fitted in a groove. He actually seemed to be in a mental aëroplane looking actually down upon the roads below.

"There is a detour you will have to take here. You turn left at a white church.[26] This stretch is dusty in dry weather, but along here," his pencil had now reached Iowa and Nebraska, "you will have no trouble at all — if it doesn't rain."

"And if it rains?"

"Well, you can get out your solitaire pack!"

"For how long?" The vision of the sort of road it must be if that man thought it impassable was hard to imagine.

"Oh, I don't know; a week or two, even three maybe. But when they are dry there are no faster roads in the country. What kind of car are you going in?"

I told him proudly.[27] Instead of being impressed by its make and power

---

25. Emily Post's friend Frank Crowninshield (1872–1947), editor of the new magazine *Vanity Fair* encouraged her to travel in late April as the Rocky Mountain passes would be clear by that time. Post, *Truly Emily Post*, 182.

26. This kind of road direction was common at the time, as there were very few sign-posts.

27. It was a custom car. In the summer of 1914 the Posts shipped the American engine to England and hired Watley's of London to build the body, which cost the massive sum of $1500. It had no doors; passengers climbed two steps from the running board. The seats were very low, only six inches above the floor, but there was plenty of legroom as Emily and her two sons were tall. It was right hand drive (although most American cars had been left hand drive for almost a decade) and had a canvas top, which needed at least two people to put in place. According to her elder son, its klaxon horn made a "noise like an infuriated bull," and the emission from the exhaust pipe "gave any pursuers a foretaste of the jet." Post, *Truly Emily Post*, 174.

he remarked: "Humph! You'd better go in a Ford![28] But suit yourself! At any rate, you can open her wide along here, as wide as you like if the weather is right." At the foot of the Rocky Mountains his pencil swerved far south.

"Way down there?" I asked. "That is all desert. Can we cross the desert?"

"Why can't you?" He looked me over from head to foot. I had felt he held small opinion of me from the start. "I only wondered if the roads were passable," I answered meekly.

"The *roads* are all right." He accented the word "roads."

"I was wondering if there were hotels."

"And what if there aren't? Splendid open dry country; won't hurt anyone to sleep out a night or two. It'd do you good! A doctor'd charge you money for that advice. I'm giving it to you free!"

On the doorstep at home I met my amateur chauffeur.

"Have you found out about routes?" he asked.

"We go by way of Cleveland and Chicago."

He looked far from pleased. "Is that so much the best way?"

"It is the *only* way," and I imitated unconsciously the voice of the oracle of the touring bureau.

One would have thought we were starting for the Congo or the North Pole! Friends and farewell gifts poured in. It was quite thrilling, although myself in the rôle of a venturesome explorer was a miscast somewhere. Every little while Edwards, our butler, brought in a new package.[29]

One present was a dark blue silk bag about twenty inches square like a pillow-case. At first sight we wondered what to do with it. It turned out afterward to be the most useful thing we had except a tin box, the story of which comes later. The silk bag held two hats without mussing, no matter how they were thrown in, clean gloves, veils, and any odd necessities, even a pair of slippers. The next friend of mine going on a motor trip is going to be sent one exactly like it!

By far the most resplendent of our presents was a marvel of a luncheon basket. Edwards staggered under its massiveness, and we all gathered around its silver-laden contents; bottles and jars, boxes and dishes, flat silver and cutlery, enamel-ware and glass, food paraphernalia enough to set before all the kings of Europe.

"I could not bear," wrote the giver, "to think of your starving in the desert."

---

28. Emily Post refers favorably to Fords on several occasions in the book; there are no such references in the *Collier's* pieces. The millionth Ford was manufactured in 1915.

29. In *Collier's* there are no references to Emily Post's butler by name or by profession. In the next-but-one paragraph he is simply called "the messenger."

Mr. B. brought us a block and tackle and two queer-looking canvas squares that he explained were African water buckets. All we needed further, he told us, were fur sleeping bags and we would be quite fixed!

Another thing sent us was an air cushion. Air cushions make me feel seasick, but the lady who traveled with us loved them. By the way, we added a passenger at the last moment. On Friday afternoon, a member of our family announced she was going with us to protect us.[30]

"The only thing is," we said, "there is no place for you to sit except in the back underneath the luggage."

"I adore sitting under luggage; it is my favorite way of traveling," she replied. And as we adore her, our party became three.

We had expected to leave New York about nine o'clock in the morning, but at eleven we were still making selections of what we most needed to take with us, and finally choosing the wrong things with an accuracy that amounted to a talent.[31] Besides our regular luggage, the sidewalk was littered with all the entrancing-looking traveling equipment that had been sent to us, and nowhere to stow it. By giving it all the floor space of the tonneau, we managed to get the big lunch basket in.[32] Then we helped in the lady who traveled with us and added a collection of six wraps, two steamer rugs, and three dressing cases, a typewriter, a best big camera and a little better one — with both of which we managed to take the highest possible percentage of worst pictures that anyone ever brought home — a medicine chest, and various other paraphernalia neatly packed over and around her. Of this collection our passenger was allowed one of the dressing cases, two wraps and a big bag. As there was not room for three bags on the back, my son and I divided a small motor trunk between us; I took the trays and he the bottom. It seemed at the time a simple enough arrangement.

On our way up Fifth Avenue, two or three times in the traffic stops, we found the motors of friends next to us.[33] Seeing our quantity of luggage, each asked: "Where are you going?"

Very importantly we answered: "To San Francisco!"

"No, really, where are you going?"

"SAN-FRAN-CIS-CO!!!" we called back. But not one of them believed us.

---

30. The cousin was Alice Beadleston, about whom no further information was found.

31. The last part of this sentence was not in the *Collier's* article.

32. A tonneau was the area where the back seats were placed in early automobiles.

33. In "Ned" Post's biography of his mother he explained that they had a final briefing in a hotel in Gramercy Park, during which Frank Crowninshield presented Emily Post with a five-pound box of Malliard's chocolates and a bunch of violets. In 1915 Emily Post was still spending most of her time in her home in Tuxedo Park, which is north-west of Manhattan, though she later moved to a cooperative apartment building at 39 East 79th Street.

II

Albany, First Stop[1]

We had intended making Syracuse our first night's stopping place. It can easily be done, but as we were so late starting — it was nearly half past one — we decided upon Albany instead. We felt very self-important; it even seemed that people ought to cheer us a little as we passed. A number of persons, especially boys, did look with curiosity at our unusually foreign type of car — solid wheels and exhaust tubes through the side of the hood always attract attention in America — but no one seemed to divine or care about the thrilling adventure we were setting out upon!

For about thirty miles outside of New York the roads grew worse and worse. Through Dobbs Ferry and Ardsley the surface looked fairly good, but was full of brittle places. Our chauffeur says the word brittle has no sense, but it is the only one I can think of to convey the sudden sharp flaked-off places that would snap the springs of a car going at a fair speed.[2]

I was rather perturbed; because if the road was as bad as this near home, what *would* it be further along? But the further we went the better it became, and for the latter seventy or eighty miles it was perfect.

The Hudson River scenery, the lower end of it, always oppressed me; I can never think of anything but the favorite fiction descriptions of the "mansions where the wealthy reside." Such overwhelmingly serious piles of solid masonry, each set squarely in the middle of a seed catalogue

---

1. See Map No. 1, p. 285 (one of Emily Post's (few) original footnotes.)

2. In the *Collier's* piece, Emily Post puts quotation marks around the word "chauffeur." As one scholar has suggested, the term "chauffeur" reflected the ambivalence some people felt about the relationship between drivers and female passengers. The word itself derived from the French word chauffer, which meant to heat or stoke up a fire or boiler, and colloquially "chauffer une femme" meant "to make hot love to a woman." Virginia Scharff, *Taking the Wheel: Women and the Coming of the Motor Age* (New York: The Free Press, 1991), 18.

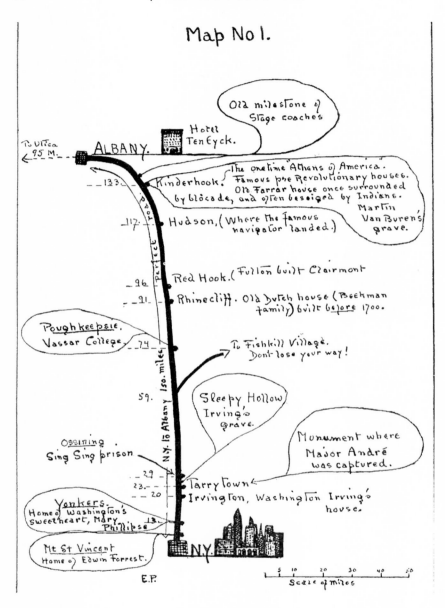

Map No I.

Old milestone of Stage coaches

Hotel Ten Eyck.

To Utica
← 95 M.   ALBANY.

--133--   Kinderhook.   The onetime "Athens of America.
                        Famous pre Revolutionary houses.
                        Old Farrar house once surrounded
                        by blocade, and often besaiged by Indians.
                                                    Martin
-117-   Hudson, (Where the famous   Van Buren's
                navigator landed.)   grave.

-96-   Red Hook. (Fulton built Clairmont

--91--   Rhinecliff. Old Dutch house (Beekman
                     family) built before 1700.

Poughkeepsie.
Vassar College.   -74-

                            To Fishkill Village.
                            Don't lose your way!

59.   Sleepy Hollow
               Irving's
               grave.

                                        Monument where
Ossining .   Major André
Sing Sing prison   was captured.

-29-
23.--   Tarry Town ←
--20-   Irvington, Washington Irving's
Yonkers.   house.
Home of Washington's
sweetheart, Mary.   -13-
          Phillipse

Mt St Vincent
Home of Edwin Forrest.

                        N.Y.

          E.P.   5 10   20   30   40   50
                                  Scale of miles

"New York to Albany," Sunday April 25, 1915. The first of Emily Post's sketch maps showing the day's journey and noting tourist sites along the way. The little hotel sketches represent what she considered a modern, even luxurious place with private baths and good food.

"Still in New York State." Although Emily Post didn't care for the lower Hudson Valley, she found the scenery further north "enchanting."

painter's dream of a pictorial lawn![3] Steep hills, steep houses, steep expenditure, typify the lower Hudson, but the scenery a hundred miles above the river's mouth is enchanting! Wide, beautiful views of rolling country; great, comfortable-looking houses with hundreds of acres about them; here, though many are worth fortunes, one feels that they were built solely to answer the individual need of their owners, and as homes.[4]

Out on a knoll, with the river spread like a great silver mirror in the distance, we christened our tea-basket. It took us five minutes to burrow down and unpile all the things we had on top of it, and five more to find in which compartment were huddled a few sandwiches and in which other box was the cake. For twenty minutes we boiled water in our beautiful little silver kettle, but as at the end of that time the boiling water was tepid, we gave it up and ate our sandwiches as recommended by the *Red Queen*

---

3. The original version of this paragraph was even more critical: after "lawn" Emily Post wrote "Since any user of the public road was allowed free and unobstructed view to the nethermost ends of the estates, and as one could scarcely imagine their giving comfort or pleasure to anyone, they must have been put there for the bewilderment and awe of the passer-by." *Collier's* September 4, 1915.

4. Emily Post had a very patrician attitude to new money and conspicuous consumption. She also had a strong preference for colonial architecture over Victorian styles.

in "Alice" who offered her dry biscuits for thirst. Then we spent fifteen minutes in putting everything away again.

"When we get out on the prairies, where *can* we get supplies enough to fill it?" I wondered. Our "chauffeur" mumbled something about "strain on tires" and "not driving a motor truck."

"It is a most wonderfully magnificent basket," said the lady who was traveling with us, rather wistfully, as she braced all the heaviest pieces of luggage between her and it.

Not counting the time out for tea, which we didn't have, it took us five hours and a half from Fifty-ninth Street, New York, to the Ten Eyck at Albany.[5] The run should have been one hundred and fifty miles, but we made it one hundred and sixty because we lost our way at Fishkill. We had no Blue Book, but had been told we only need to follow the river all the way. At Fishkill the road runs into the woods and the river disappears until it seems permanently lost! We wandered around and around a mountain in a wood for about ten miles before we discovered a signpost pointing the way to Albany!

Fortunately we had telegraphed ahead for rooms at the Ten Eyck, or they would not have been able to take us in. The hotel was filled to overflowing with senators and assemblymen, but we had very comfortable rooms and delicious coffee in the morning before we left for Syracuse.[6]

PREPARATORY EXPENSES

6 Repub. staggered tires, 6 tubes, and put on[7]	$347.04
Warner speedometer[8]	$51.00

---

5. The Ten Eyck (named for a prominent local family) was the finest hotel in Albany at the time, and the unofficial headquarters of the New York Republican Party. It became part of the Sheraton group in the mid-1950s. It was demolished in the late 1980s and its forty-foot bar was transported to Staunton, Virginia where it graces the Depot Grille in the restored train station.

6. In the original version Emily Post wrote "At the Ten Eyck we found good accommodations—two rooms with a bath between for $7, and a single room with a bath for $3. The hotel is comfortable and well run, but furnished in the heaviest mid-American period of shiny red mahogany, crimsons, yellows and browns. We had unusually good coffee and toast for breakfast and at ten o'clock left for Syracuse." *Collier's* September 4, 1915.

7. Staggered tires are still used to give greater traction on soft or uneven surfaces.

8. The Warner Electric Company, which still makes speedometers, was founded by Arthur Pratt Warner. His achievements, apart from patenting a speedometer, include being the first official timer of the Indianapolis 500, and becoming in 1909 the first private individual to purchase an airplane. The Overland was the first car to have a speedometer as standard equipment, and the Cadillac was second. Edwin Post had to have one fitted to his car.

First Day's Run, New York to Albany [Sunday April 25, 1915][9]

Personal

New York   Lunched at home
Albany   Ten Eyck Hotel

2 hallboys carrying up luggage	$ .50
Dinner, for three	$4.60
Tip	$ .50
"Movies"	$ .30
Postcards	$ .10
Stamps	$ .10
Soda water	$ .30
Telephone home	$ .90
Double room and bath (hotel full, couldn't get three singles)	$5.00
Single room (no bath)	$2.00
Coffee and toast for two (in room)	$ .80
Tip	$ .20
Breakfast (E. M.)	$ .70
Tip	$ .25
Luggage carried down	$ .50
Tip, chambermaid	$ .75

Motor

New York.   49th Street Garage

15 gals. gas	$2.70

160 miles (should have been 150)

Albany   Albany Garage Co.

18 gals. gas	$2.70
Storage	$1.00
Washing	$1.50
1 gal. oil	$ .80

---

9. I have added the travel date to each of her expense lists. She only gave one date, mentioning that she was stopped by mud in Rochelle, Illinois, on May 6–7, but the dates were calculated by the number of days the car was put in storage, or the number of nights she spent in hotels.

III

A Breakdown

Only two hundred miles from home and a breakdown! We had left Albany early in the morning and were running happily along over a road as smooth as a billiard table. Everything went beautifully until we were about twenty miles from Utica when our "chauffeur" said he heard a squeak. Gloom began to shadow his features. Half a mile further, the squeak became a knock and gloom deepened. He stopped the engine, got out and looked under the hood, lifted the cranking handle once or twice, and threw his hands up in a gesture of abject despair. His lips framed all sorts of words but all he said aloud was: "It's a bearing!" He looked so utterly dejected that in my sympathy for him (starting out on such a trip with a mother and a cousin and neither of us of the slightest use to him) I forgot that we were all equally concerned in whatever this misfortune about a "bearing" might be.

"Couldn't we *try* to get to a garage?" timorously asked the one in the back.

Our "chauffeur" shook his head. "Not without wrecking the engine. There is nothing for it but to be towed to a machine shop."

"And then?" I asked.

"That depends—" was his ambiguous answer, and we said nothing more.

Is there anything more exhilarating than an automobile running smoothly along? Is there anything more dispiriting than the same automobile unable to go? The bigger and heavier it is, the worse the situation seems to be. You might get out and push a little one, but a big car standing stonily silent portends something of the inexorability of Fate.[1]

And there we sat. Presently an old man came jogging along in a

---

1. Much of this dialogue was reworked for dramatic effect by Emily Post, as the original version in *Collier's* contained very little of this detail.

buggy.[2] "Any trouble?" He grinned as the owner of a horse always does
grin under such circumstances. But after a few further exasperating
remarks, he offered kindly, "Say, son, I'll drive you to a good garage down
the road; there are others a mile nearer, but Hoffman and Adams' place at
Fort Plain is first class."[3]

There had been nothing in our informer's conversation to give us
great confidence in his recommendation but the garage turned out even
better than he said. There was a first-rate machine shop and an expert
mechanic in charge of it, who peered into our engine dubiously:

"If it was only a Ford or a Cadillac," said he, "I could fix you up right
away![4] But a bearing for that car of yours'll like as not have to be made.
Can you get one in New York, do you think?"

An unusual and "special" car may be very smart-looking and be particularly easy to trace if stolen, but in a breakdown a make of popular type
would be best — a Ford ideal. You could buy a whole new one at the first
garage you came to, or maybe get a missing part at the first ten-cent store.
We discovered the difficulty, or inconvenience rather, of repairing ours,
within twenty-four hours of leaving home.

The telephone service at Fort Plain was hopeless.[5] For over four hours
we tried to get the agency in New York; even then it was doubtful whether
they would have the part. Meantime the engine had been taken down and
the cause of the burnt-out bearing discovered to be a broken oil pipe. They
mended that and our "chauffeur" was a little more cheerful when he discovered that they had all the necessary tools and things to make a new bearing by hand, which they started to do. The lady who was traveling with us
and I walked round and round the town. We sent picture postcards by the
dozen quite as though we had arrived where we had intended to be. We
discovered a restaurant where we could, if it should be necessary, return

2. In *Collier's* he was driving a white horse, not a buggy.
3. Twenty-two-year-old Roland Hoffman, who had studied at Syracuse University, took
over the Fort Plain Motor Company in 1914. He was local distributor for Ford motorcars,
tractors and trucks, and the Lincoln motorcar. Later, after a distinguished wartime career
in naval aviation, he became supervisor of the nearby town of Minden, where he was an
energetic advocate of road improvement. *History of the Mohawk Valley 1614–1925* Vol. III
(Chicago S.J. Clarke, 1925): 549–50.
4. There was no mention of Fords or Cadillacs, either in this paragraph or the next, in
the original version.
5. Although telephone systems were still spotty, the first transcontinental line between
New York and San Francisco opened on January 25, 1915 with a ceremonial telephone call
from Alexander Graham Bell to his old friend and collaborator Thomas Watson. The line
was made of two metallic circuits; it used 2,500 tons of hard-drawn copper wire and 130,000
telephone poles. AT&T had an exhibit at the Panama-Pacific International Exposition to celebrate the new line.

Map No 2.

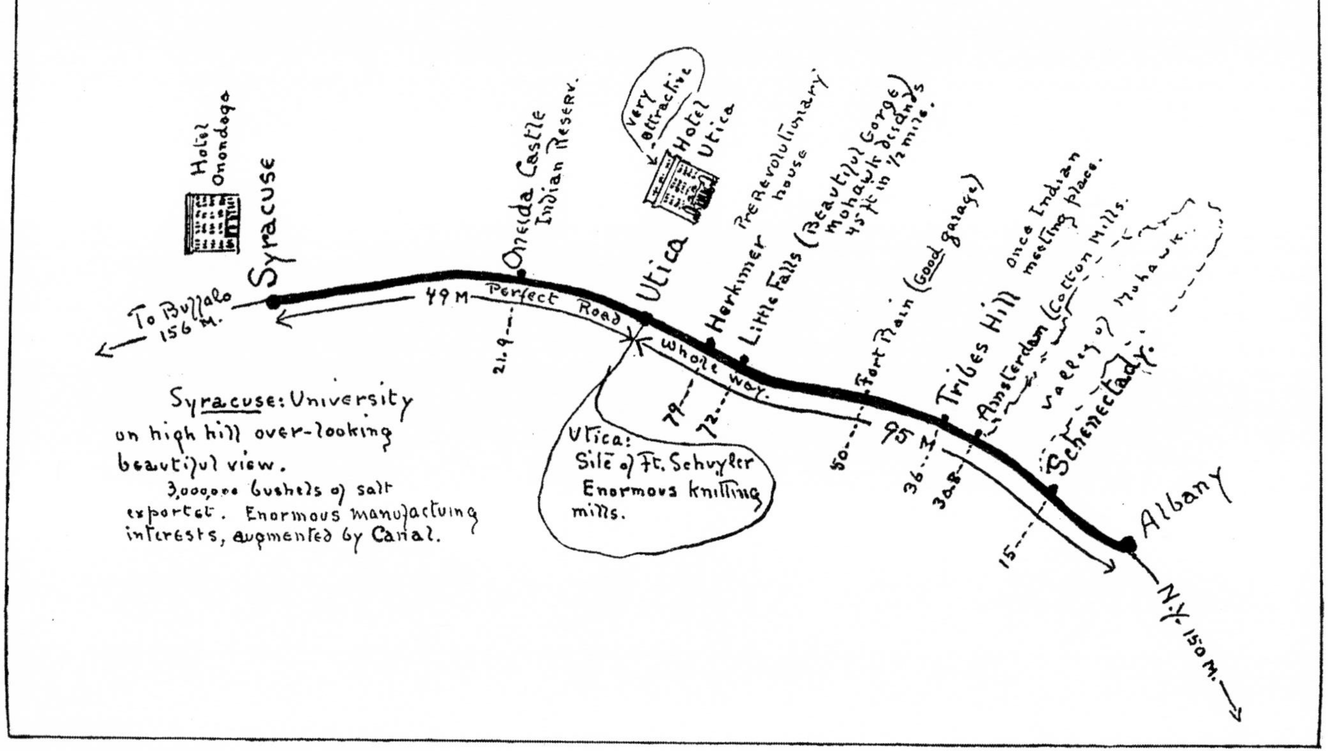

N.Y. 150 M.

Albany

Schenectady.

15

Mohawk

Amsterdam (cotton mills.

Tribes Hill. once Indian
meeting place.

34.8

36

Fort Plain (good garage)

96

Little Falls (Beautiful Gorge)
Mohawk Besides
H.S.H. in Parish.

60

Herkimer
Pre-Revolutionary
house

Whole Way

71

74

Utica

Hotel
Utica

Very
attractive.

Utica: Site of Ft. Schuyler
Enormous knitting
mills.

Perfect Road

Oneida Castle
Indian Reserv.

21.9

49 M.

Syracuse

To Buffalo
158 M.

Hotel Onondaga

Syracuse: University
on high hill over-looking
beautiful view.
3,000,000 bushels of salt
exported. Enormous manufacturing
interests, augmented by Canal.

for lunch, and a news stand where we fortified ourselves with chocolate and magazines. After which reconnoitering we returned to the garage prepared to stay where we were indefinitely. Mr. Hoffman made us comfortable in the office, where I found excitement in the workings of a very gorgeous and complicated cash register. It had all sorts of knobs and buttons in every variety of color, and was altogether fascinating! I wonder if anyone has ever opened a store for the mere joy of playing on the cash register. I wanted to set up a shop at once![6]

Finally New York telephoned they had a bearing, so we decided to go to Utica by train. Someone told us—I can't remember who it was—that beyond Albany the nearest good hotel was the Onondaga at Syracuse; but as we would surely have to stop at some poor hotels we though we might as well get used to a lack of luxury first as last, so we took the train for Utica, to wait there until our car should be repaired.[7]

Notwithstanding our altruistic intention to accept cheerfully whatever accommodations offered, our delightful surprise might be imagined when we entered the beautiful, wide, white marble lobby of the brandnew Hotel Utica! Our rooms were big and charmingly furnished. One had light blue damask hangings, and cane furniture; another mahogany and English chintz; each of them had its own bathroom with best sort of plumbing.[8]

The food is very good and reasonable as to price. One dinner, for

---

6. The second half of this paragraph, starting "The lady who was traveling..." was not in the *Collier's* article. By 1915 the National Cash Register company (NCR), which was based in Dayton, Ohio, dominated the market; although other materials, including cast-iron and wood were sometimes used, and finishes ranged from nickel-plate to even silver and gold-plate, the vast majority were made of brass. On the eve of World War I NCR ran the largest brass foundry in the world. Emily Post was, however, seeing cash registers at the end of an era; after 1916 brass and bronze were appropriated for the war effort, and after the war machines became much plainer and more utilitarian.

7. In the original version "a lack of luxury" read "a certain amount of discomfort."

8. The fourteen-story Renaissance Revival style Hotel Utica opened in 1912, and closed in 1972, when it was threatened with demolition. It reopened, however, in 2001, after a three-year $12 million renovation, which restored the hotel's ornate mahogany public spaces and enlarged many of the guestrooms, adding even more up-to-date plumbing, namely whirlpool baths. Emily Post's original *Collier's* description had an extra paragraph here: it reads: "The rates are about the same as in New York. An enormous room with twin beds (as they are called here) and bath is $6 a day; a big single room and bath $5; a smaller but equally attractive room with bath, $2.50. The food is unusually good, reasonable as to price, and well served." *Collier's*, September 4, 1915.

Opposite: "Map no. 2 Albany to Syracuse," April 26 and 27, 1915. This journey took two days, as the car broke down near Fort Plain and Emily Post, her son and cousin had to spend a night in Utica.

instance, was a dollar and thirty cents for each of us, including crêpes Suzette, which were delicious![9] There was music during dinner, and afterward dancing, As in most places outside of Broadway, they still call every sort of dance that is not a waltz the "tango."[10]

Sitting in the lobby for a little while in the evening, we noticed that the clerk at the desk, instead of showing the blank indifference typical of hotels on Fifth Avenue and Madison Avenue, greeted all arriving guest with a hearty "How do you do?" They also gave us souvenirs. A little gilt powder pencil, a leather change purse, and a gilt stamped leather cardcase. We felt as though we had been to a children's party.

Our "chauffeur," who went back to Fort Plain at daybreak, returned with the car in the late afternoon, so we were able to go on again after a delay of only a day and a half.

Second Day's Run, Albany to Fort Plain (Monday April 26 and Tuesday April 27, 1915)

Personal

Fort Plain, N.Y.

Lunch for three	$1.50
Tip	$ .30
Chocolate, postcards, etc.	$ .40
3 R.R. tickets to Utica	$2.22

Utica. Hotel Utica

3 fares Utica Hotel omnibus	$ .45
Telephone home	$1.20
Dinner (delicious) for three	$3.50
Tip	$ .40

9. Crêpes Suzettes were popularized by Henri Charpentier, John D. Rockefeller's chef, some time in the 1890s.

10. The provinces were, it seems, more up-to-date than Emily Post suggests, as "tangomania" had only recently arrived in New York, having taken Paris by storm in 1912. On the other hand, she was not happy about the bed linen: another paragraph that did not appear in the book version reads: "In all particulars except one the quality and accommodation is that of the Plaza, the Belmont, or the Vanderbilt in New York. The exception is the room linen. To pay $5 or $6 for rooms and find cotton pillow cases on the beds! If the sheets and pillow cases feel fuzzy, the towels, on the other hand, are of that stiff and shiny variety that feels like wrapping paper. But everything is in the best of taste and spotlessly fresh." *Collier's* September 4, 1915.

Tip, 1 hallboy (most of luggage left in car)	$ .25
"Movies"	$ .30
Soda water	$ .30
Double room (very big and lovely; did not wire ahead and could not get three singles with baths)	$ 6.00
Single and bath (small but attractive)	$ 2.50
Coffee for two (in room)	$ .90
Tip	$ .20
Breakfast (E. M.)	$ .90
Tip	$ .25
Telephone home	$ 1.20
Lunch (for two)	$ 1.60
Tip	$ .50
Valet, pressing one Suit, E.M.	$ 1.00
Hired motor	$ 3.00
Tip	$ .50

Second night and morning Utica about the same as above.

Motor

Fort Plain

Broke bearing; towed to Hoffman & Adams' garage	$ 3.00

Hoffman & Adams' Garage at *Fort Plain*

New bearing valves	$ 9.09
Time labor	$12.30
9 gals. oil	$ 1.15[11]
Gaskets, telephone etc.	$ 3.00

(A remarkably good garage; intelligent, efficient
    and good-natured men.)

Utica. Hotel Utica garage.

10 gals. gas	$ 1.20
2 qts. oil	$ .40
Washing	$ 1.50
Storage	$ 1.00

(Wind shield broken in garage.)

---

11. This was an error in the book; it should read nine quarts.

IV

Pennsylvania, Ohio and Indiana

Erie is a nice, homelike little city, full of business; and our hotel the Lawrence, very good.[1] There was an irate man at the desk this morning. "Say, what kind of a hotel do you run? That dancing went on until three o'clock this morning! It's an outrage!" The clerk was sorry, and willingly arranged to have the guest put in a quiet room, but he bit off the end of a cigar viciously and went out still storming about the disgrace of allowing such a performance in a reputable hotel.

"He ought to take a trip to little old New York if he thinks dancing till three is late," said a by-stander.

"He'd better go back to the farm and go to roost with the chickens!" answered another.

From Albany the roads have been wonderful, wide and smooth as a billiard table all the way. There were stretches of long straight road as in France — much better than any in France since the first year theirs were built.[2] One thing that we have already found out; we are seeing our own country for the first time! It is not alone that a train window gives one only a piece of whirling view; but the tracks go through the ragged outskirts of town, past the back doors and through the poorest land generally, while the roads become the best avenues of the cities, and go past the front entrances of farms. And such farms! We had expected the scenery to be uninteresting! No one with a spark of sentiment for his own country could remain long indifferent. Well-fenced lands under perfect cultivation; splendid-looking grazing pastures, splendid-looking cows, horses, houses,

---

1. The original version read "plain" rather than "homelike."
2. Here Emily Post remarked, "No wonder New York is called the Empire State!" *Collier's* September 4, 1915.

barns. And in every barn, a Ford.³ And fruits, fruits, fruits! Miles and miles and miles of grapevines as neatly trimmed and evenly set in rows as soldiers on parade.

"It looks like Welch's grape juice!" we said and laughed. It was!⁴

So much for the country. The towns— only the humanizing genius of Julian Street could ever tell them apart.⁵ Small Utica dressed herself in taupe color, big Syracuse wore red with brown trimmings. The favorite hues were brown and red, though one or two were fond of gray, but all looked almost exactly alike. Each had a bustling and brown business center, with trolley cars swinging around the corners, pedestrians elbowing their ways past big new dry-goods stores' windows, and automobiles driving up to the curbs; each had a wide tree-bordered residence avenue, with block-shaped detached houses, garnished with cupolas and shelf-paper trimmings.⁶ The houses of Utica had deeper gardens than most, and there was a stable at the rear of nearly every one on the proverbial Genesee Street. Syracuse, like the cities in Holland, was picturesquely crossed by canals and, like the thriving industrial center it is, by — this is just our personal opinion — all the freight trains in the world! It took us almost an hour to dodge between the continuous parade of box, refrigerator, and flat cars! Of the salt, for which Syracuse is so celebrated — the marshes were to the north of our road — we saw not an ounce. Perhaps those millions of freight cars were full of it.⁷

For a surprise we came upon Geneva, a perfect little Quaker, sitting on her own garden lawn at the edge of the road leading west. Facing an

---

3. In *Collier's* this read "And in every barn, an automobile."

4. Welch's Grape Juice, the pasteurized juice of Concord grapes, was first produced as a non-alcoholic communion wine in 1869. It reached a much wider public at the Chicago Worlds' Fair in 1893, and in 1913 and 1914 scored two huge publicity coups when Secretary of State William Jennings Bryan served it at a formal diplomatic dinner, honoring the outgoing British ambassador, and when Navy Secretary Josephus Daniels forbade the use of alcoholic beverages on navy ships, substituting Welch's Grape Juice. Both decisions garnered amused and scornful attention from cartoonists and columnists.

5. Julian Street (1879–1945), playwright and author, traveled through America in 1914, also commissioned by the editor of *Collier's*. As the outbreak of war in August 1914 closed Europe to American travelers, Street resolved to "see America" and to see it at work, rather than at play. He wrote about the grain elevators in Buffalo, the coal docks in Cleveland, and the stock yards in Chicago. He also visited the Ford plant at Highland Park and talked to prostitutes in Cripple Creek. See Julian Street, *Abroad at Home: American Ramblings, Observations and Adventures* (Garden City, New York: Garden City Publishing Co., 1914).

6. The first half of this sentence, as far as the semicolon, was not in the original *Collier's* article.

7. The four sentences beginning "Syracuse, like the cities in Holland..." were not in the original *Collier's* article. Although Syracuse was famous for its salt works, the industry may have been declining when Emily Post visited, as production ended in the 1920s.

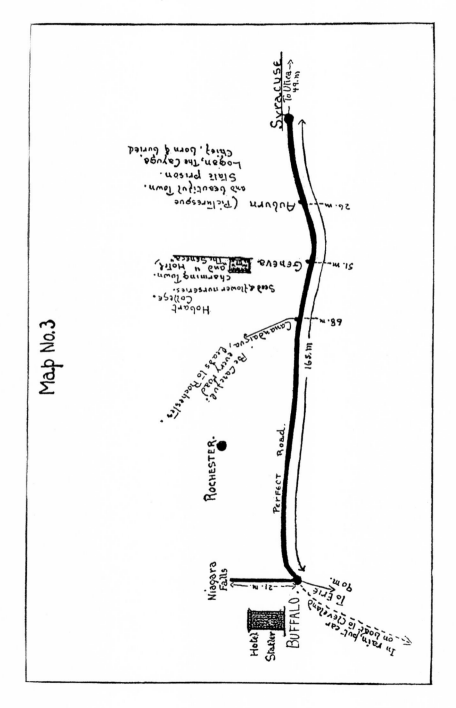

Map No. 3

old Puritan church across a square of green, stood a row of little houses that suggested the setting of a play like "Pomander Walk."[8] To the mon- eyed magnates of the mansions of the lower Hudson, to the retired trades- men residing in some of the red and brown residences of the various Genesee avenues, the demure little square of huddled houses of Geneva might seem contemptibly mean. Yet the mansions left us cold, while the little houses indescribably warmed our hearts. It was like the unexpected finding of a bit of fragile and beautiful old porcelain in a brickyard. We expected to see the counterpart of one of the heroines of Miss Austen's novels come out of one of the quaint little doorways.

We would have liked to find a tea shop on the square, for it was lunch time and we hated having to turn into Main Street and make our choice between several unprepossessing hotels. Geneva was certainly a town of unexpected contrasts. Although the little houses around the corner were so adorable, the Hotel Seneca from its façade of factory brick, sitting flat on the street, never for a moment warned us of an interior looking exactly like the illustrations in *Vogue!* White woodwork, French blue cut velvet, delicate spindly Adam furniture, a dining room all white with little square- paned mirror doors, too attractive! [9] Luncheon was delicious and well served by waitresses in white dresses, crisp and clean.[10]

Our great surprise has been the excellence of the roads and the hotels, and our really beautiful and prosperous country. Going through these miles after miles of perfect vineyards and orchards, these wonderfully kept farms, it seems impossible that in New York City are long bread lines, and

---

8. *Pomander Walk,* a play by Louis N. Parker (1852–1944), was produced on Broadway in 1910–11. Its celebration of olden times was echoed in 1921 by developer Thomas Healy when he commissioned architects King and Campbell to construct a row of apartments between 94th and 95th Streets in Manhattan's upper West Side. Still called Pomander Walk, it is now an expensive gated community. The houses admired by Emily Post were probably the row houses near Pulteney Park on South Main Street, Geneva.

9. The Hotel Seneca was originally founded in 1897 by Samuel K. Nester and called the Nester. It was refurbished in 1913, when it became the Hotel Seneca and was for many years regarded as the best hotel in town. Seen in old photographs, it was a six-story building over- looking the lake, and although one side was indeed flat, the street front had numerous bay windows. It was demolished in 1982 to make way for a senior citizens' housing project.

10. The hotel restaurant was said to be of gourmet quality, and people came from Buffalo and New York City to buy the bread rolls made in its brick oven. The oak bar is now in the Hobart and William Smith campus social building. The information about Geneva in this and the two previous notes is from Karen D. Osburn, archivist at the Geneva Historical Society.

Opposite: "Syracuse to Buffalo," Wednesday April 28, 1915. They went via Geneva, which Emily Post found "a charming town."

"One of the exciting things in motoring is wondering what sort of a hotel you will arrive at for the night." Alice is sitting in the back of the car; the strange shape on her head is a veil, designed to shield her from dust and sun. Emily Post swore by her veil, though she admitted it did not look very beautiful.

that in other parts of our great country there is strife, hunger, poverty and waste.[11]

In Buffalo we stopped at the Statler, a commercial hotel with a much advertised and really quite faultless service that carries the idea of personal attention to guests to its highest degree.[12] When you register, the clerk reads your name and invariably thereafter everyone calls you by it. In fact

11. In 1915 economist Wilford Isbell King published *The Wealth and Income of the People of the United States* in which he noted the increasing disparity of wealth in the nation. In 1910 the richest 1.6 percent of U.S. families received 19 percent of the national income, a proportion that had almost doubled since 1890. Average per capita income for the richest two percent of the population was $3,386 per year, while the poorest 65 percent averaged $197.

12. The Buffalo Statler was opened in 1907, the first hotel in the chain built by Ellsworth M. Statler (1863–1928). It was to set a new standard in hotels: it was the first built with a private bath for every room, it had facilities for traveling salesmen, and the kitchens were near to the dining rooms so as to avoid cold food. His slogan was "A Room and a Bath for a Dollar and a Half." Most of Statler's later hotels were designed by the New York architectural firm of George W. Post & Sons, (who were not related to Emily Post). Statler shared the Progressive Era's passion for efficiency and standardization: bed linen had the same size hem at top and bottom to save the chambermaid's time, while double sheets were distinguished from single sheets by the depth of their hems. See Rufus Jarman, *A Bed for the Night: The Story of the Wheeling Bellboy, E. M. Statler, and his Remarkable Hotels* (New York: Harper, 1952).

they did even more than that. I had wired ahead for rooms and as soon as I went up to register, the clerk, whose own name was printed and hung over the desk, said: "Your room is No. 355, Mrs. Post!" I had no idea where Room 355 was, but I felt as though I must have occupied it often before — as though in fact it in some personal way belonged to me. A decidedly pleasant contrast to a certain New York Hotel where, after stopping four months under its roof, the clerks asked a guest her name![13]

The Buffalo hotel publishes a little pamphlet called the "Statler Service Codes." It contains advice to employees, an explanation of what is meant by good service, a talk about tipping and a talk to patrons. A few of its sayings, copied at random, are:

"At rare intervals some perverse member of our force disagrees with a guest. He maintains that *this* sauce was ordered when the guest says another. Or that the boy *did* go up to the room. Or that it was *a room* reserved and not dinner for six. Either may be right. But no employee of this hotel is allowed the privilege of arguing any point with a guest."[14]

"A door man can *swing* the door in a manner to assure the guest that he is in *His Hotel*, or he can *sling* it in a way that sticks in the guest's crop and makes him expect to find at the desk a sputtery pen sticking in a potato."

After giving every thought to the guest's comfort, the end of the little book asks fairness on the part of the guests. Such as, not to say you waited fifteen minutes when you waited barely five; or not to object if the clerks can't read your signature if you write in hieroglyphics.

In the morning at the Statler, a newspaper is pushed under your door and on it is a printed slip saying "Good morning! This is your paper while you are in Buffalo."[15] And when you are ready to leave instead of calling, "Front! Get 355's baggage!" the Statler clerk says, "Go up to Mrs. Post's room and bring down her things!"

I certainly liked it very much. And I am sure other people must feel the same.

If the hotel tried to make us pleased with ourselves, we were not allowed to keep our self-complacence long. When we went to Niagara, we passed a sort of taxidermist's museum; its windows at least were full of stuffed beasts. The proprietor, standing in front of it, tried his best to make

---

13. None of this information about the Statler, the visit to the Syracuse pottery or the trip to Niagara Falls was in the original *Collier's* piece.

14. He used to say, "No body has the right to insult one of my guests but me, and I won't." Quoted in Jarman, *A Bed for the Night*, 4.

15. To allow for delivery of the newspaper, Statler hotel doors left five eighths of an inch clearance.

us "step inside and see the mummied mermaid" and his museum of the greatest educational wonders of the world. When we showed no interest in his collection he burst out with:

"If you're going to remain as ignorant about everything you come to, as you are about this wonderful museum, traveling won't educate you any!"

Put a little differently, it might have hit a mark. We had ourselves been saying, only a little while before, that we were undoubtedly missing lots of interesting things because we did not quite know how or where to see them. Yet, though we are still ignorant about the "wonders" of that particular museum, we are not always so indifferent. We have tried to look out for points of historical value and we have found many things of great diversion to ourselves. In Utica, for instance, we hung for hours over the railings of an exhibit of china making by the Syracuse pottery manufacturers. There is an irresistible fascination in watching the potter shaping pitchers, and the decorators putting decalcomania on plates and drawing fine gilt lines. The facility with which experts in any branch of industry use their hands is a marvel and a delight to me. I could stand indefinitely and watch a glass-blower, or a potter or a blacksmith, or a paper hanger — anyone doing anything superlatively well.[16]

I am not thinking of describing the world's wonder of wonders, Niagara Falls, because everyone knows they are less than an hour's run from Buffalo, with a splendid wide motor road leading out to them, and because their stupendous beauty has been described too often.[17]

There were four bridal couples with us in the elevator that took us down to go under the Falls.[18] One of the brides was apparently concerned about the unbecomingness of the black rubber mackintosh and hood that everyone puts on, for her evidently Southern husband said aloud:

"Don't you fret about it, Nelly, you look real sweet in it, 'deed you

---

16. The Syracuse Pottery Company was founded in 1885. Decalcomania was a late 18th century technique for decorating furniture and accessories with prints in imitation of oriental lacquer work. Relief decorations are formed by cutout prints stuck to a painted surface and varnished or placed under glass and varnished from behind, imitating reverse painting.

17. One of the first Americans to link romance with Niagara Falls was Theodosia, daughter of vice president Aaron Burr, who visited in 1801 with her husband-to-be, along with five packhorses; two years later Jerome Bonaparte, brother of Napoleon, traveled there with his bride. By the middle of the nineteenth century Niagara was a favorite honeymoon destination, partly inspired by a popular song "Niagara Falls."

18. Tourists were walking behind the Horseshoe Falls as early as 1818 when Thomas Barnett gave out certificates to those who had ventured behind "The Sheet of Falling Water." While Emily Post's companions were wearing unbecoming black rubber waterproofs, modern tourists get "souvenir" yellow raincoats.

do!" Whereupon each of the other three patted around the edge of the hood where her hair ought to be, and glanced a little self-consciously at the arbiter of her own loveliness.

Later, the young Southerner linked his arm in that of his bride lest she go too close to that terrific torrent of drenching water. The other three pairs walked gingerly through the soaking rock galleries in three closely huddled units. And the rest of us looked at them with that smiling interest that one irresistibly feels for happy young couples on their honeymoon.

On Sunday evening in Buffalo a man who looked as though he had been lifted out of a yellow flour barrel had come into the lobby of the hotel. We could not tell whether he was black or white or even human. A clerk, seeing us staring, remarked casually: "Oh, he's just a motorist who has come from Cleveland. Gives you some idea of the roads, doesn't it?"

THIRD DAY'S RUN, UTICA TO BUFFALO WEDNESDAY APRIL 28, 1915.

Personal

Lunched *Geneva*. Hotel Seneca

Lunch for 3 (very good and beautifully served)	$3.00
Tip	$ .35

Buffalo. Hotel Statler.

2 hallboys carrying up luggage	$ .50
Dinner (for three)	$3.95
Tip	$ .40
3 single rooms (very nice and each with bath)	$7.50
Tip, chambermaid	$ .75
Telegram to Erie	$ .26
Sundries	$ .80

Motor

Geneva

2 gals. oil	$1.20
(218 miles)	

Buffalo. Hotel Statler Garage

New glass in windshield	$4.00
Storage	$1.00
2 gals. gas	$2.60[19]

---

19. This is a mistake in the original; it should read 20 gallons of gas.

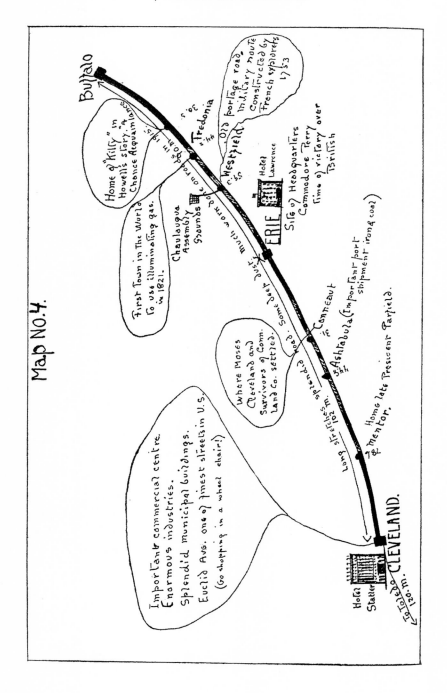

We started the next day therefore in a rather disturbed frame of mind, and soon saw how on a Sunday, when every motorist is out, he had looked as he did. Even on Monday the dust was so thick that the wind blew it in great yellow clouds, sometimes making it impossible to see ahead. But most of the way it blew to the left of us, leaving us fairly clean and not enveloping us unless we had to pass another car going our own way. As we had gone out to the Falls in the morning, we did not leave Buffalo until about two o'clock, but in spite of bumpy roads and dust so thick that it made us swerve a little, we reached Erie easily at a little after six.[20]

We left Erie the next day at two o'clock and arrived in Cleveland at seven — which was as fast as the Ohio speed limit of twenty miles an hour would allow.[21] The road was much the same as it had been the day before. Forty miles of the whole distance was rather rough and very dusty; the rest was good, a little of it splendid.

At Mentor, about twenty-three miles before Cleveland, we came to a number of beautiful places that must have been the out-of-town homes of Cleveland people.[22] The houses, many of them enormous, were long, low and white; not farmhouses and not Colonial manor houses, but a most happy adaptation of both; dignified, homelike, imposing and enchanting.[23]

The remark of the man at the museum in Buffalo irresistibly recurs to me. We certainly won't be "educated" if our chauffeur can help it! He is exactly like the time lock on a safe. Only instead of being set for an hour, he is set for distance. At Erie, for instance, he throws in his clutch, "Cleveland?" he asks, and snap! nothing can make him look to the left or the right of the road in front of him.[24]

---

20. The distance between the two cities is a little less than one hundred miles.

21. The Posts were clearly sticking to the speed limit, as the distance between Erie and Cleveland is 102 miles.

22. Emily Post was partly correct in her assumption, but many businessmen moved to Mentor after 1891, when a number of Cleveland banks and insurance firms relocated their corporate headquarters to the township to avoid the city's higher taxes.

23. One of the lovely white ones is the Garfield house, where the President's widow still lives. [An original Post footnote.] Republican James Abraham Garfield (1831–81), 20th president of the United States, was shot by a disappointed office-seeker. His widow Lucretia outlived him by thirty-seven years, dying in 1918 at the age of eighty-five. She spent part of her time in Pasadena to avoid the mid-western winter.

24. In this Ned Post was the absolute opposite of the writer Theodore Dreiser who traveled many of the same roads in 1916, and stopped whenever the fancy took him. In western New York he went skinny-dipping in a willow grove, and described it lyrically: "The sky, between the walls of green wood, was especially blue. The great stones about us were   →

Opposite: "Buffalo — Lake Erie — Cleveland" via Niagara, Thursday April 29 and Friday April 30, 1915.

"The crowd in less than a minute. A photograph taken "out of the window" in Cleveland" as an admiring crowd of men gathers around the Posts' car.

"Oh, look! That's the house where President Garfield —"
Zip! we have passed it!
"Wait a minute, let me see that inscription —"
We are half a mile beyond! We arrive in Cleveland, when click goes the lock and he stops dead, and nothing will make him go further.

The food at the hotel in Cleveland, also a Statler, was so extraordinary good that I asked where the maître d'hôtel and his chefs had come from. I thought that possibly on account of the war they had secured the staff of Henri's or Voisin's or Paillard's in Paris, and was really surprised to hear the head chef was from Chicago and the maître d'hôtel from New York.[25]

---

all slippery with a thin, green moss, and yet so clear and pretty, and the water gurgled and sipped. Lying on my back I could see robins and bluejays and catbirds in the trees about." Theodore Dreiser, *A Hoosier Holiday* (New York, Lane, 1916), 140.

25. The Cleveland Statler had opened in 1912: civic leaders, impressed by his Buffalo hotel, invited E. M. Statler to build what was to become the city's leading hotel. A sixteen-story edifice with 800 rooms, the Cleveland Statler became a model for the hotel industry. The interior designer was Louis Rorimer (1897–1957) who went on to design interiors for Statler hotels throughout the country into the 1930s. For more information, see Leslie Pina, *Louis Rorimer: A Man of Style* (Kent, Ohio: Kent State University Press, 1990). Voisin's restaurant in Paris was much liked by writers including Guy de Maupassant, Willa Cather and Ian Fleming; while Aleister Crowley, the English occult writer, took author Arnold Bennett to Paillard's in 1911, and profoundly impressed the latter by the sumptuousness of the service and the deference of the maître d'.

The dining-room service was quite as good as the food. We did not wait more than a moment before they brought our first course, and as soon as we had finished that our plates were whisked away and the second put before us. Never, even in France, have we had better or more perfectly cooked chicken casserole, and the hollandaise sauce on the asparagus was of the exact smooth, golden consistency and flavor that it ought to be, instead of the various yellow acids, pastes, and eggy mixtures that too often masquerade under the name. Our waiter brought in crisp, fresh salad and expertly and quickly made his own dressing. He was in fact a paragon of his kind, serving all of our meals without that everlasting patting and fussing and fixing that most waiters go through with until what you have ordered is so shopworn and handled and cold that it is not fit to eat. Can anything be more unappetizing than to have a waiter, or two of them, breathing over your food for half an hour?

Personally I hate hotel service. I hate to be helped. In our own houses even children of six resent it. I often wonder, why do we submit to having the piece we don't want, in the amount we don't want, put on the part of the plate we don't want it on, covering it with sauce if we hate sauce, or giving us the dryest wisps if we like it otherwise, by a waiter who bends unpleasantly close? Why do we have everything we eat pinched between the fork and spoon in that one-handed lobster-claw fashion, and endure it in silence? All of this is no fault of the waiter, who, after all, is trying to do the best he can in the way that has been taught him. But why is the service in a hotel so radically different from all good service in a private house?

Cleveland, "the Sixth City" — and she likes you to have her know her rating — is certainly prosperous-looking and in many ways beautiful.[26] She has wide, roomy streets with splendid lawns and trees and houses. A few of the older mansions are hideous but enormous, comfortable, and well built. They look like the homes of people with no end of money who are content to live in houses of American architecture's darkest period because they are used to them and often because their fathers lived in them. There is no suggestion of the upstart in their ugliness. The whole city impresses one as having a nice fat bank account and being in no hurry to spend it. The municipal buildings, however, are superb, and the newer dwelling houses all that money and taste can make them, but almost best of all, I liked the shops.[27]

---

26. The remark about "Sixth City" was not in the Collier's piece, but was certainly made much of in Julian Street's 1914 book; see *Abroad at Home* 44–47.

27. The public buildings were part of the ambitious City Beautiful era Group Plan of 1903, which designed the first major civic center outside Washington D.C. Seven public →

In a big new one on Euclid Avenue, two elderly ladies with much-befeathered bonnets were ensconced in a double rolling chair like those of the Atlantic City boardwalk. An attentive young man was pushing them around among bronzes and porcelains. Stopping before a shelf of samples he asked: "Are any of these at all like the coffee cups you are looking for, Mrs. Davis?"[28]

Mrs. Davis was so absorbed in the conversation with her friend that the clerk had to repeat his question three times before her purple feathers bobbed toward the coffee cups casually.

"Coffee cups?" she added absently. "I don't think I care about any today, thank you. But you might drive us through the linen department and the lamp shades. The lamp shades are always so pretty!" she added to her friend, exactly as though, after telling her coachman to drive around the east side of the park, she had remarked upon the beauty of the wisteria.

"Does that lady drive about town in a rolling chair?" I asked of the man who was waiting upon us.

"Oh, those chairs are ours," he answered. "We have them so that customers can visit with each other and shop without getting tired. One of the clerks will be glad to push you about in one. It is a very pleasant innovation," he added, and out of courtesy he did not say for whom.

Cleveland is also the city of three-cent car fares—in fact, three cents in Cleveland is almost as good as five cents in other cities. Lemonade three cents, moving pictures three cents, a ball of pop-corn three cents—a whole counter full of small articles in one of the big stores. Let's all move to Cleveland![29]

One thing, though, struck us most particularly in the hotels of Utica and Cleveland; the people didn't match the background. Dining in a white marble room quite faultlessly appointed, there was not a man in evening

---

buildings were to be built surrounding a 500' wide central mall. By the time of Emily Post's visit in 1915 only the Federal Building and the Cuyahoga Country Courthouse were in place; the scheme was not completed until the early 1960s.

28. This was probably Halle Brothers' store, which was diagonally across the street from the Statler. Founded in 1891, the Euclid Avenue store was built in 1910, and doubled in size in 1914. My thanks to Tom Wolf at the Ohio Historical Society for a wealth of fascinating information about Cleveland in 1915.

29. Wealthy industrialist Tom Johnson (1854–1911), who was influenced by "single-tax" reformer Henry George, was elected mayor of Cleveland in 1901, campaigning on "home rule, 3-cent fare, and just taxation." Although Johnson was no longer alive, his 3-cent legacy continued on the city-controlled street railways, and, according to Julian Street, in city-controlled dance halls where "the usual rate is cut: fifteen cents will buy five dances in the municipal dance halls, instead of three." *Abroad at Home* 55–56.

clothes and not a single woman smartly dressed or who even looked as though she had ever been! Men in unpressed business suits, women in black skirts and white shirtwaists are appropriate to the imitation wood or plaster walls of some of the eating places we have been in, but in a beautiful hotel like the Statler in Cleveland, and especially in the evening, they spoil the picture.

FOURTH DAY. BUFFALO TO CLEVELAND. BROKEN BY STOP-OVER IN ERIE. THURSDAY APRIL 29 AND FRIDAY APRIL 30, 1915

Personal

Lunch at *Niagara Falls*	
(At R.R. lunch counter to save time)	$ .50
Tip	$ .20
Erie, Pa. Hotel Lawrence.	
Hallboys up and down	$ 1.00
Chambermaid	$ .75
Dinner	$ 4.95
Tip	$ .50
3 single rooms with baths	$ 9.00
Coffee and toast (in room) for one	$ .65
Breakfast, C. and E. M.	$ 1.60
Tip	$ .25
Telegrams and sundries	$ 1.00
Lunch (for three)	$ 3.15
Tip	$ .35
Cleveland. Hotel Statler	
Dinner (three)	$ 4.80
Tip	$ .50
Theater (three)	$ 6.00
Ice-cream sodas	$ .30
3 rooms with baths (lovely)	$13.50
Coffee in room (2)	$ .80
Tip	$ .20
"Club" breakfast, E. M.	$ .75
Tip	$ .25

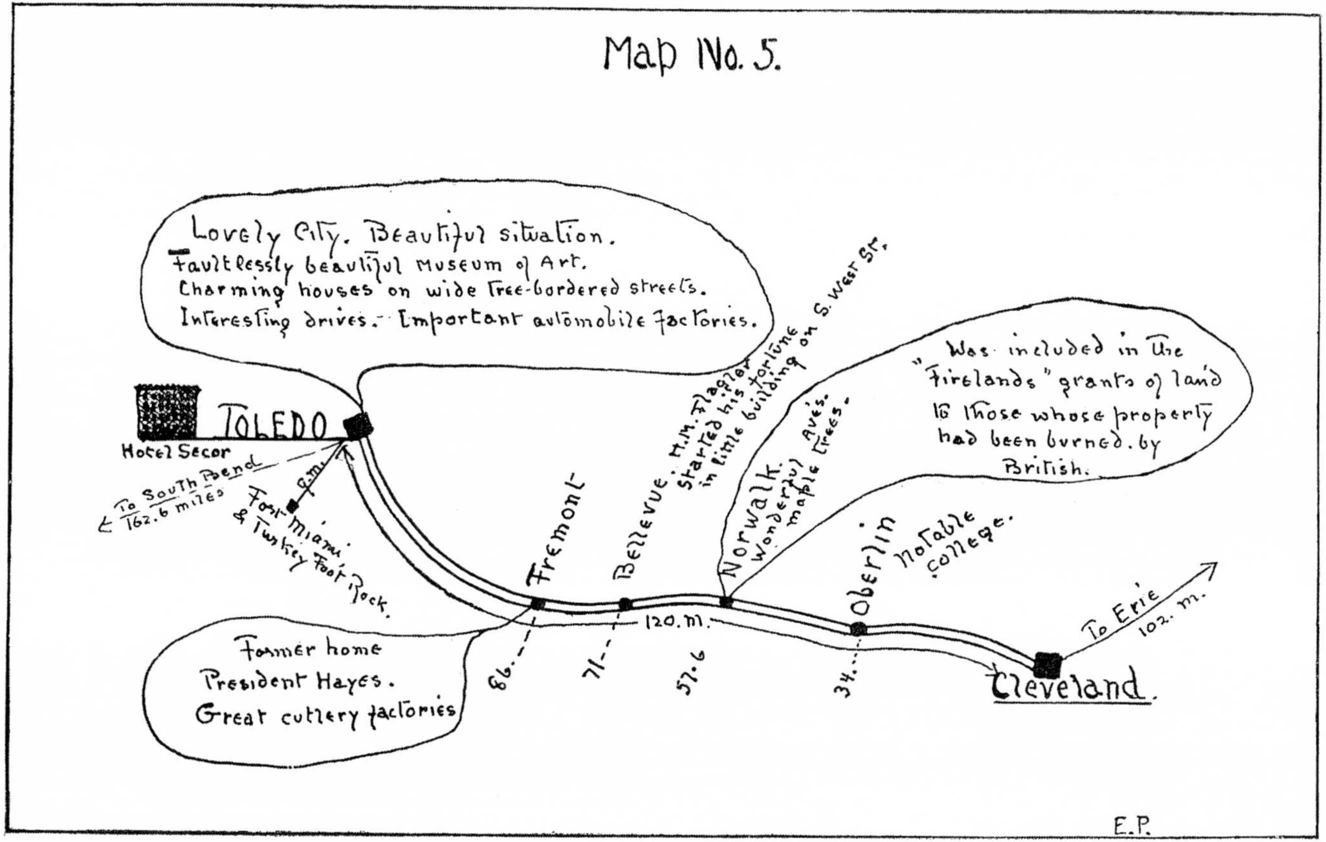

Map No. 5.

Cleveland.

To Erie 102m.

Oberlin College.

34.

Norwalk. Wonderful Aves. - maple trees.

57.6

120 m.

Bellevue Sherd. H.M.Flagler started his fortune in little building on S. West St.

71.

Fremont.

98.

Toledo

Hotel Secor

To South Bend. 162.6 miles ←

Fort Miami. & Turkey Foot Rock.

Lovely city. Beautiful situation. Faultlessly beautiful museum of Art. Charming houses on wide tree-bordered streets. Interesting drives. - Important automobile factories.

Former home President Hayes.

Great cutlery factories.

Was included in the "Firelands" grants of land to those whose property had been burned by British.

E.P.

Valet, press two suits, (E. M.)	$2.00
All tips— 2 boys up	$ .50
Down	$ .50
Chambermaid	$ .75

Motor

Drove out to *Niagara Falls*, back after lunch,
and to *Erie, Pa*, 93 miles.
Erie. Star Garage.

Storage	$1.00
10 gals. gas	$1.30
2 gals. oil	$1.20

(Very nice garage.)
Cleveland, 102 miles
Hotel's Garage.

Storage	$1.00
10 gals. gas	$1.30
1 qt. oil	$ .20

Toledo, 120 miles.

From Cleveland to Toledo the roads are very much like those of France, they have wonderful foundations but badly worn surfaces. Much the best hotel in Toledo is the Secor, and the restaurant, which made no attempt at imitating French cooking, was good.[30]

There was a most beautiful art museum in Toledo, a small building pure Greek in style and set like a jewel against pyramidal evergreens. It is quite the loveliest thing we have seen.[31]

Because of Ohio's speed restrictions, twenty miles fastest going and eight for villages, etc., one must either spend days in crawling across the state or break the law. As is usually the case with unreasonable laws, few keep them, or else the motoring Ohioans interpret their speed laws rather

---

30. The Secor Hotel, which was built in 1908, was named in honor of Toledo banker and businessman Jay K. Secor (1872–1921). It is on the National Register of Historic Places, and now houses offices and the Toledo School for the Arts.

31. Founded in 1901 by glass manufacturer Edward Libbey and his wife Florence Scott Libbey, the Toledo Museum of Art soon outgrew its original building, and the one Emily Post so much admired was opened in 1912. Designed by Edward B. Green and Harry W. Wachter, the classical revival building remains the core of the museum. In the *Collier's* version Emily Post adds: "If its collection is in any way worthy of its exterior, it is valuable indeed. We could not stop to go in it because we were going to South Bend."

Opposite: "Cleveland to Toledo," Saturday May 1, 1915.

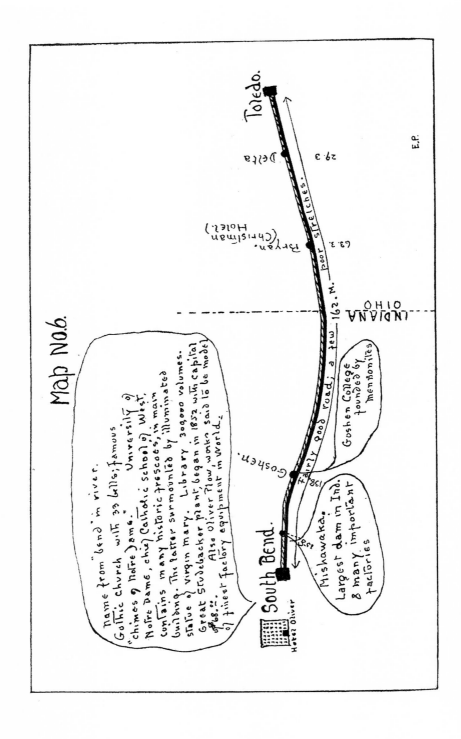

Map No.6.

Toledo.

Delta

29.3

63.3 Bryan.
(Christman
Hotel.)

poor stretches.

162. M.

OHIO
INDIANA

Fairly good road, a few

Goshen College
founded by
Mennonites

Goshen.

138

Mishawaka.
Largest dam in Ind.
& many important
factories

South Bend.

Hotel Oliver

Name from "bend" in river.
Gothic church with 33 bells; famous
"chimes of Notre Dame."   University of
Notre Dame, chief Catholic school of West.
contains many historic frescoes, in main
building. The latter surmounted by illuminated
statue of virgin mary.   Library 300,000 volumes.
Great Studebacker plant, began in 1852 with capital
of 68.∞   Also Oliver Plow works said to be model
of finest factory equipment in world.

E.P.

liberally. Of the hundreds of motors we met in Ohio, especially near Cleveland, which is one of the biggest automobile centers in the country, scarcely one, even within the city limits, was going less than twenty-five miles an hour.

However, as it is not courteous for the stranger to dash lawlessly through faster than the twelve-mile average prescribed by law, the run from Toledo to South Bend, a distance of one hundred and sixty-two miles, will take from twelve to fourteen hours. The road is good, most of it, but sandwiched between occasional poor stretches.

FIFTH DAY'S RUN, CLEVELAND TO TOLEDO
SATURDAY MAY 1, 1915

Personal

Cleveland
Lunched Statler	$ 3.75

Very reasonable! Most delicious food

Toledo. Hotel Secor
Dinner	$ 3.40
Tip	$ .40
"Movies"	$ .30
Ice-cream soda	$ .30
Telegrams, newspapers, etc	$ .80
3 rooms, 2 baths	$10.50
Coffee and toast (for two)	$ .70
Tip	$ .20
Usual tips, hallboys.	$ 1.00
Chambermaid	$ .75
Telegram to *South* Bend	$ .26

Motor

Toledo. United Garage.
Storage	$ .75
12 gals. gas (15c.)	$ 1.80
Wash and polish	$ 1.50
Fill grease cups	$ .75
Pair of pliers	$ .50

Opposite: "Toledo to South Bend," Sunday, May 2, 1915.

We lunched at Bryan at the Christman Hotel.[32] It was here that I heard a new retort courteous. I had dropped a veil; a youth picked it up. I said, "Thank you." He replied politely, "Yours truly!"

The Oliver, "Indiana's finest hotel," at South Bend is good, clean, well run, with a Louis Quatorze dining-room in black and white. The black and white craze is raging here quite as much as in New York.[33]

SIXTH DAY'S RUN, TOLEDO TO SOUTH BEND (SUNDAY MAY 2, 1915)

Personal

Lunch *Bryan*

Christman Hotel (3)	$2.25
Tip	$ .25
South Bend. Hotel Oliver.	
Dinner	$4.10
Tip	$ .40
3 rooms, 3 baths	$9.00
Coffee and toast (2), Breakfast (1)	$1.90
Usual tips	$1.75
Sundries	$ .80

Motor

South Bend. Lincoln Garage.

Storage	$ .75
1 gal. oil	$ .80
17 gals. gas	$2.38

---

32. The hotel, built by Phillip Christman, opened in 1895 and was demolished in 1979.

33. The one hundred and thirty-six room Oliver opened in 1899, and claimed to be one of America's finest hotels, not just the finest in North Bend. Its lobby was marble and two thousand people attended its gala opening. It was demolished in 1967: its site is now occupied by the Downtown Holiday Inn.

V

Luggage and Other Luxuries

Never in the world did people have so much luggage with nowhere to put it and nothing in it when it is put! Each black piece is bursting! Yet everything we have with us is the wrong thing and just so much to take care of without any compensating comfort. We have gradually eliminated everything we could until now we have just enough for three hallboys on our arrival and three porters on our departure to stagger under. Then too, although possibly all right for a man and wife, sharing the same motor trunk with a son is inconvenience unimagined! If the trunk is put in my room, he finds himself somewhere on another floor or at the end of an interminable corridor unable to get his pajamas without entirely redressing. If the trunk is in his room I have to hunt for him, get his key, and bring the trays to my room.[1] Packing one trunk in two rooms at once is even more difficult. Consequently he has in desperation bought a "suit-case."[2] It is orange-colored, made of paper, I think, and it also makes one more lump of baggage to be carried up and down and packed on top of our traveling companion.

The thermometer was at about thirty when we left home, so I could think of nothing but serge coats of heavy weight, plaited skirts also nice and warm, sweaters of various thicknesses, and fur coats.[3] There came almost a break in a heretofore happy family when I insisted that over the Rocky Mountains our "chauffeur" would need his heaviest coat. He refused

---

1. In the *Collier's* version, Emily Post calls for a hallboy, who does all this hunting on her behalf.
2. According to the Merriam-Webster dictionary, the word suitcase was first used in 1897. It is, therefore, odd that Emily Post needs to describe it in such detail. In *Collier's* she calls it a "dress-suit" case.
3. Plaited is an old form of pleated.

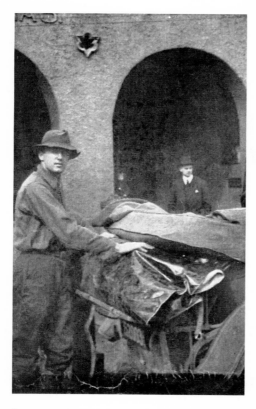

"Stowing the luggage": Ned Post in his traveling outfit of khaki flannel shirt and breeches, wondering where to put everything.

to take a coonskin — Heaven praise his intuition on that! — but obligingly brought a huge ulster.[4] We had not gone fifty miles from New York when the sun came out hot and has ever since then been trying to show how heat is produced in the tropics. Our car is loaded down with wraps for the Rockies, and in this sweltering heat not one thin dress have I brought.

In every way my clothes are a trial and disappointment. A taffeta afternoon dress that was intended to give me a smart appearance whenever I might want to look otherwise than as a bedraggled tripper comes out of the trunk looking like crinkled crepon.[5] I thought of pretending that it *was* crinkled crepon, but its crinkle was somehow not right in evenness or design. There is also a coat and skirt of a basket weave material that I had made especially to be serviceable motoring. I don't know what sort of dresses would have packed better, but I *am* sure none could be worse. In fact, I unhesitatingly challenge these two of mine against the most perishable clothes that anyone can produce, that mine will wrinkle more and deeper and sooner than any others in existence.

I have, however, found one small article that I happen to have brought, a great success, and that is a lace veil with a good deal of pattern — one of those things that make you look as if something queer was the matter with your face — unless there *is* something the matter with your

4. An ulster was an overcoat without sleeves. The garment was popular between 1830 and 1910.
5. Crepon is a heavy crepe fabric with lengthways crinkles.

face, in which case it takes all the blame.[6] In doing the same thing every day you find you shake down to a rather regular system. As we come into the outskirts of a city where we are to spend the night, I take off, in the car, my goggles and the swathing of veils that I wear touring, and put on the lace one. The transformation from blown-about hair and dusty face to a tidy disguise of all blemishes is quite miraculous. Dusters are ugly things, but as every woman who motors knows, there is nothing so practical.[7] I don't think personally that silk ones can be compared for sense and comfort with those of dust-colored linen or cotton. Silk sheds the dust perhaps a little better, but wrinkles more. At all events, I find that by putting my lace veil on and taking my duster off, I can walk up to the desk and register without being taken for a vagrant. The lady who was traveling with us is one of those aggravating women who stay tidy. She keeps her gloves on and her hands dustless. But even she saw the transforming possibilities of a lace veil and soon bought one too.

Hotels, however, are very lenient in the matter of the appearance of guests, because of all the begrimed-looking tramps, our "chauffeur" after driving ten hours in the sifting dust is the grimiest. The only reason he is not taken for a professional driver is because no one would hire anyone so disreputable-looking.

In one hotel, though, a grimy working mechanic having gone up in the elevator and a strange, perfectly turned out person having come down, the confused clerk asked where the chauffeur went and did the new gentleman want a room?

6. Neither this rather delightful and self-deprecatory paragraph, nor the two following paragraphs, was in the *Collier's* article!

7. A duster was a long, lightweight garment that protected motorists' clothing from the dusty roads.

VI

*Did Anybody
Say "Chicken"?*[1]

Sometimes we take luncheon with us and sometimes we don't. If we do, we see nice, clean-looking places on the road, such as the Parmly at Plainsville between Erie and Cleveland and the Avelon at Norwalk between Cleveland and Toledo; if we don't we find nothing but hotels of the saloon-front and ladies'-entrance-in-the-back variety.[2]

Between South Bend and Chicago we had not intended to stop, but found ourselves rather hungry and unwilling to wait until about three o'clock to lunch in Chicago. We looked in the Blue Book and saw the advertisement of a restaurant a few miles ahead. "Mrs. Seth Brown. Chicken dinners a specialty." That is not her real name.

The very words "chicken dinner" made us suddenly conscious that we were ravenous.

"Do you remember the chicken dinners at the different places near Bar Harbor?" reminisced the lady-who-was-traveling-with-us. I am not going to call her that any more! It is too long to say. I will call her "Celia" instead. It is not her name, but it is an anagram of it, which will do as well. Also a repetition of our "chauffeur" sounds tiresome, and his own initials of E. M. would be much simpler.

Anyway, all three of us conjured up visions of the chicken that was in a little while going to be set before us.

"Country chickens are so much better than town ones!" said Celia. "They are never the same after they have been packed in ice and shipped,

---

1. Only the barest details of the dreadful chicken dinner were revealed in the *Collier's* article; what here takes a chapter was described in about four sentences. This version is much livelier as well as more dramatic.
2. Emily Post is referring to the Parmly Hotel in Painesville, Ohio.

and I do wonder whether it will be broiled, with crisp fried potatoes, or whether it will be fried with corn fritters and bacon!"

"— And pop-overs," suggested E. M.

"Couldn't we drive a little faster?" I asked. For by now my imaginations had conjured up not only the actual aroma of deliciously broiled chicken, but I was already putting fresh country butter on crisp hot pop-overs. But in my greediness for the delectable dinner that was awaiting us, I lost my place in the Blue Book. Nothing that I could find any longer tallied with the road we were on, and it took us at least half an hour to find ourselves again. By the time we finally reached the little town of delectable dinners we were so hungry we would have thought any kind of old fowl good. But search as we might we could not discover any place that looked even remotely like a restaurant, There was a saloon, and a factory, and some small frame tenements. Nothing else in the place. Inquiring of some men standing on a corner, one of them answered, "The ladies' entrance of the saloon is Mrs. Seth Brown's place, and the eating's all right." We were very hungry and the lure of chicken being strong, also feeling that perhaps the interior might prove better than the entrance promised, we went in. In the rear of a bar was a dingy room smelling of fried fat and stale beer. There were three groups of perfectly respectable-looking people sitting at three tables. A barkeeper with a collarless shirt, ragged apron, and a cigar in his mouth, sat us at a fourth table with a coffee-stained cloth on it, rusty black-handled cutlery, and plates that were a little dusty.

"What y'want?"

"Do you serve chicken dinners?" I asked.

"D'ye see it advertised?"

"Yes, in the Blue Book."

"Y'c'n have dinner," he said as though he was inclined against his inclination to live up to his advertisement.

E. M. was drawing water out of the well to fill the radiator tank. Celia and I began wiping off the plates and forks on the corners of the tablecloth.

At the table nearest us were four men and a woman. One of the men kept hugging the woman, who paid no attention to him. Two of the others went continually back and forth to the bar, while the fourth was occupied solely with his food. At another table was a family motoring party, and at the third, a second family, with a baby that cried without stopping and a little child who screamed from time to time in chorus.

Our chicken dinner proved to be some greasy fried fish, cold bluish potatoes, sliced raw onions, pickled gherkins, bread and coffee.

We ate some bread and drank the coffee. If we had been blindfolded it wouldn't have been so bad.

There is one consoling feature in such an incident, that although it is not especially enjoyable at the time, it is just such experiences and disappointments, of course, that make the high spots of a whole motor trip in looking back upon it. It is your troubles on the road, your bad meals in queer places, your unexpected stops at people's houses; in short, your misadventures that afterwards become your most treasured memories. In fact, after years of touring, I have in a vague, ragged sort of way tried to hold on to what might be called a motor philosophy. Anyway, I have found it a splendid idea when things go very uncomfortably to remember — if I can — what a very charming diplomat, who was also a great traveler, once told me: that in motoring, as in life, since trouble gives character, obstacles and misadventures are really necessary to give the *trip* character! The peaceful motorist, who has no motor trouble or weather trouble or road trouble has a pleasant enough time, but after all he gets the least out of it in the way of recollections. Not that our one disappointment about our chicken dinner is meant to serve as a backbone of character for this trip, neither do I hope we shall run into any serious misadventure, but I really quite honestly hope that everything will not be so easy as to be entirely colorless.

I was turning these thoughts over in my mind as we sped on to Chicago and they suggested a most discouraging possibility, which I immediately confided to Celia:

"Suppose so little happens that there will be nothing to write about? No one wants descriptions of scenery or too many details of directions as to roads or hotels, and supposing that is all we know?"

"You could make some up, couldn't you?" said she sympathetically.

"Do you think that I could tell you a lot of things that never happened and that you would believe me?" I asked.

She answered positively: "Of course you couldn't."

"Then I'm certain nobody else would believe me either."

"No, I don't suppose they would," she agreed, but suddenly she suggested: "I tell you what we could do. We could stop over in little places and pass those where we mean to stop — and we can in many ways make ourselves uncomfortable, if you think it necessary for interesting material."

But our conversation turned at that point into admiration of our surroundings; for we had come into a long drive through a park on the very edge of the Lake that is the beautiful, welcoming entrance to Chicago.

VII

The City of Ambition

We arrived yesterday at "America's most perfect hotel." We are still a little overawed. So far we have only been in hotels that have prided themselves on being the "best hotel in the state" or "the best hotel in the Middle West," but Chicago's pride throws down the gauntlet to America, North and South, and coast to coast. I have never heard that Chicago did anything by halves! "The world will take you at your own valuation." Maybe the maxim originated in Chicago.

America's best hotel looks like a huge tower of chocolate cake covered with confectioner's icing. If it were cake, it might easily be the biggest piece of chocolate in the world, but for "America's best" — probably because the word "best" in America has also come to mean also "biggest" — the Blackstone seems rather small. Still, I don't think it boasts of being anything but the finest and foremost, most perfect and complete hotel in the Western Hemisphere.[1]

The lobby as you enter is it very like the thick chocolate center of the cake and gives a slightly stuffy expression that is felt in no other part of the really beautiful interior. The cerise and cream-colored dining-room, in which for afternoon tea they take up the center carpet and remove some tables, leaving a hollow square of gray marble tiling to dance on, is the most beautiful room I have ever seen anywhere, not excepting Paris. The white marble simplicity of the second dining-room also appealed to me, and the upstairs halls are like those in a great private country house.

---

1. Considered Chicago's best example of a turn-of-the-century Beaux Arts luxury hotel, the Blackstone was completed in 1910. It became known as the "Hotel of Presidents," serving as host to a dozen U.S. Presidents, including Woodrow Wilson, Theodore Roosevelt, Franklin D. Roosevelt, and John F. Kennedy. The Blackstone was the location of the famous "smoke-filled rooms" where Warren G. Harding was chosen as the compromise Republican nominee for President in June 1920. This rather jaundiced account of the Blackstone (in this and the next four paragraphs) was not included in the *Collier's* piece.

The restaurant we find for its standard of high prices not very good. The food at the Statler in Cleveland was the best we have had anywhere, and the prices were half. Perhaps we ordered, by luck, the Statler's specialties and the dishes that the Blackstone prepares least well.

The room service, however, is well done, with a lamp under the coffee pot and a chafing dish for anything that ought to be kept hot. Yet my coffee this morning had a flavor not at all associated with memories of best hotels, but reminiscent of little inns that one stops at in motoring through France, Germany, or Italy. There should have been a sourish bread and fresh flower-flavored honey to go with it. It leaves a copperish taste in the mouth long afterward.

In defense of the management, I ought to add that we take our coffee at the abnormally early hour of seven, and the coffee for such as we is probably kept over in a copper boiler from the night before. Still, ought this to happen in the best hotel, even if only of the Western Hemisphere?

Our rooms high up and overlooking the lake are lovely, perfectly appointed, and with an entrancing view of moonlight on the water. The furnishings of the bedrooms are very like those of the Ritz hotels, and the prices are reasonable considering the high quality of their accommodations. The three-dollar-and-a-half rooms are small, light, and completely comfortable; for seven dollars one can have a big room overlooking the lake, both of course including bathrooms with outside windows and all the latest Ritz-Carlton type of furnishings, and — I must not forget — linen sheets and pillow cases, the first real linen we have seen since we left home! Also the reading lamp by my bed has a shade, pink on the outside and lined with white and a generous flare, that I can read by.

At the Statler in Cleveland there was an exceedingly pretty bed table lamp with a silk shade on it of Alice blue and a little gold lace, but one might as well have tried to read by the light of a captured firefly tied up in blue tissue paper. I tried to get the shade off but it was locked on — to prevent guest from ironing or stealing the shade or the bulb? At any rate, since nothing could part the cover from the fixture, and reading in the blue, glimmering gloom was impossible, I was obliged to get to sleep by watching the members of a club in the building opposite smoking and lounging, exactly like the drummers downstairs — downstairs in Cleveland, not here.[2]

The ubiquitous drummer is not in evidence as he was in northern New York, Indiana, and Ohio. The people down these stairs are more like the

---

2. A drummer was a traveling salesman, presumably because he had to drum up business.

people one sees in the hotels in New York, Boston, or Philadelphia. In the other cities we have come through there were traveling men to the right of us and traveling men to the left of us, and cigars— segars, looks more like it — tilted in the corners of their mouths. Traveling men standing and leaning, traveling men leaning and sitting, but always men in cigar smoke, talking and lounging and taking their rest in the lobbies.[3]

Like the drummers, I shall soon have all the hotels in the country at my finger ends; the advantages, disadvantages, and peculiarities of each. Already I could write a treatise on plumbing apparatus! The Statler in Cleveland had an "anti-scald" device. I read about it in the "service booklet" afterward. The curious-looking handles and levers occupying most of a white-tiled wall at the head of the bathtub so fascinated me that I had to try and see how they worked. I pulled knobs and pushed buttons that seemingly were for ornament only, until suddenly a harmless-looking handle let loose a roaring spray of water that came from every part of the amateur Niagara at once. My bath was over before I had meant it to begin, and I got undressed afterward instead of before. But I like the bathrooms with running ice-water faucets,[4] and I love to examine the wares in the automatic machines, also placed in the bathrooms. They look like a miniature row of nickel telephone booths, each displaying a bottle or box through the closed glass door, each with a slot to drop a quarter in and a knob to pull your chosen box or bottle out with. The tantalizing thing about them is that they hold very little of use to me. I don't like the kind of cold cream they carry; the toothbrushes are usually sold out, and razors and shaving soap don't really tempt me.[5]

There are paper bags in the closets to send your laundry away in and a notice that all washing sent to the desk before nine in the morning will be returned by five in the afternoon. If only they could run an owl laundry, taking your things at nine in the evening and returning them at five

---

3. Two more grumpy paragraphs, which were not in *Collier's*: Emily Post did not have a good time at the Blackstone. "Segars" suggests cheap cigars.

4. E.M. Statler explained he was inspired to do this by his experiences as a bellhop at the McLure Hotel in Wheeling, West Virginia, where he spent much of his time taking pitchers of ice water to the thirsty traveling salesmen staying here. See Jarman, *A Bed for the Night*, 3.

5. Julian Street was much more appreciative of his hotel rooms: he described his room at the Statler in Buffalo providing "a clothes brush; a card bearing on one side a calendar and on the other side a list of all the trains leaving Buffalo and their times of departure; a memorandum pad and pencil by the telephone; a Bible (placed in this hotel by the Gideons), and a pincushion, containing not only a variety of pins (including a large safety pin), but also needles threaded with black thread and white, and buttons of different kinds, even to a suspender button." *Abroad at Home* 34.

Map No.7.

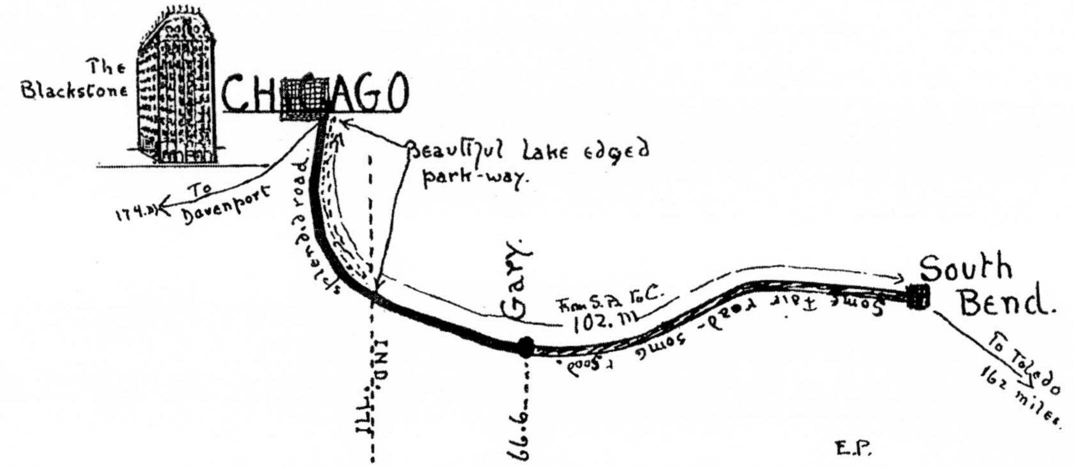

The Blackstone

CH(I)(C)AGO

To Davenport
174 M.

Beautiful lake edged
park-way.

Splendid road.

IND.

ILL.

Gary

66.9

From S.A.F.C.
102 m.

Some fair road.

Some fair road—some good.

South
Bend.

To Toledo
162 miles.

E.P.

in the morning, it would be much more convenient for people who arrive at night and leave in the early dawn.

I should like to make a collection of hotel signs, such as plates on the bedroom doors saying, "Stop! Have you forgotten something?" And in the bathroom the same sentiments and an additional "How about that razor strop?"

While waiting for my change in one of the big department stores I overheard the following conversation between two women directly beside me:

"So you like living in the city, do you?" said one.

"Sure!" answered the other. "You can run into the stores as often as you feel like it. And if you get lonesome you can go to the movies or a vaudeville show, or you can walk up Michigan Avenue and see the styles— there's always something going on in the city."

"I dare say you get used to it and feel you couldn't give it up. But what I could never get used to is one of them flats. Now out at home, we've got a fifteen-room house, all hardwood floors—"

"What d'you want all that room for? You've only got to spend money to furnish it and elbow grease to care for it. You need two girls or more. Now, we've got a flat all fixed up nice and cozy and one girl takes care of it easy."

"Well, I guess it's all right, but if I had to bring my babies out of the good country air and put them in a flat, I think they'd die!"

Opposite: "South Bend to Chicago," Monday May 3, 1915.

VIII

A Few Chicagoans

The disappointing and unsatisfying thing about a motor trip is that unless you have unlimited time, which few people ever seem to have, you stop too short a while in each place to know anything at all about it. You arrive at night and leave early in the morning and all you see is one street driving in, and another going out, and the lobby, dining room and a bedroom or two at the hotel.

Happily for us, we have been staying several days in Chicago, and, while we can scarcely be said to know the city well, we have met at least a few glimpses of her life and have met quite a few of her people.

Last evening at a dinner given for us, our hostess explained that she had asked the most typical Chicagoans she could think of, and that one of the most representative of them was to take me in to dinner. "He is so enthusiastic, he is what some people would call a booster," she whispered just before she introduced him.

In books and articles I had read of persons called "boosters," and had thought of them as persons slangy as their sobriquet; blustering, noisy braggarts, disagreeable in every way. I think the one last night must have been a very superior quality. He was neither noisy nor disagreeable; on the contrary, he was most charming and seemed really trying not to be a booster at all if he could help it.[1]

He began by asking me eagerly how we liked Chicago. Had we thought the Lake Shore Drive beautiful? Were we struck with Chicago's smallness compared to New York? I told him we had, and we were not. He thereupon generously but reluctantly admitted — the list is his own — that probably New York had more tall buildings, more wholesale hat and ribbon

---

1. Although the term "booster" meaning an enthusiastic supporter, had been in use since 1890, the term "boosterism" was coined in 1913.

houses, a bigger museum of art, a few more theaters, and yes, undoubt-edly, more millionaires' palaces, but — he suddenly straightened up — "Chicago has more real homes! And when it comes to beauty, has New York anything to compare with Chicago's boulevard system of parks edged by the lake and jeweled with lagoons? And yet she is the greatest railroad cen-ter in the whole world. And let me tell you this," he paused. "New York can never equal Chicago commercially! How can she? Look on the map and see for yourself! From New York to San Francisco, north to the lakes and south to Mexico— that's where Chicago's trade reaches! What is there left for New York after *that*? She can, of course, trade north to Boston and south to Washington, but she can't go west, because Chicago reaches all the way to New York herself, and there is nothing on the east except the Atlantic Ocean!"

After dinner we were taken to the small dancing club, a one-storied pavilion containing only a ballroom with a service pantry in the back, that a few fashionables of Chicago built in a moment of dancing enthusiasm. Although we met comparatively few people and had little opportunity to talk to anyone, I noticed everywhere the same attitude as that of my com-panion at dinner. The women had it as much as the men. As soon as they heard we were from New York they began to laud Chicago.

Mrs. X., one of their most prominent hostesses and one of the most beautiful and flawlessly turned out people I have ever seen, instead of talk-ing impersonalities as would a New York woman of like position, plunged immediately into the comparison of New York's shoreline of unsightly docks with view across her own lawn to the Lake. Imagine a typical host-ess of Fifth Avenue greeting a stranger with: "How do you do, Mrs. Pitts-burgh; our city is twice as clean as yours!" However, I felt I had to say something in defense of mine, so I remarked that the houses on Riverside Drive faced the Hudson, and across a green terrace, too.[2]

"Oh, but the Palisades opposite are so hideously disfigured with signs," she objected, "and besides none of your really fashionable world lives on your upper West Side.

Having staked out our fashionable boundaries for us, she switched the topic to country clubs. Had we been to any of them?

We had been given a dinner at the Saddle and Cycle Club, and we had to admit it was quite true that New York had nothing in its immediate vicinity to compare with the terrace on which we had dined, directly on

---

2. Mrs. X was robably the famous Bertha Honoré (Mrs. Potter) Palmer (1850–1918), who lived overlooking the lake. I am indebted to John K. Notz, Jr., for much information on Chicago.

the Lake, and apparently in the heart of the wilderness, although the heart of Chicago was only a few minutes' drive away.[3]

"You must come out to Wheaton and lunch with us tomorrow!" Mrs. X. said. You could tell from her tone that she was now speaking of her particularly favorite club. "I think they will be playing polo, but anyway you must see what a beautiful spot we have made of it, and there wasn't even a tree on the place when we started — we have done everything ourselves."[4]

Doing things themselves seemed to me chief characteristic of the Chicagoans. A "do-nothing" must be the most opprobrious name that could be given a man.[5] Nearly all of Chicago's prominent citizens are self-made — and proud of it. Millionaire after millionaire will tell you of the day when he wore ragged clothes, ran bare-footed, sold papers, cleaned sidewalks, drove grocers' wagons, and did any job that he could find to get along. And then came opportunity, not driving up in a golden chariot, either! But more often a trudging wayfarer to be accompanied long and wearily. You cannot but admire the straightforwardness— even the pride with which these successful men recount their meager beginnings, as well as the ability that always underlies the success.[6]

Another thing that impressed us was that cleverness is rather the rule than the exception, and the general topics of conversation are more worth listening to than average topics elsewhere. For instance, their city is a factor of vital interest to them, and therefore their keenness on the subject of politics and all municipal matters is equaled possibly in English society only. They are also interested in inventions, in science, in all real events and affairs, both at home and abroad. At least this is what we found there, and what I am told by many people who have spent much time in Chicago.

To compare Chicago with Boston is much like comparing a dynamo

---

3. The Saddle and Cycle Club was founded in 1895 by a group of young Chicagoans including lawyer Victor M. Elting. The introduction of the safety bicycle and of pneumatic tires made the sport safe and comfortable, and cycle clubs sprang up all over the western world. By the time Emily Post visited the Saddle and Cycle Club had evolved a social side; it still exists at 900, West Foster Avenue, Chicago, where it has tennis courts, ice rinks, and a concert arena.

4. This was the prestigious Chicago Golf Club, (incorporated 1893, and the site of the first USGA Open Championship in 1897), which was (and is) situated just off the Warrenville Road in Wheaton. Robert Todd Lincoln, son of President Abraham Lincoln, was the club's president from 1905–06. A map of the club produced for the 1928 Walker Cup matches shows the polo field in the middle of the course; the polo field was created sometime between 1910 and 1914. It was, and remains, one of Chicago's most prestigious golf clubs. I am indebted to Jamie Kelly of the Wheaton History Center.

5. This and the next three paragraphs were added for the book version.

6. Horatio Alger was clearly alive and well in Chicago.

with a marble monument, yet paradoxically there is a strong similarity between the two. There is no public place where people congregate. Both are cities of homes, and hotel life has little part in the society of either. Boston society is possibly the most distinguished in America — and Boston front doors will never open to you unless you have cultivation and birth to the extent of proving satisfactorily who your grandparents were. Chicago, of course, cares not at all, in a Boston sense, who your grandfather was so long as he was not a half-wit who transferred his mental deficiency to you. Boston society is distinguished and cultivated. Chicago society interesting and stimulating. At least that is what the people I have met in these two cities seem to me.

But to go back to the evening of our first dinner party in Chicago: the attitude of everyone rather puzzled and not a little amused me, and after I had gone to bed I lay awake, and their remarks, especially those of the man at dinner, recurred to me and I began to laugh — then suddenly stopped.

The mere bragging about the greatness and bigness of his city was not the point; *the point was his caring.* The Chicagoans love their city, not as though it were a city at all, but as though it were their actual flesh and blood. They look at it in the way a mother looks at her child, thinking it the brightest, most beautiful and wonderful baby in the whole world. Tell a mother that Mrs. Smith's baby is the loveliest and cleverest prodigy you have ever seen, and her feelings will be those exactly of Chicagoans if you tell them anything that could be construed into an unfavorable comparison. They can't bear New York any more than the mother can bear Mrs. Smith's baby. At the very sight of a New Yorker they nettle and their minds flurry around and gather up quickly every point of possible advantage to their own beloved Chicago. Not for a second am I ridiculing them any more than I would ridicule the sacredness of a man's belief in prayer. Their love of their city is something wonderful, glorious, sublime. They don't brag for the sake of bragging, but they champion her with every last corpuscle in their heart's blood because they so loyally and tremendously care.

I wonder, is it their attitude that has affected us, too? Otherwise why is the appeal of Chicago so much more personal than that of other cities we have come through, so that even we are feeling quite low-spirited because tomorrow we leave for good! To be sure, the Blackstone is a beautiful and luxurious hotel, and we are not likely to meet its double again between here and the Pacific Coast, but it is not that, neither is it that we have any sentiment for the city or those that dwell therein. We have no really close friends here, we have met only a few people — in fact we are ordinary tourists merely passing through a strange city, running into a few acquaintances as people are sure to run into occasional acquaintances almost everywhere.

I don't think I can explain this personal and sudden liking that I feel for Chicago. Once in a very great while one meets a rare person whom one likes and trusts at first sight, and about whom one feels that to know him better would be to love him much.

To me Chicago is like that.

I don't suppose a New Yorker ever wants to live anywhere else, but if sentence should be passed on me that I had to spend the rest of my life in Chicago I doubt if I would find the punishment severe. There is something big, wholesome, and vitalizing out here. It is just the sort of place where one would choose to bring up one's children, the ideal soil and sun and climate for young Americans to grow in. New York is a great exotic hot-house in which orchids thrive; but the question is this: in selecting a young plant for the garden of the world, is an orchid the best plant to choose?

IX

Tins

If E. M. were put in charge of the commissary department we would be given hardtack and water — his suggestions as to food never go any further. I, on the other hand, feel impelled toward chocolate in the way a drunkard is impelled toward rum, and if the supplies were left to me I should fill every thermos with chocolate ice-cream soda water and the sandwich boxes with chocolate cake. But Celia, having little opinion of hardtack and still less of chocolate, which she declared was making me as fat as butter, suddenly took the matter of food supplies into her own hands. Although she acknowledged that she had invited herself upon the expedition in the first place, and that she had agreed to sit under the luggage at the back, she protested that a heavy hamper full of silver and crockery and nothing to eat in it was an inhumanly heavy weight to put her up against, and she would like to arrange things differently.

Of course we told her that if she felt like rising above her surroundings it was not for us to hold her down. So without any more ado she shipped the beautiful lunch basket home by freight and dragged me out with her to buy a more practical substitute. Her first purchase was a large, white, tin breadbox — just an ordinary box with a padlock, neither lining nor fixtures.

"What for?" I asked.

"To put things in," said she. "It is going to be padlocked and it is going to stand flat on the floor of the tonneau and stay there, and not tumble over me! Also we won't have to have it lugged up to our room at night or carted down in the morning."

"Excellent!" I agreed enthusiastically. "Let's have paper plates and five-cents-a-dozen spoons and throw them away and not have to fuss with anything to be washed."

At a ten-cent store we bought only three knives, but dozens of plates and spoons and enough oiled paper to wrap sandwiches for an expedition.[1] Then we went to a beautiful grocery store near the hotel and laid in a supply of everything imaginable that comes in china, glass or tin! Chicken, ham, tongue, pheasant in tubes like tooth paste, pâté de fois gras in china, big pieces of chicken in glass, nuts, jam marmalade, and honey.

One article of food that we had tried to find ever since leaving New York was still unobtainable. Neither brittle bread nor protopuffs had ever been heard of west of New York, and our Chicago grocer looked as blank as the rest.[2] Either New York women are the only ones who worry about keeping their figures or else the women of other cities stay slim naturally![3] Nothing but good, rich, fat-producing bread and butter to be had, to say nothing of chocolate! And our waist-bands getting tighter every day! Not E. M.—he being very young is as lathlike as ever.

Having bought everything else, we repeated our question, was he *sure* he had no gluten or Swedish bread, no dry, flourless bread of any kind! No, he had only hardtack, and then produced—round packages of brittle bread!

Wonderful! We were so delighted we fairly floundered on it. "Bring us more; we are going to cross the continent; we must have lots of it!" I said greedily. Then we hurried home and waited for our supplies to arrive.

Finally came a big basket, bulging. Had we really bought all that? But it was only the beginning. Bread, bread, and more bread! Bales of it! It was I who had ordered "lots of it." Celia looked sorry for me.

"It looks like rain! We could shelter the car under it," was all that I, idiotically, could think of. And in my absent-mindedness I broke open one of the bales. It was certainly Swedish bread, the nicest, crispest imaginable, and then I took a bite. Caraway seeds!

---

1. This was Woolworth's—see the accounts at the end of this chapter for what Emily Post's purchases cost. Frank Winfield Woolworth opened his first store in 1879, and by the time his company was incorporated in 1911 he had one thousand stores. See Karen Plunkett-Powell, *Remembering Woolworth's: A Nostalgic History of the World's Most Famous Five-and-Dime* (New York: St. Martin's Press, 2001). The wonderful shopping list in the second part of this paragraph was not in the *Collier's* article, and the details about protopuffs (see below) and caraway seeds were also added for the book version.
2. Brittle bread is a southern dish, of very thinly rolled dough (often incorporating sour cream) baked into wafers. It is not clear what protopuffs were, but the context suggests they and brittle bread were popular with the diet-conscious.
3. The craze for slimming was of relatively recent date. Although the first popular diet book appeared in England in 1863, it was not until the mid–1890s that advertisements for products proclaiming their efficacy in weight loss started appearing in newspapers and magazines. Ingredients in these products included laxatives, purgatives, arsenic, strychnine, washing soda and Epsom Salts. The first American book to link calorie counting to weight loss was Dr. Lulu Hunt Peters' *Diet and Health, with Key to the Calories*, which was published in Chicago by Reilly and Lee in 1918.

In our family some ancestor must have been done to death on car-away seeds. The strongest of us becomes a queer green at even so much as a whiff of one. Celia ran out into the hall as though I had exclaimed "Snakes!" And I, like the one who had just been bitten, followed unstably after her.

"Is there a bat in your room?" asked the floor clerk, sympathetically.

"N-o, —car-a-way s-seeds," said Celia, all in a tremble.

"We none of us can bear them — and they are in the bread," I explained.

"Caraway seeds?" exclaimed the bewildered floor clerk. "Oh, but I like caraway seeds very much!"

"Do you?" we gasped. "Well, then if you will send a staff of porters into Room 202, you can have enough to last all your life! You can stack a whole mountain of it around your desk and eat your way out."

It rained all last night and drizzled on and off all morning. As every-one has warned us against muddy roads west of Chicago, we sat with our faces pressed to the windows overlooking the Lake, feeling alternately hopeful and downcast and asking each other questions in circles. Might we try to get on? Had we perhaps better unpack and stay? Twice the sun struggled out and we sent down for the porters to come for our luggage, but both times when they arrived it had begun to rain and we sent them away again. By twelve o'clock, having finally decided to stay over a day, E. M. went to the Saddle and Cycle Club to lunch with some friends. Celia and I were about to go down to the restaurant for our own luncheon when the breadbox caught her attention. I saw her lift the cover and look wist-fully at the two neatly tied white paper packages and three brightly shin-ing thermos jars that were on top. Expecting to start early in the morning we had the night before ordered a luncheon put up. And now what were we to do with the food?

"It was so expensive!" she said wistfully. "The pâté sandwiches were sixty cents apiece and they will be horrid and dry tomorrow!"

"And the lobster salad was a dollar and a half — and that certainly won't keep!"[4]

"And we don't even know whether it is good or not!" she almost wailed, but quite as quickly she exclaimed happily: "Lets picnic here!"

"Here?" I said vaguely, looking about at the rose silk hangings and the velvet carpet.

"Why not? It is ever so much more comfortable here than it would

4. These were certainly high prices, as they seldom paid more than 75 cents each for lunch. In the earlier *Collier's* version ice cream took the place of lobster salad.

have been out on a dusty roadside. Besides, we really ought to see how our commissary department works. We ought to be sure we haven't any more caraway seeds!" she shivered.

A few minutes later we had spread our picnic on the floor and were having a perfect time. Also while we were about it we thought we had better sample the various things we had bought the day before.

"There is no use," said the food expert, "in carting about a lot of stuff that we don't like!" So we opened and tasted a tin of this and a jar of that until we were surrounded with what looked like the discards of a canning factory. Suppose our New York friends who had exclaimed at our going without any servants could see us now!

I was just jabbing a hole in a can of condensed milk with a silver and tortoise-shell nail file when someone knocked at the door.[5] Without a thought of the picture we were presenting to the probable chambermaid, I called, "Come in!" but was too busy to look up until I heard a sort of gasp and a man's voice stammered:

"I only came to see — to see if Mrs. Post — if there was anything I could do to — serve —"

"Miller!" It was the head waiter of one of the dining rooms downstairs — a man who had for several years been second head waiter in a celebrated New York hotel and who had once been a butler for a member of our family. The expression on his face was one of such surprise, bewilderment, apology, shame and humility that I found myself explaining:

"We were to have picnicked along the road, but it rained. And so we have picnicked —! It is very simple!"

"Yes, madam," he agreed, stoically. But it was not until I had assured him that we never picnicked more than once a day indoors and had given him permission to order our dinner at what time and wherever he pleased, and most particularly after I refused to allow him to send a waiter to put the room in order and be a witness to the family's eccentricities that he became his urbane, impassible self once more.

Tonight I suppose we will have to deck ourselves out in our best bibs and tuckers and sit through a conventionally complete dinner at the most prominent table in the dining-room so that Miller may suffer no loss to his proper pride.

---

5. Gail Borden was granted a patent on condensed milk in 1856, the same year Louis Pasteur began his experiments on milk.

SEVENTH DAY'S RUN,
SOUTH BEND TO CHICAGO
MONDAY MAY 3 1915.

The travelers stayed in Chicago for three nights, leaving on May 6.

Personal

Chicken dinners and tip	$1.75

Chicago. The Blackstone

4 bellboys (or porters) luggage up	$1.00
Dinner for 2 (E. M. out) and tip[6]	$4.00
Theater (2)	$5.00
Telegram	$ .52
Coffee (2) and tip.	$1.10
Breakfast, E.M	$ .90
Tip	$ .25
Lunch (2)	$2.60
Tip	$ .30
Beautiful big double twin beds and dressing room	$7.00
Lovely small, single room and bath (E. M.)	$3.50
Laundry	$4.75
Valet	$2.00
Tailor, pressing two dresses	$2.00

Average one day's expenses, less extras than above.
Extras bought in Chicago:

Supply of potted meats, etc.	$9.35

At Woolworth's:

Kettle	$ .10
4 doz. plates	$ .20
Oiled paper	$ .10
2 doz, spoons	$ .10
Solid alcohol, lamp, saucepan (complete)	$1.25
Bread box	$3.45
Padlock	$ .30

Motor

Chicago. "Down Town" Garage.

---

6. Only dinner and lunch we had in the hotel. [An original Emily Post footnote]

Storage, three days	$2.25
Ground valves	$6.75
2 spark plugs	$2.00
Wash and polish (3 days)	$6.00
17 gals. gas (13c)	$2.21
2 qts. oil	$ .40
20 gals. gas	$2.60
1 gal. oil	$ .80

X

Mud!![1]

We have struck it!

It looks pretty much as though our motor trip to San Francisco were going to end in Rochelle, Illinois.

Thirty-six miles out of Chicago we met the Lincoln Highway and from the first found it a disappointment. As the most important, advertised and lauded road in our country, its first appearance was not engaging. If it were called the cross continent *trail* you would expect little and be philosophical about less, but the very word "highway" suggests macadam at the least. And with such titles as "Transcontinental" and "Lincoln" put before it, you dream of a wide straight road like the Route Nationale of France, or state roads in the East, and you wake rather unhappily to the actuality of a meandering dirt road that becomes mud half a foot deep after a day or two of rain![2]

Still we went over it easily enough until we passed De Kalb.[3] After that the only "highway" attributes left were the painted red, white and blue signs decorating the telegraph poles along the way. The highway itself disappeared into a wallow of mud! The center of the road was slightly turtle-backed; the sides were of thick, black ooze and unmanageably deep, and the car was *possessed*, as though it were alive, to pivot around and slide backward into it. We had no chains with us, and had passed no places where we could get any. Apart of the difficulty of keeping going on chain-

---

1. As noted earlier, Emily Post was traveling in the wettest spring anyone could remember.

2. Carl G. Fisher's original (and not very inspired) name for his proposed road was the Coast-to-Coast Rock Highway: the more patriotic Lincoln Highway was a reaction to Congress's proposed expenditure of $1.7 million on a memorial to Abraham Lincoln in Washington D. C.

3. See map No. 8, page 392. [An original Emily Post footnote]. In addition to having one of the "seedling miles" of the Lincoln Highway, De Kalb claims to be the birthplace of barbed wire.

less tires our only danger, except that of being bogged, was in getting over
the bridges that had no railings on their approaches. The car chasséd up
every one, swung over toward the embankment, slewed back on the bridge,
went across that steadily, and dove into the mud again! It certainly was
dampening to one's ardor for motoring. If the Lincoln Highway was
like this what would the ordinary road be after it branched away at Sterling?

A little car on ahead was slithering and sliding around too, although
it had four chains on it, but it did not sink in very far and it was getting
along much better than we were — so much better in fact, that at the end
of a few miles it slowly wobbled beyond our sight.[4]

Finally we turned a bend and there was a little car on ahead. Not the
same one however. This one evidently had no chains and was coming
toward us drunkenly staggering from side to side. Gradually the lower half
of it was hidden by the incline of an intervening bridge, then suddenly it
disappeared altogether. When we arrived at the bridge ourselves we saw
the car in a deep ditch almost over on its side. The occupants of it, a man
and a small boy, were both out and nothing, apparently, was hurt. The
small boy was having a heavenly time paddling around in mud way above
his knees, and the man called up to us cheerfully:

"'Twas m'own fault; I hadn't ought to 'a' come without chains on! No
use for you to stop, thank you! You couldn't help any and we'd only block
th'road between us. A team'll be along before long!"

Regretfully we left them and slipped and slid and staggered on for
some miles more.

"Oh," said Celia in the back, "how are we ever going up *that*?" "That"
was an awful embankment ahead which to look at made me feel as if I had
eaten nothing for a week. It was steep, narrow, turtle-backed, with black
slime, and had a terrifying drop at either side of its treacherous and
unguarded edges. The car went snorting up the incline until, nearly at
the top point where the drop was steepest, it balked and slid toward the
edge —!

"This is the end," I thought, wondering in the same second if any of
us would fall clear. For one of those eternity-laden moments we seemed
to hang poised on the brink. Then E. M. seemed almost to lift the huge
weight of the machine around bodily and compel it in spite of its help-
lessness to crawl up, up, up on the bridge.

Glancing back at Celia, after we were safely over, she looked about as

---

4. The next two paragraphs were not in the original *Collier's* article.

chalky and weak-kneed as I felt. A short distance further, however, we ran on the brick pavement of a town. The ragged red-brick buildings of the street we turned into were not very encouraging and we feared that again the Blue Book's hotel description might be one of those "complimentary" ones, consisting of its paid advertisement. E. M. urged our trying to get chains and going on to Davenport, but Celia and I had all the motoring in mud that we cared about. No matter how squalid the town, or how poor the accommodations, we meant to cross no more bridges like that last one until the roads dried! Then we made two turns like the letter Z and found ourselves in the sweetest, cleanest, newest little town imaginable. Its streets were all wide and smoothly paved with brick, and its houses, mostly white, were set each in a garden of trim and clipped green. There was a new post-office of marble magnificence and a shopping center of big-windowed, fresh-painted, enterprising stores, but no hotel except a dingy ramshackle tavern that we took for granted was the one mentioned in the guide book. We wondered if one of the neat, sweet little houses might perhaps take us to board instead.

In front of a garage was a man with a blue coat and brass buttons, and "Fire Chief" on them.[5] We asked if he knew anyone at whose house we could stay until the road dried. He looked at us and then at the car in a quizzical sort of way.

"Oh, y-es," he drawled. "You could put up at Mrs. Blake's, I guess."

We asked the way to Mrs. Blake's and then happened to remark that it was curious a town as up to date as this one had no good hotel. He lost his drawl immediately. "No good hotel? Well, I just guess there *is* a good hotel! The Collier Inn is just across that street and around the corner. It's a fine hotel."[6]

We cheered up instantly. But why hadn't he told us that sooner? He thought that "considerin' we had asked for a boarding-house, mebbe the hotel was too high-priced for us, but it was a fine hotel if we didn't mind the cost."

I don't know how we had missed it. It was a fair-sized yellow brick

5. The Fire Chief was George "String" Henzie, and the fire truck, a 1912 American La France model, was stored in the 1884 City Hall, which is now the town museum. My grateful thanks to Betty A. Barnes of the Flagg Township Historical Society for this and much more information on Rochelle.

6. Samuel Whitaker, who in 1914 went *Across The Continent in a Ford* (Done into print by his former pals at the Dean-Hicks plant at Grand Rapids, Michigan, 1915), also stayed in the Collier Inn in Rochelle, a place he liked: "Rochelle is a town after my own heart. A very pretty and prosperous looking city of 3500 inhabitants. The structures are mainly brick, the stores all neat and well kept and quite up-to-date." *http://www.wellswooster.com/ ford/phoenix.htm.* He made no comment on the hotel.

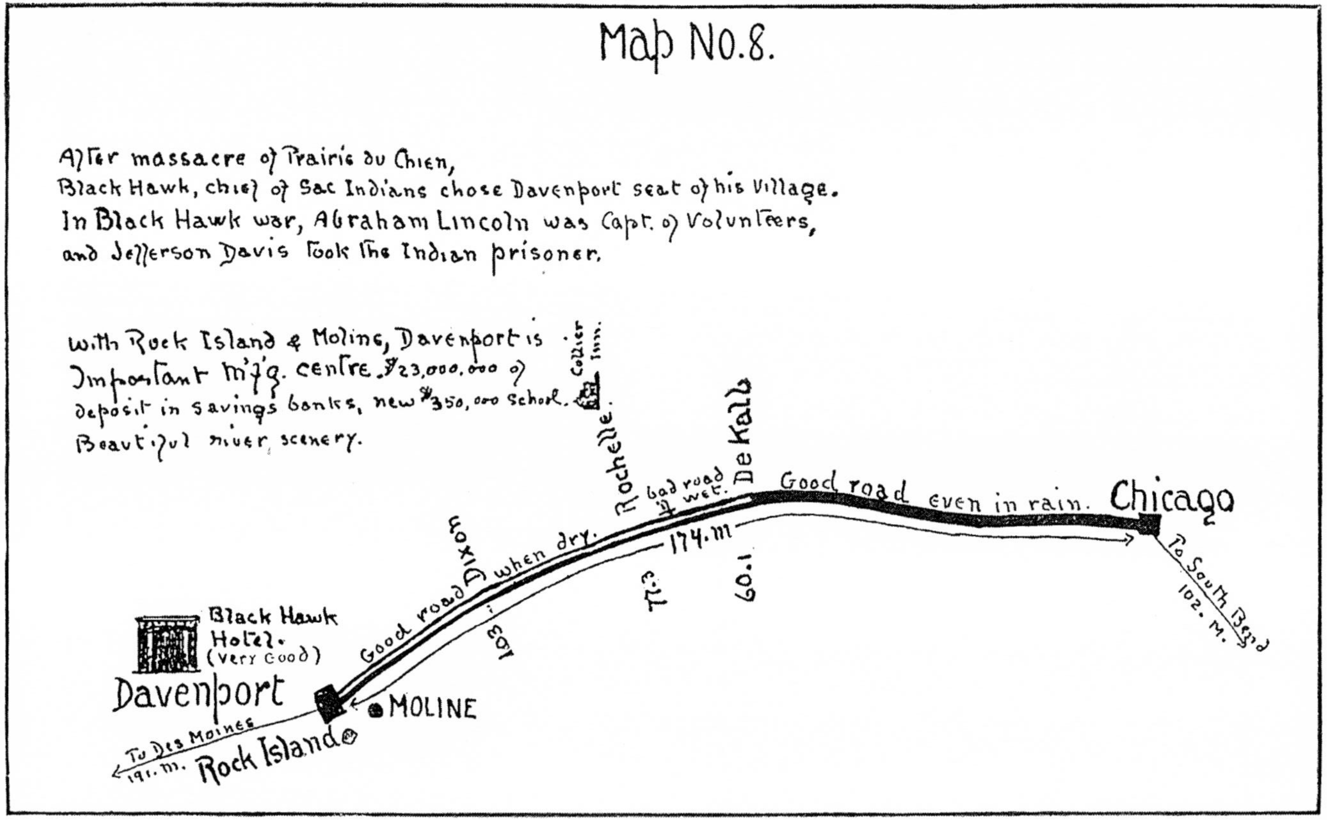

Map No.8.

After massacre of Prairie du Chien, Black Hawk, chief of Sac Indians chose Davenport seat of his village. In Black Hawk war, Abraham Lincoln was Capt. of Volunteers, and Jefferson Davis took the Indian prisoner.

With Rock Island & Moline, Davenport is important mfg. centre. $23,000,000 deposit in savings banks, new $350,000 school. Beautiful river scenery.

Chicago

To South Bend 102. M.

Good road even in rain

De Kalb

bad road when wet

60.1

174. m.

Rochelle

77.3

Dixon

good road when dry

103

MOLINE

Davenport

Black Hawk Hotel (Very Good)

Rock Island

To Des Moines 181. m.

building on a corner, a rather typical small-town commercial hotel. I went in expecting dingy darkness. The lobby looked like the office in a Maine summer resort. I asked — not that I for a moment expected to get it — for rooms with baths. The proprietor said, "Certainly," and showed me three new little rooms, each with a new little bathroom attached.

I returned to my companions grinning like a Cheshire cat. It seemed to us as though we had found a veritable Ritz![7]

---

7. The Collier was a three-story hotel with fifty rooms, bay windows on the corner, and a porch at the side.

Opposite: "Chicago to Davenport." This one hundred and eighty-mile journey took two and a half days from Thursday May 6 through Saturday May 8 because of the muddy conditions near Rochelle.

XI

In Rochelle

Twenty-four hours in a town like this and we feel as though we knew it and the people intimately. In many ways it suggests a toy-land town. Its streets are so straight and evenly laid, its houses so white and shining, its gardens so green, its shops so freshly painted, its displays in the windows so new, and its people so friendly.[1]

"Strangers in town!" they seem to say to themselves as they look at us, but instead of looking at us in a "wait until we know who you are before we take any notice of you," they seem quite ready to smile and begin a conversation.

Our most particular friend, as well as our oldest acquaintance, is the fire chief. E. M. has, of course, one or two other particular friends in the garage. If he can only find a mechanic or two to talk to, he is perfectly happy.[2] Celia's and my chief diversion has been going to the moving picture theaters, which is evidently the fashionable thing to do here. In the evening we saw three real theater parties. One of them was a very important affair; they met in the lobby and went down the aisle two by two; the ladies all had many diamonds, brand-new white-kid gloves quite tight, picture hats, corsage bouquets and boxes of candy.[3]

Celia and I had neither gloves nor hats on, and when we ran into the theater parties, we felt almost like urchins that had been caught wander-

---

1. Neither this nor the following three paragraphs were in the original *Collier's* piece.

2. As John A. Jakle has pointed out, motoring "encouraged different forms of social encounter." Emily Post's usual social circle almost certainly lacked fire chiefs. Her son Ned clearly became part of a "motoring fraternity" which included garage mechanics and other motorists, while Emily Post herself was at least marginally drawn into this fraternity. John A. Jakle, *The Tourist: Travel in Twentieth-Century America* (Lincoln: University of Nebraska Press, 1985), 104.

3. Emily Post went to the Majestic Theater, which was built in 1912, remodeled in 1915, and destroyed in a fire in the early 1940s.

ing into the foyer of the Metropolitan Opera House. Like our hatred of
caraway seeds, our love of hatlessness must be a family failing. In Chicago
two different papers took the trouble to mention E. M.'s carelessness in
the matter of head-covering. "Scorning to wear a hat even on occasions
when it is generally considered to be convenable," said one. The other
described him as "such a disciple of fresh air that he was seen driving a
big racing machine on Michigan Avenue without a hat!" Yet isn't it a popular supposition that the West is freer from conventions than the East?

The rain has finally stopped and this morning the sun is trying hard
to shine. To do much good it will have to shine steadily for about three
days. We walked to the end of the brick paving down one of the streets a
little while ago and looked at the black wet Lincoln Highway leading to
Sterling.

On our way back we met our friend the fire chief.

"Been to look at the mud?" asked he, cheerfully. "It isn't a bit bad now.
You ought to see it when it's muddy! Why, it took me eight hours to go
twenty-one miles! I did have to get a team of horses to pull me out of one
bog, but otherwise I got through all right."

"Didn't you strain your engine?" I asked him. "Oh, yes," he said cheerfully; "I guess I did, but I couldn't help that."

"Well, maybe you couldn't," I agreed, then added with confidential
finality, "but I tell you what we're going to do! We're going to put ours on
a nice, dry, comfortable freight car tomorrow morning and ship it past the
mud district — which is probably the width of the continent."

His warmth of manner fell suddenly to zero. I feared we had in some
way offended him because we thought his state muddy. "Of course it is a
lovely country to grow things in," I added quickly, "but you see we want
particularly to get to San Francisco, and the surest way is by freight."

But we could not put the broken conversation back together again.
In fact, our friend the fire chief doesn't smile any more. Our other friends,
the garage men, also look at us askance — in fact in some way we seem to
have lost our popularity.

Eighth Day's Run, Chicago to Rochelle Thursday May 6, 1915.

They stayed in Rochelle for two nights, May 6 and 7, 1915.

Personal

Rochelle, Ill. Collier Inn.
   (Typical day)
   (No bellboys)
   3 telegrams ... $1.48
   3 rooms with bath, one at $3,two at $2.50, including board ... $8.00
   Tips to waitress ... $ .75
   Tip to chambermaid ... $ .50
   "Movies," etc. ... $ .80
Left *Rochelle*, May 8

Motor

Stopped by mud at *Rochelle, Ill.*,
77 miles, May 6–7.
   Rochelle. Garage next door to Inn.[4]
   Storage, two days ... $1.00
   Wash car ... $1.50
   Chains (2) ... $3.60
   8 gals. gas ... $1.20

4. This was Lazier's Garage, "Home of the Studebaker," on the corner of Main and 4th Avenue. For a photograph of it, as well as of the post office, the Majestic cinema, the Collier Inn and the Ogle Inn, possibly the "ramshackle tavern" rejected by Emily Post, see *Rochelle "The City of Progress"* (S.P. Herrick for the Rochelle Chamber of Commerce, 1922, reprinted by the Flagg Township Historical Society, Rochelle, Illinois, 1988).

XII

The Weight of Public Opinion[1]

We know now what is the matter! They think we are quitters! They are so filled with a sense of shame for us that we are beginning to feel it ourselves. In spite of our original intention to go only as far as roads were good and accommodations were comfortable, we feel that we are somehow lacking in mettle, that we are sandless, to say the least.

To explain that we are not crossing the continent as a feat of endurance is useless; having started to motor to the West, our stopping this side of the place we set out for is to them incomprehensible.

"Why, *that* car ought to go through anything!" is all any of them can think of saying to us.

Our friend the fire chief stood glowering out in front of the garage all morning. I think he would have gone to great lengths to prevent our machine's incarceration in a freight car. The proprietor of the garage gave us his opinion: "Of course we drive pretty light vehicles around here, and yours is heavy and your wheels are uncommon narrow, but that engine of yours sure ain't no toy! I'd go through it if I was you! I wouldn't quit for a little *mud*! No, sir!"

"And only a *little mud* at that!" scornfully echoed the fire chief.

"And supposing we slide off one of those bridges, or turn turtle in a ditch?" asked we.

The chief scratched his head, but his determination was undaunted. "She'd be kind of heavy to fall on you," he grinned. "All the same, if that car was mine, I'd go right on plumb across Hell itself, I would!"

---

1. Very little of this chapter appeared in the original *Collier's* article, though the basic point remains: that the people of Rochelle thought they were quitters, and that when they eventually changed their minds the town turned out to see them off.

To finish what you have begun, to see it through at whatever cost, that seems to be the spirit here; it is probably the spirit of the West, the spirit that has doubled and trebled these towns in a few years. The consideration as to whether it is the wisest and most expedient thing to do, has no part in the process of their reasoning. That is exactly the point.

> Theirs not to reason why,
> Theirs not to make reply,
> Theirs but to do and die.[2]

Only they do not seem to die. They thrive gloriously.

All the same, if this country of ours ever gets into the war there will be the making of a second Balaklava regiment in a town in Illinois beginning with an R and a certain fire chief should make a gallant captain.

But magnificent as is their indomitability as a quality of character; for us, for instance, to wreck a valuable car, which we might never afford to replace, for the sake of saying that we were not stopped by any such trifle as mud seems more foolhardy than courageous. Nevertheless, they have in some way imbued us with their spirit to such a degree that we have countermanded the freight car, and although the mud is not a bit better, have put chains on and are going to start.

Enthusiasm was no name for it! The town turned out to see us off; the fire chief drove out his engine in all its brass and scarlet resplendency. The ban of our cowardly leanings toward freight cars was lifted and they saw us off on our muddy way rejoicing![3]

We are glad to have seen this little town. Maybe the contagion of its enthusiasm will remain with us permanently.

The mud, by the way, lasted only ten miles. The celebrated Lincoln Highway parted from us at Sterling and as soon as we left it, the ordinary, unadvertised River to River road that we had dreaded was splendid all the rest of the way to this beautiful hotel, the Black Hawk, in Davenport, Iowa.[4]

I was in a perfect flutter of excitement about crossing the Mississippi

---

2. Part of Alfred, Lord Tennyson's poem *The Charge of the Light Brigade* (1854), though Emily Post has reversed the first and second lines.

3. The town is still proud of its association with Emily Post. A story in the *Rochelle News-Leader* on December 30, 2001, was headed "Former Resident Researches Emily Post's Account of Trip to Rochelle," and describes work done by Sheridan A. (Rusty) Glen. The Historical Society also mounted a small exhibit on Emily Post's journey in the Town Hall.

4. The Black Hawk Hotel (which cost an estimated $800,000 to build) was brand new when Emily Post arrived; at that time it was seven stories high: four more floors were added in the 1920s, giving it four hundred rooms. Numerous celebrities, from Richard Nixon to Jack Dempsey, later stayed there, and after some vicissitudes it reopened in 1979 as the premier hotel in downtown Davenport.

though I have scarcely the courage to tell the unbelievably idiotic reason why![5] It was Mrs. Z., who had crossed the continent an uncountable number of times, who told me in all seriousness that the middle of the United States was cut unbridgeably in two by the Mississippi! Nothing spanned this divide except a railroad bridge, and the only way motorists had ever crossed was on the trestles in the middle of the night, against the law and at the risk of their lives! The bridges, needless to say, are many and quite as crossable as Manhattan to Brooklyn. The river itself is yellow as the Tiber, but its banks, devoid of factories and refuse collections, were enchantingly lovely, sloping and vividly green; a little like the upper Hudson, or still more, Queenstown Harbor in Ireland.

Davenport is evidently a gay resort. A friendly elevator boy detained E. M. and whispered: "Say, mister, there's a cabberay going on tonight on the island.[6] They'll be vaudeville, tangoing and a band!"[7] He must have put E. M.'s lack of enthusiasm at our door, for he added: "The fun doesn't start until late. You could easily take them," pointing toward us, "to a movie first. The Princess is high class and *re*fined. You take it from me and fix it to stay for a while. You'll find we're some lively town!"

EIGHTH DAY'S RUN, CONTINUED.
ROCHELLE TO DAVENPORT
MAY 8, 1915

Personal

Lunched *Rochelle.*
Davenport, Iowa. Black Hawk Hotel.

Dinner (3)	$3.40
Tip	$ .40
Hallboys, luggage up and down	$1.00

---

5. At this point, the original *Collier's* article said: "Two seemingly educated and otherwise intelligent New York women told me that the middle of the United States was cut in two unbridgeably by the Mississippi."

6. This was either Rock Island or Suburban Island; the latter was renamed Credit Island after the Davenport Board of Park Commissioners purchased it in 1918. See Marlys Svendsen, *Davenport 1836–1986: A Pictorial History* (Davenport: G. Bradley, 1986).

7. This is, of course, the early twentieth-century usage of gay as "lively." Just before Emily Post arrived in town, the local newspaper reported that it had been serenaded by Water's Concert Band, which was traveling with "The World at Home" Carnival and was "one of the best heard in Davenport for many a day." The *Davenport Democrat and Leader* (May 5, 1915), 11.

(Went down to riverbank and spent *nothing*.)[8]
Enormous twin-bed room and bath, very attractive
    furnishing $4.50
Single room and bath $1.50
(Best rooms for least price of any hotel we encountered)
Breakfast $ .60
Tip $ .25
Coffee and toast (2) $ .80
Tip $ .20

Motor

Davenport. Black Hawk Hotel's garage.
    10 gals. gas $2.20
    1 gal. oil $ .75
    Storage (night charge) $ .50
    Wash car $1.50
Started on road of mud to *Des Moines.* We went to
Cedar Rapids, but as it is out of the course between
Davenport and does not belong on this route, it is omitted.
There was an A1 garage there, but our experience in mud cost:
    Vulcanizing 3 tires $2.25[9]
    Taking off radiator, repair gear case $5.60
    Car in shop (no storage) wash $2.00
    20 gals. gas $4.40
    1 gal. oil $ .75

---

8. Davenport is one of the few cities on the Mississippi not to have a dike in place to prevent flooding, and the scenic view of the river meant that many people would stroll along
its banks. My thanks to Kevin Knoot, Special Collections Archivist of the State Historical
Society of Iowa, for this and other information on Davenport.
   9. Vulcanization is defined by Merriam Webster as "the process of treating crude or synthetic rubber or similar plastic material chemically to give it useful properties (as elastic-
ity, strength, and stability)."

XIII

Muddier!

The morning looked gray but having gone easily enough the day before with chains on, we no longer worried about a little rain. Nevertheless, we left our beautiful rooms at the Black Hawk in Davenport, Iowa, the best accommodations at the most reasonable rates that we have yet had, with a regret that has since been doubly intensified.

For seventy-five miles beyond Davenport the road was excellent; not macadam, but a wide, dustless surface of natural clay. The country was very much like that in southern New York and eastern New Jersey — a rolling picturesque landscape of green fields, beautiful trees and streams. As there were black clouds gradually coming up behind us, and we had as usual forgotten to bring any food except our tinned collection, it seemed wiser when we got to Iowa City to buy some sandwiches rather than stop at the Hotel Jefferson, and give the black clouds a chance to catch up.[1] At an eating-place that had a sign on it: "Every Sort of Sandwiches Ready," a gum-chewing youth leaning against the shelves behind the counter pushed a greasy bill of fare toward me. From a list of chicken, ham, tongue and cheese sandwiches, I ordered three chicken — we could not do with less and I doubted if we'd care for more. They hadn't any chicken! "Ham, then?" There wasn't any ham! "Tongue?" The youth thought if we weren't in a hurry he might be able to get some canned tongue at the grocer's down the street; the only sandwiches he had ready were of cheese laid between huge hunks of bread and each garnished with a radish skewered on the top with a toothpick!

Celia meanwhile by chance discovered an apartment called "Woman's Rest Room" where she got some delicious homemade coffee-cake and rolls. Those with our own potted meats or jams were, of course, all anyone could

---

1. The Hotel Jefferson on Washington Street in Iowa City now belongs to the University of Iowa and houses, among other things, the American Studies Department.

89

ask. That is always the difficulty — a stranger in town has no idea where to go for anything.

From a point about ten miles beyond Iowa City the story of that dreadful day ought to be written in indigo of the darkest shade. It was such an experience as to dampen your enthusiasm as an adventuring motorist forever; but that leaves you at least a great appreciation of Pullman trains, or even old-fashioned stage coaches — any means of conveyance that can keep going, right end first.

Our delay in foraging had given the black clouds time to gain on us. But after observing them uneasily for a mile or two, we felt confident that we were keeping ahead of them, until about ten miles further, at which point we had a puncture — our very first — and the rain caught us. We debated whether we had better go back to Iowa City or whether we should try to run one hundred and thirty miles in the rain to Des Moines.

E. M. was not at all enthusiastic about going on. In fact he had not wanted to leave Davenport. As he is certainly not apt to care about weather we ought to have paid exceptional attention to his dubiousness. But he only said something about a strain on his engine, to which I paid no great attention — as I feel perfectly confident that no matter what happens, he is not going to let that engine get hurt very much if it is in his power to prevent it. The engine is to him what Chicago is to Chicagoans, the very child of his heart; its every little piece of steel or aluminum as personally precious to him as a baby's tooth or curl is to its doting parent. We can all be tired or hungry, wet or cold, or broiling and thirsty, it means nothing to him as long as that engine is comfortably purring under its bonnet. But the slightest complaint on its part, the faintest squeak or grumble, the smallest thing that he feels may disagree with it, and he is unspeakably miserable.[2]

However, the rain seemed to be only a drizzle, and the roads looked so hard and splendid, we concluded it would surely take many hours of downpour to get them in a bad condition — if in fact they were likely to be much affected at all. So although as a precaution E. M. put on chains, we went on in tranquil ignorance of the Nemesis that lurked in waiting.

As an illustration of what rain in Iowa can do, twenty-five minutes of drizzle turned the smooth, hard surface of the road into the consistency of gruel. Not only that, but as though it were made in layers, and the top layer slid off the under layers and the under layers slipped out between, or the reverse. Our wheels, even with chains on, had no more hold than revolving cakes of soap might have on slanting wet marble. The car not

---

2. This paragraph was not in the *Collier's* article. In line with her generally Anglophile position, Emily Post is using the British term for a car's hood.

only zigzagged sideways, backwards, every way but forward, unless some unexpected obstacle or pitfall loomed or yawned in our path, in which case it was seized with an impetuous desire to plunge to destruction. We saw two unfortunate automobiles already landed in the ditch.[3] One, luckily, was being hauled out by a team, but the second was on a lonely stretch of road, and embedded far above the hubs. Its occupants peered out at us sympathetically, as they saw we were utterly powerless to help. We were just balancing this way and that, and for a while it looked as though we were going to park ourselves beside them. We could only call out as we finally slithered by, that we would send back a team from a town ahead — if we ever got to one.

At the end of an hour of this swerving, crawling misery, we had a second puncture. There was a barn near by, and the farmer, a German, let us drive in and change the tire under cover. We asked if there was any town nearer and less out of our course than Cedar Rapids. Or would he himself, or perhaps one of his neighbors, take us in? No, he did not want any boarders in his house; he said it with quite a surly manner; his neighbors had no liking for strangers, either. Cedar Rapids was our nearest place.[4]

In contrast to the kindness with which he had motioned us to come into his barn in the first place, it struck us that he was on closer acquaintance, surprisingly curt. But it was not until afterwards, in the light of later experience, that we realized his manner had become intentionally unfriendly.

The tire changing went very quickly, and in a few minutes we were on the road again. Celia and I ate our luncheon, but E. M., struggling with the zigzagging car, had no thought for food and ate only a mouthful or two that I fed him as he drove. It was by now pouring hard and we seemed to be making less and less progress. One thing, we now quite understood what our friend the fire chief meant when he said the road around Rochelle was only a little muddy. Without hesitating a moment we would be willing to swear the mud championship of the world belongs to Iowa. Illinois

---

3. Material from this point through the next two paragraphs was not in the original account; American attitudes toward Germans had perhaps hardened in the months between original publication and the appearance of the book.
4. Emily Post had probably met members of the Amana Colonies of Pennsylvania Dutch, who spoke, and still speak German, and who were under considerable local suspicion during World War I. This was the time, as textbooks tell us, that all things German were suspect; when sauerkraut was renamed Liberty Cabbage and some orchestras refused to play Beethoven. See Joan Liffring-Zug Bourret *Life in Amana 1867–1935: Reporters' Views of the Communal Way* (Iowa City, Iowa: Pennfield Press, 1998), which contains a reprint from a local newspaper suggesting that while the colonists insisted they were loyal Americans, other Iowans considered them "as German as if they actually were on German soil." My thanks to the reference staff at Cedar Rapids public library for this information.

mud is slippery and slyly eager to push unstable tourists into the ditch, but in Iowa it lurks in unfathomable treachery, loath to let anything ever get out again that ventures into it. Our progress through it became hideously like that of a fly crawling through yellow flypaper — as though it were a question of time how soon we would be brought to an exhausted end, and sink into it forever!

At the end of two hours more, we had gone ten miles. Cedar Rapids was still nearly twenty miles away. *Twenty miles!* Could anyone in a life-time go so far as that? Could any machine hold out so endlessly? In another hour we had gone only four miles further, and by no means sure of our road, and then came a third puncture! It was one of those last straws that seem to finish everything. You think you just can't live through it and struggle more. Much better give up and *lie* down in the fly-paper and stay there. We were at the top of a fairly steep hill, so that we might perhaps be able to go on again, but to see E. M., already exhausted, and not a soul to help him, get out again into that drenching rain — he had no raincoat and the mud was over his shoetops — and we had started on the trip in the first place because he had been ill — I could easily have burst into tears. Which exhibition of courage would have helped the situation such a lot!

Meanwhile he was having a hopeless time trying to jack the car up. There was no foundation for the jack to stand on, so that it merely bur-rowed down into the clay. Some men lounged out of the one house near by. They were Germans. All the inhabitants seemed to be German. They approached with seeming friendliness, but on closer inspection of us, their demeanor noticeably changed. There was something in our appearance they did not like. I thought perhaps they resented our car's waltzing, or thought that E. M.'s jack was harmfully puncturing the surface of their beautiful road. Two of them shrugged their shoulders and all of them looked at us in impassive silence that was neither friendly nor polite. Then a younger man appeared who came forward as though to offer to help, but stopping to look inquisitively at the radiator top, he too, grew sullen. And then we understood! The emblem of the Royal Automobile Club of Lon-don was put on when we were in England last year; and as it is very pretty, we happen never to have taken it off, and the men were Germans![5] That's

---

5. In the original version, Emily Post said the emblem was "soldered on" rather than "very pretty" which was why they had never taken it off. The Royal Automobile Club (not to be confused with the modern RAC which provides automobile services) was founded in 1897, and by 1911 occupied splendid premises on the site of the old War Office on London's Pall Mall. When war broke out in 1914 the building was put at the disposal of the armed services: the Pall Mall facility practically became an officers' club, and the British Red Cross Society used a portion of it.

why they wouldn't help us. We had asked for a piece of plank that one of them was holding; the man carried it away. Finally, when that dreadful tire was at last on, they would not even tell us the way until I asked in German. Then one of them laconically pointed it out.

Hot, tired, and soaked as a drowned rat, E. M. for three and a half hours longer guided the steaming, floundering and irresponsible machine until at last by supreme effort he got us to Cedar Rapids.

XIV

One of the
Fogged Impressions

Somewhere we read a sign "Cedar Rapids suits me. It will suit you." Of course after those last six hours of mud-wallowing agony C-e-d-a-r R-a-p-i-d-s simply spelled Heaven. But after we were dry and warm and fed — such is the ingratitude of human nature and tourist — we would have very gladly gone away again.[1]

> I do not like thee, Doctor Fell,
> The reason why, I cannot tell —[2]

explains our feelings rather perfectly. We were tired; at least E. M. was exhausted, and Celia and I were tired probably in sympathy. Also it is always disappointing to start out for a place and not be able to get there, and little things sometimes sum up a feeling of depression quite out of proportion to their importance.

We went over bad pavement, and came to some more that was torn up, so that the city had an upheaved effect. It was all drenched in rain, and the little we saw of it looked ugly and brown, and finally our rooms were completely sapping to joyfulness of spirit. Perhaps if we had come from a hotel less attractive than the Black Hawk in Davenport, we should not have so keenly felt the contrast, but the rooms we were in depressed us to the

---

1. This sentence originally ended "if anything but motoring in the mud had been the alternative."

2. "...But this I know, I know full well/ I do not like you, Dr. Fell." Thomas Brown (1663–1704) English satirist, author of *Dialogues of the Dead*, produced his famous poem while a student at Christchurch College, Oxford, on the demand of Dean John Fell. An extemporaneous translation of Martial's Thirty-third epigram, "Non amo te, Sabidi," it apparently saved him from rustication. Brown is buried in Westminster Abbey near his friend the playwright Mrs. Aphra Benn.

verge of melancholia.[3] Dingy bottle-green paper, a stained carpet, a bath-room in which the plumbing wouldn't work, a depressing view of a torn-up street! I wandered around the cow-path surrounding my big bed in my narrow room, looked out at the weeping sky, and wondered whether we were going to have this sort of thing all the way — these dust-filled hideous rooms, cleaned only by a carpet sweeper; these sooty, ugly, busy, noisy towns.[4] And the meals — those anemic chilled potatoes, beans full of strings, everything slapped on plates any which way, and everything tast-ing as though it had come out of the same dishwater!

Whenever I am far away from home and uncomfortable, I think of the story Eleanor Hoyt Brainard once told me. After a long chapter of mis-adventures on one of those dreadful journeys where she missed the good boat and rocked about on a little one, failed to get accommodations at the places she counted on, and as a last straw took a wrong continental train, and finally too exhausted to sleep was settling herself for the night in the corner of a third-class day coach, she began to cry. "Oh, dear!" she sobbed, "its just come over me we have a perfectly good home! And I wonder *why* we don't stay in it more!"[5]

When my article appeared in *Collier's*, a Cedar Rapids newspaper arose in wrath and said we must have put up at a third-rate hotel. I agree with its rating, but was told it was the best in town. I do realize, however, that it is a very distorted judgment that appraises a town by a few rooms in an hotel. Unless you stay in a city long enough to know some of its peo-ple, to learn something about its atmosphere and personality, your opin-ion of it is as valueless as your opinion of a play would be, after seeing only the posters on the outside of a theater. Yet if you are a transient tourist, it is the room you are shown into that necessarily colors your impression of that city. If your room is fresh and clean and comfortable, you give the attributes of newness, cleanness and up-to-dateness to the city itself. An ugly, down-at-heels, uncomfortable hotel makes you think the same of the city. You can't help it, can you? Besides which we had come to see the country and not stop, rained in, for indefinite periods in towns that differed in no way from dozens of others in the East. It was the West, the

---

3. At this point Emily Post had originally waxed nostalgic about the "little inns of France, Austrian Tyrol, or Switzerland, with their shining spotlessness redolent of hours and hours of soap and water scrubbing, their simple fare, but so appetizingly flavored and served."

4. Portable electric vacuum cleaners were in their infancy: William H. Hoover set up his company in 1908, to manufacture a machine invented by his wife's cousin the previous year.

5. Inquiries of the Brainard family (who have Hoyts as part of their lineage) have failed to identify Eleanor Hoyt Brainard. In the original version, Emily Post ascribed this sen-tence to herself and her cousin Alice.

real great, free, open West we had come to see. Ranches, cowboys, Indians, not little cities like sample New Yorks.[6]

At the hotel there was a large Bakers' Convention. A suggestively domestic affair in more ways than one, since many had brought their wives. As though in an advertisement of the nourishing quality of a wheat diet, men and women were nearly all pleasingly plump. We noticed, also, that every man without exception had a solitaire diamond ring on his wedding-ring finger. Sometimes the wife had only a wide gold wedding-ring, but her husband was in diamonds. I don't know whether bread is a specialty of Cedar Rapids, or whether an effort was made to do particular honor to the bakers, but bread was the one thing on the menu that proved to be really good.[7]

There were two bakers and their wives, elderly couples, who sat at the table next to us. One of the wives had a wretched cough and the other was rather deaf; and to the combination we owe an anecdote that I hope they did not mind our over-hearing, or my repeating.

It seems the husband of the wife who had the cough, sent for a doctor who had been out night after night on serious cases until the poor man was completely exhausted. In order to listen to the patient's breathing he put his head on her chest and told her to "count four." The husband came into the room and heard his wife counting "One hundred and forty-six — one hundred and forty-seven —" and the doctor sound asleep!

It was in Cedar Rapids, too, that our waitress told us about an automobile she had just bought, to drive out in the evenings! As a newspaper afterwards printed in criticism of my above remark, "Tips in the West may be larger than the earnings of dyspeptic authoresses in the East!"[8]

---

6. *Collier's* did not print readers' letters, so angry responses would either appear in local newspapers, as described here, or in letters to the editor, which were never published. A search of the *Cedar Rapids Gazette* for the weeks following publication of the second *Collier's* article was fruitless, but my thanks to the reference staff of the Cedar Rapids Public Library for their efforts.

7. The anecdote about the baker's wife and the doctor was not in the *Collier's* article.

8. The original conclusion to this paragraph read: "Thus has the fad found its way into every crevice of the country!"

XV

A Few Ways of the West

Just as the good roads turned into mud slides in a few minutes, a few hours of sun and wind transformed them into good ones again. After only two days' delay we went back over the scene of all our misery and the distance out of our way that had taken us nearly six hours, we skimmed over in less than one, returning to our Des Moines road with a little delay and no misadventure.[1] (Our non-interruptible chauffeur paying no attention to the suggestion of stopping to taste the famous springs at Colfax.)[2]

When we arrived in Des Moines, as E. M. wanted to take the car to a garage to have some things fixed, Celia and I went out by ourselves on foot. The first vehicle we say had a sign on it "Jitney, 5 cents."[3] Never having been in one, and not caring a bit where it took us, we promptly got in.

"Now, what are we going to see?" asked Celia, not addressing anyone in particular.

"Strangers?" questioned the driver affably, turning around.

"Yes," said Celia, "what can we see from your car?"

"Well, there's the Capitol — I go right by that, and the finest buffaloes in the State are less'n a block further out. You could go see the buffaloes and then walk back to the Capitol."

"Excellent!" we agreed.

The buffaloes were stuffed in a case at the museum, but they must

---

1. Very little of this chapter was in Emily Post's original *Collier's* article. The new material begins here and continues until the paragraph dealing with the "topsy-turviness" of Des Moines.

2. Colfax, named after Colfax Schuyler who became vice president of the United States under U.S. Grant, is twenty miles east of Des Moines. After mineral springs were discovered there in 1875 hotels were built and it became a "little Carlsbad," at least until the water ceased to flow.

3. The term jitney is slang term for a nickel. Around the turn of the century, many five-cent bus services sprang up throughout the country, and the fare gave rise to the name.

certainly have been among the finest in the world when they were alive. We also saw some stuffed prairie dogs. But out here you need not go in a museum to see them! After the museum we walked through the Capitol, a fine building splendidly situated on a height overlooking the city and its dome newly gleaming with gold.[4] When we were descending the many steps of the Capitol's terrace, we saw the same jitney driver who had brought us there, and his car being empty, he drew up expectantly at the curb. Not wanting, however, to return to the spot we had started from, we suggested that he take off his sign and drive us about by the hour.

He grinned broadly. Sure he would! Also he augmented his price with equal alacrity. Then rolling up his "5–cent" sign, and surveying his unplacarded machine in evident satisfaction, he said jauntily:

"I tell you! The cops'll think I'm the showfer of a *millionaire*! When you're nothing but a jitney you stay behind here, and you don't go there! But you bet they'll let me through *now* all right!"

As a jitney he had been trundling along briskly, but now assuming all the characteristics of those who are hired by time instead of by distance, he never let the speedometer go above eight miles an hour; tried his best to keep it at six and stalled the engine about every hundred yards, until at the end of a very little while of halting and creeping we found his tin-kettle tramp machine acute punishment. We told him that if he would only go quickly, we would willingly pay for a second hour's drive at the end of twenty minutes. But nothing we could any had any effect on him. He kept on at the same dot-and-go-one creep. Finally, in desperation, Celia shrieked:

"If you don't get us home at once, it will be too late! You will have to take us to the asylum!"

He looked around at Celia like a scared rabbit, and in her frenzied countenance found evidently no reassurance, for he took us home at a speed that broke the traffic regulations—even for the "showfers of millionaires!"

In a few of our impressions, Des Moines had an eccentric topsy-turviness as though we had stumbled into the pages of "Alice in Wonderland." At the Chamberlain, an old-fashioned General Grant style of hotel, the elevator boys sit on chairs *in the center* of the elevator and the guests stand.[5] When I asked to have a cup of coffee and toast sent to my room the next

---

4. The state capitol building was completed in 1886, and the dome was regilded in 23 carat gold in 1905, and "recently" before 1915. My thanks to Joan Arnett, Tour Guide supervisor, Iowa State House, for this information.

5. The Chamberlain Hotel was built around 1896. It was on the corner of 7th Street and Grand Avenue, on the site of the former Westminster Presbyterian Church. In August 1915,

morning at half-past seven, the head waitress raised her eyebrows and explained:

"If you will tell the clerk at the desk, he will have your room called at whatever hour you say."

"I don't want my room called," I protested, "I want you to send my coffee up to me at seven-thirty."

She looked vaguely puzzled. Then in a moment she said, with obvious intention to be kind: "Don't you think you better just leave a rising call? Because maybe you will feel all right in the morning and'll want to come down for your breakfast."[6]

We also found another original idea in hotel service. At the Chamberlain we were told that our rooms would be two dollars and a half apiece, but our bill was two-fifty for one and five-fifty for the other two. When I asked why, the clerk said: "Didn't you have the door open between?"

"Certainly we did."

"Well, you see," he explained, "that makes the room *en suite,* so it is fifty cents extra."

The interest people take in population is very amazing to us. Ask any New Yorker the city's population and two out of five will shrug their shoulders. Ask anyone out here — man, woman or child — you will get on the spot the figures of the last census — plus the imagined increase since!

At random I asked two young girls looking in a milliner's window. In the midst of their exclamations about the "swellness" of a black and white hat they answered in unison, "Eighty-six thousand, three hundred and sixty-eight."

"A Mrs. Simson had twins this morning — that makes eighty-six thousand, three hundred and seventy, doesn't it?"

"Why, yes— that's so," beamed one of them.

"But six deaths would make it six less!"

For a moment they looked disconcerted, then the other answered brightly: "Oh, the deaths'll come off the next census taking, and there'll be *ever* so many births before that!"

Des Moines newspapers were full of the glory of their city. "Enterprise, confidence, civic pride are what makes the citizenship of our city!" "Des Moines is ever going forward!" are sentences we read. "Nothing the matter with Des Moines!" was the title of a leader in one of them. What

---

some three months after Emily Post's visit, it was the center of much excitement when the judges, who were occupying rooms in the Chamberlain, spent half the night deciding who had won the first Des Moines Speedway race.

6. The next nine paragraphs were also additions to the *Collier's* account.

was the matter with Des Moines, we wondered. The article did not tell us. It only said: "With our new thirteen-story building and the new gilded dome of the Capitol, Des Moines towers above the other cities of the State like a lone cottonwood on the prairie."

However, levity aside, when Des Moines has completed the parkway in front of the Capitol, and built up all of the embankment like the stretch that is already finished, the city with its civic center will be one of the most beautiful and perfect in the world. Already a community of beautiful buildings and houses, one day Des Moines will probably put up a last word in hotels. Maybe Des Moines, being a city of homes, doesn't care about hotels! Don't think from this that the Chamberlain is poor! It is a perfectly comfortable and well-run hotel, but not truly representative of this fine city.[7]

In a little hotel the other day a waitress rushed out of the dining-room and shouted to the clerk behind the desk at which I was standing:

"Say, have you seen Charlie?"

"Who wants him?"

"Miss Higgins."

"Excuse me a minute," said the clerk, as he went to look for Charlie, the proprietor, for Miss Higgins, the waitress!

Most of the hotels so far have been comfortable and nearly all clean. One of the exceptions has a story, and because of the story I cannot bear to tell its name. "A new house," the clerk we left in the morning told us, "doing a big business. Yes, you had better telegraph ahead for rooms."[8]

Escorted by negro bellboys we entered a terra cotta and green lobby, the walls and ceilings of which protuberated with green and orange and brown and iron and gold and plaster, and all smudged with many wipings in of soot.

The clerk, or proprietor, was a ray of welcoming attentiveness. Yes, indeed, he had saved rooms with baths for each of us, he was the pink of personal neatness and we hoped the bellboys' color had not been chosen with a purpose. Our rooms, however, were brown and sooty, and in my bathroom I wrote the word "dirt" on the washstand with my finger and it showed like a rut in the road. We went down to dinner not expecting much. And, had surprisingly good food in a spotlessly clean dining room! When I went to bed the electric lights would not turn on, and as no one answered the bell I gave up ringing and went to bed in the dark. The ther-

---

7. Perhaps the people of Des Moines had objected to the description of the Chamberlain, so Emily Post added these two sentences.
8. The story of this unnamed hotel, complete with its racial and ethnic slurs, was not in the original article.

mometer was about ninety-five; everything felt gritty, and in front of my eyes blinked mockingly an intermittent electric sign which in letters six feet high flashed all through the night about a snow-white laundry!

I was awakened by a waiter with my breakfast, which couldn't have been better; clean silver, unchipped china, and the best coffee and toast we had had anywhere! Evidently the man who ran the restaurant was good, and whoever ran the chambermaid was bad, and whoever decorated the place in terra cotta, green, bronze and crimson was criminal! The nice man at the desk was evidently the proprietor; we wondered whether to tell him about the electric light and the bells that did not work, and the good-for-nothing chambermaid, but decided that either he knew it and could not help it or that he did not know it and did not want to! When I went to the office to pay our bill he was so really attentively interested in our welfare that I found myself saying politely: "We have been very comfortable."

The man's look of wistfulness changed to one of pitying perplexity: "You have been comfortable! Here?" He smiled as one would smile at a child who was trying to say it did not mind the splinter in its finger.

"I had a delicious breakfast," I found myself saying enthusiastically. "Really I did. The best toast I have had since I left my home."

"Did you?" He seemed pleased and interested. "You were lucky."

His expressionless, dry tone and impersonal smile would have made Hodge in "The Man from Home" even more famous.[9]

"Don't you mind my feelings," he said, "you needn't try to pretend my house is first-class or even second! I've seen good hotels, and I know!" He leaned over the desk and away from one of the "shoe men." "It's about fourth-class; that's *just* about what it is."

"There is just one thing the matter—" I hesitated.

"*One*, which one?"

"A dirty chambermaid."

"Oh, they're Polacks! Housekeeper can't break them in! They are something like cats; they don't take to water! No, ma'am, there is a big difference between this house and the ones in New York City, I know that; but all the same," and the first look of pride crept into his face, "this hotel's the best in the city. The others'd tumble to pieces if you stepped in 'em."

A great deal of Iowa is uncultivated, picturesque, with grazing lands, many trees, —chiefly beautiful cottonwood, — and streams, and much prettier than Illinois, although Illinois was to me interesting because of the immense flat farms of grain, and the houses in groups, like being placed

---

9. William T. Hodge starred in the Broadway play *The Man from Home* in 1908–09. It became a Hollywood movie in 1915.

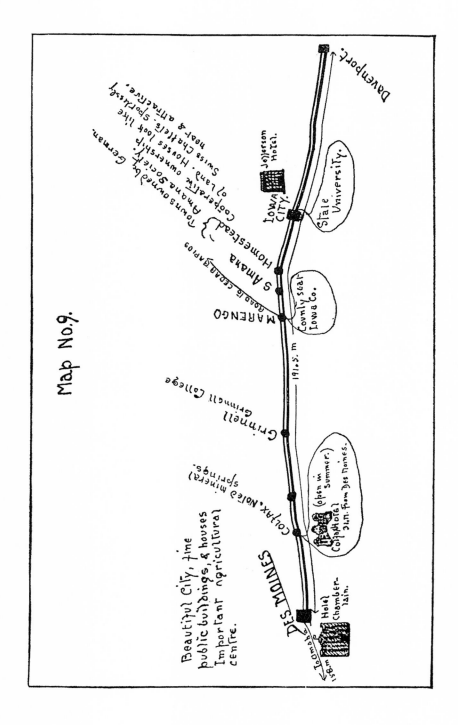

Map No. 9.

Davenport.

Jefferson Hotel.

IOWA CITY.

State University.

S. Amana } Homestead } Town-owned by Amana Society. Co-operative ownership of Land. Houses look like Swiss Chalets. - sportless, neat, & attractive.

German.

MARENGO

Good & Cedar Rapids

County seat Iowa Co.

191.5. m

Grinnell College

Colfax, Noted mineral springs.

(open in Summer.) Colfax Hotel 31m. from Des Moines.

DES MOINES

Beautiful City, fine public buildings, & houses Important agricultural centre.

Hotel Chamberlain.

Toombs 158.m

at the hub of a wheel, the farms spreading out like the spokes. The houses were like those in New England, white with green shutters and well built. All of this great Western country is rich on its face value, and it is little surprise to be told of the wealth reputed to these landowners.

Every town through the Middle West seems to have a little grill of brick-paved streets; a splendid post-office building of stone or brick or marble; a court-house, but of an older period generally; and one or two moving picture houses; two or three important-looking dry-goods stores, and some sort of hotel, and in it a lot of drummers in tilted-back chairs exhibiting the soles of their shoes to the street.

[Emily Post omitted details of her enforced detour to Cedar Rapids, an experience she clearly wanted to forget, and did not name the hotel she described in such lurid detail.]

NINTH DAY'S RUN, DAVENPORT TO DES MOINES VIA CEDAR RAPIDS

Personal

Des Moines. Chamberlain Hotel.

Tips, bellboys etc., as usual	$1.75
Drive in the converted jitney	$5.00
Dinner (3)	$3.75
Tip	$ .35
Breakfast	$ .75
Tip	$ .25
Sundries	$ .80
Coffee and toast (in room) (2)	$1.10
2 single rooms (bath between)	$5.50
1 single room and bath	$2.50
Lunch to take with us	$2.25
Ice cream	$ .30

Motor

Des Moines. Bernhard and Turner Auto Co.

Vulcanizing tire	$ .75
Storage	$ .50
20 gals. gas (22c.)	$4.40
2 qts. oil	$ .30

Opposite: "Davenport — Cedar Rapids — Des Moines," Sunday May 9 and Monday May 10, 1915.

XVI

Halfway House

Where, Oh, where is the West that Easterners dream of — the West of Bret Harte's stories, the West depicted in the moving pictures?[1] Are the scenes no longer to be found except in the pages of a book, or on a cinematograph screen? We have gone half the distance across the continent and all this while we might be anywhere at home. Omaha is a big up-to-date and perfectly Eastern city, and the Fontanelle is a brand-new hotel where we are going to stay over a day in order to luxuriate in our rooms.[2]

One act of cruelty, however, I hereby protest against; they sent to our rooms a tempting bill of fare — a special and delicious-sounding luncheon at only sixty cents! When we hurried down to order it, we were told it was sold solely to the traveling men in their café, Celia and I not admitted. E. M. said it was as good as it sounded — much interest was that to us! Also that he sat at a table with a traveler for the Ansco Photographic Company.[3] E. M. had some very poor films we had taken, and after luncheon

---

1. Francis Brett Harte (1836–1902) was born in Albany, NY, and went to California in 1854, where he worked as a compositor in San Francisco. During his time as Secretary of the US Mint in San Francisco (1864–70) he published a number of poems, and founded the *Overland Monthly* (1870) to which he contributed stories such as *The Luck of the Roaring Camp* and *The Outcasts of Poker Flat*. Westerns became one of the staples of the silent film era. Tom Mix, a former rodeo champion, made more than one hundred westerns between 1910–17 before he moved to the Fox studios and became a superstar. One of his roles in 1915 was as *The Man from Texas* in which he played a cowboy who fought cattle rustlers, dealt with a dishonest sheriff, and killed his sister's betrayer.

2. The newly-opened fourteen-story Fontanelle was Omaha's grandest hotel for many years.

3. The name of Ned Post's lunch companion is not known, but Ansco, the company he worked for, was founded in 1841 by Edward Anthony who was trained as a daguerrotypist by Samuel Morse; the firm grew to be one of the biggest photographic companies in the United States. In 1881 Anthony started producing cameras for the general public under an advertising slogan "Photography for the Millions." In 1907 his firm merged with another well-established company, Scovill and Adams, and the name was shortened to Ansco. In 1927 they merged with Agfa, the German photographic firm, which became Agfa-Ansco.

his new friend made him some prints. The results were little short of marvellous. If it was the paper — why does anyone ever use any other? If it was the man, Oh, why doesn't he open a hospital for the benefit of weak and decrepit amateur films.[4]

On the subject of food, the cumulative effect of a traveling diet is queer. After many days of it you feel as though you had been interlined with a sort of paste. Everything you eat is made of flour, flour, and again flour. A friend of ours took a trip around the world going by slow stages. After a month or two her letters were nothing except dissertations on the state of the cleanliness of hotels and the quality of the food. Alas! We are getting the same attitude of mind. Ordinarily the advantage of motoring is that if you don't like the appearance of the hotel you come to, you can go on. Out here where one stopping place is fifty or a hundred miles away from the other, that is not possible, unless you are willing to drive nights and days without a pause, or sleep along the roadside and be independent of hotels altogether. We are not traveling that way — yet.[5]

Omaha, as everyone knows, is divided from Council Bluffs by the coffee-colored Missouri. How can as much mud as that be carried down current all the time and leave any land above, or any river below?

It seemed to us that Council Bluffs and Omaha were comparatively not unlike Brooklyn and Manhattan. Council Bluffs is much the smaller city and the Bluffs from which it takes its name are not steep river embankments as we had supposed, but a high residence-crowned hill behind and above its innumerable railroad stations. Nothing, by the way, seems more typical of American towns than to have a "residential district" on the "heights."

Omaha, as I said before, is an impressively up-to-date city with many fine new buildings, important dwellings and beautiful avenues on which, last but not least, motors are made hospitably welcome. In nearly all Eastern cities automobiles are treated as though they were loitering tramps; continually ordered by the police to "keep moving along." In Omaha they avenues are so splendidly wide that they can afford chalked-off parking

---

The trademark was later purchased by the Haking Company of Hong Kong, which makes inexpensive photographic products.

4. This paragraph and the next were not in the original *Collier's* article.

5. What has been called "gypsying" or family automobile camping was popular at the time Emily Post wrote. A response to President Theodore Roosevelt's call for the "strenuous life" as well as a reaction to Victorian gentility, numerous middle-class Americans took to the road in the 1910s. See Warren Belasco, "Commercialized Nostalgia: The Origins of the Roadside Strip," in David L. Lewis and Laurence Goldstein, eds., *The Automobile and American Culture* (Ann Arbor: University of Michigan Press, 1991), 105–122.

places in the center of the streets where motors can stand unmolested and indefinitely.[6] If only New York and Boston had the space to follow their example!

Much as New Yorkers go to Sherry's or the Ritz, Omaha society seems to come to the Fontanelle to dine.[7] On Sunday evenings, we are told, it is impossible to secure a table unless ordered long in advance. Even on an ordinary evening, the dining-room of the Fontanelle looked like an "Importers' Opening." A few women looked smart, but a number suggested the probability of their having arrayed themselves to take part in tableau vivants, or an amateur fashion parade.[8]

A young girl with pink tulle draped around the lower half of her face bent the top edge down gingerly while she ate a few mouthfuls, and then carefully arranged it across the tip of her nose again. It seemed to be another example beside that of banting for thinness, of *faut avoir faim pour etre belle*.[9]

A quite plump matron had on a high-necked dress of white satin hooped around the hips, and trimmed with black velvet; another wore black charmeuse,[10] the neck and sleeves and picture hat outlined with three-quarter inch diameter pearl beads, but the prize for eccentricities of costumes went to a man in a black-and-white checked suit, black-and-white striped socks and tie, and a white stiff shirt with black mourning border on the collar and cuffs and down the front seam. You can't get away from the black-and-white craze anywhere; people will paint the fronts of their houses in black-and-white stripes if the obsession goes any further.[11]

---

6. The *Collier's* article had a photograph of this wondrous parking.

7. Sherry's hotel, an elaborate twelve-story building designed by Stanford White, opened in 1898 at Fifth Avenue and Forty-fourth Street, just opposite Delmonico's. Its sumptuous dining room was a meeting place for the rich and famous. Cesar Ritz (1850–1918) was a European hotelier who employed the famous chef Auguste Escoffier at the Ritz in Paris. He also part-owned other restaurants, including the Carlton in London, and his name became a synonym for luxury in terms such as "ritzy" or "putting on the Ritz." After his death his widow sold the Ritz-Carlton name, which became a franchise.

8. Apart from the remark about how a really chic woman never looks as though she was trying to make an effort, the rest of this (very lively) chapter was not to be found in *Collier's*.

9. Literally: "a woman must be hungry to be beautiful." William Banting (1797–1878), a 205 lb., five feet five inch tall English funeral director and cabinetmaker (whose other claim to fame was making a coffin for the Duke of Wellington) published the first weight-loss pamphlet, "A Letter on Corpulence Addressed to the Public," in 1863. In it he described how he had reduced his weight by 46 lbs., and his waist by twelve inches, by following a low-carbohydrate diet. His system was followed in America and he shares with Captain Boycott and Louis Pasteur the distinction of his name becoming a verb.

10. Charmeuse is an opaque silk with a shiny satin finish.

11. Emily Post was exaggerating a little, as a glance at *Gimbel's Illustrated 1915 Catalogue*

Among the appropriately and well-dressed women one was superlatively smart. This one was really perfect, from the direction in which her hair was brushed to exactly suit the outline of her hat, to her perfectly shaped patent leather shoes. Her costume is not much to describe: a severely simple gun-metal-colored taffeta one-piece dress with a white organdie collar and sleeves of self-colored chiffon, a wide-brimmed black straw hat turned up at one side of the back with a black bird. The distinctive effect was due more to the way it was worn than to the costume. You felt that it belonged to her almost in the way that a collie's fur belongs to him; it was as much a part of her, as her perfectly done hair or her polished fingernails. How few women pay attention to the effect or outline that their heads make! Nine women out of ten — more, forty-nine out of fifty — seemingly gather their hair up on a haphazard spot on their heads and fasten it there almost any way. Sit in any theater audience and look at them! And yet a paradox; a really chic woman never gives the appearance of having made an effort. Her hair suggests dexterity, not effort, and though she may have on a four-hundred-dollar creation of jet or white velvet she looks as though she happened to put on a black dress or a white one, but never as though she had put on *the* black or *the* white one. This dissertation, by the way, belongs by no means solely to Omaha, but to every city where women follow fashions. New York women are quite as prone to be content with being mannequins for the display of their clothes rather than take greater pains to select clothes that are a completion of their own personalities — the last leaf left for the American woman to take out of the book of her Parisian sister.

Quite by chance on our last evening, we ran across Mrs. K. in the corridor of the Fontanelle; and the next moment we found ourselves in a little fragment of Omaha Society — with a capital S. Had it not been for one topic of conversation I should probably not mention the incident, as we had merely a glimpse of a few well-bred people that offered little matter for comment. The topic was the famous cyclone of three years ago.[12] Among the stories they told us, was one of Mrs. R., the one whose appearance I had so admired earlier in the evening. Three years ago she arrived home from Paris with seventeen trunks full of trousseau, and as soon as

---

(New York: Dover, Reprint edition, 1994) will show: although there were undoubtedly black and white garments on display, navy blue, rose and tan also featured, as did plain white dresses.

12. A cyclone tore through Iowa, Illinois and Nebraska at 5.45pm on Easter Sunday, March 23rd, 1913. In Omaha alone it left 115 dead, 2000 ruined homes and more than $8 million worth of damage. Mrs. R. was more fortunate than two of her Farnum Avenue neighbors who died in the storm.

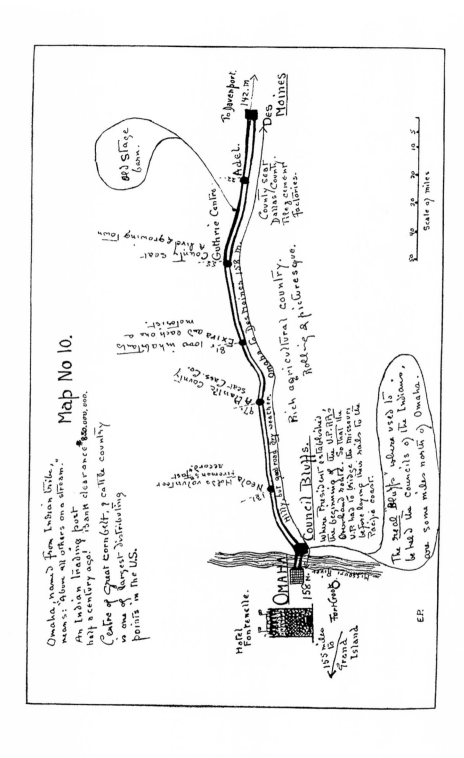

Map No 10.

Omaha, named from Indian Tribe, means: "Above all others on a stream."

An Indian Trading Post half a century ago! Bank clearance $850,000,000.

Centre of Great Corn Belt, a cattle country is one of largest distributing points in the U.S.

Hotel Fontenelle.

OMAHA 158 M.

Fort Crook

155 miles to Grand Island

Missouri River.

Council Bluffs.

Hilly, but good road by weather.

Where President established the beginning of the U.P.RR. Overland route. So that the U.P. had to bridge the Missouri before laying their rails to the Pacific coast.

The "Real Bluffs" where used to be held the Councils of the Indians, are some miles north of Omaha.

Omaha to Des Moines 158 m.

Rich agricultural country. Rolling & picturesque.

131. Neola Hed a volunteer fireman's post record!

97½ Atlantic County seat Cass Co.

81 Iowa wholesale Extra 2¢ each on a motorist.

58 County seat! a live & growing town

Guthrie Centre

County seat Dallas County. Tile & cement factories.

Adel.

142. m

To Davenport.

Des Moines

Old Stage (barn.)

Scale of miles

50   40   30   20   10   5

E.P.

her things could be unpacked she spread them around a big room, in imitation of a bazaar, so that her particular friends might view them. Instead of her friends, however, arrived the Cyclone! It tore off the entire bay window; caught up dresses, hats, lingerie, wraps; whisked them through the open space where the window had been, and festooned the topmost branches of the trees all down Farnum Avenue with fragments of French finery.

Scarcely a garment was ever worth rescuing, as each was pierced through and through by the branches that skewered it fast.

Mrs. K's own story of the cyclone, I give as she told it. "It did not seem very amusing at the time, but one of the funny things to look back upon was what happened to Father! The storm came from the south. Father started across the living-room, which has both north and south windows, just as the cyclone struck. The windows burst out, the furniture flew around the room and literally out of the north window. Father made a sort of vortex in the middle and everything swirled like a whirlpool around him. When we got to him he was tightly bound up in the rugs, portières, and curtains, which completely prevented his moving; but also protected him snugly from flying glass. He was prostrate, of course, and lightly resting on his chest was a large picture of the Doge's palace.[13]

Whatever damage the cyclone did has long been obliterated, and Omaha now presents a beautifully in order exterior and enjoys an evidently gay social life; two features of which are the new Hotel, and the Country Club — neither of them likely to grow much moss on their ballroom floors.[14]

But to go from the triviality of the mere social side to the deeper characteristics of the Omahans. There is something very inspiring, very wonderful in the attitude of the West. The pride in their city, the personal caring, that we met first in Chicago, is also the underlying motive here. One hears much of the ambitious Western towns, but I think the word not quite right; it is not mere ambition, but aspiration, that is carrying them forward. One of the editors of a leading paper said yesterday:

"The making of a great city depends less on the men who are in office than on those who have no office, and who want none. It is the spirit of

---

13. A portiere is a curtain hanging over a doorway.
14. The Omaha Country Club, a golf and social club, was founded in 1899 northwest of the city center near 52nd St. and Military Avenue; it moved to its present site in 1927.

Opposite: "Des Moines to Omaha," Tuesday May 11, 1915. They stayed two nights at the Fontanelle in Omaha.

the people that makes a city go forward or leaves it standing still. The spirit that is essential to progress, in Omaha as everywhere, is one of unity, harmony and good will. Combined with this there must be energy, enterprise, confidence in the future, civic pride and devotion. No city, however well favored otherwise, can make the progress its opportunities call for, if its people are forever quarreling among themselves, envious of one another's good fortune, seeking each to build himself up by tearing some other down. It is shoulder to shoulder, in mass formation, that great armies advance. Rancor, hatred, suspicion, pettiness, that cause division in the ranks, are as deadly as the other extreme where indifference, greed, lack of respect for the other man's rights, produce dry rot."

Nor are these merely editorial embroideries of speech. They are the actual sentiments, not only thought, but for the most part lived up to.

Tenth Day's Run, Des Moines to Omaha

They stayed in Omaha for two nights, arriving on Tuesday May 11 and leaving on Thursday May 13, 1915.

Personal

Omaha. Hotel Fontanelle.

(Typical day)	
Hallboys, porters, chambermaid	$ 1.75
Dinner (3)	$ 3.80
Tip	$ .40
3 single rooms and baths (at $3.50) (lovely)	$10.50
Coffee (1)	$ .30
Tip	$ .15
Breakfast (E. M.)	$ .50
Tip	$ .20
Lunch, ladies' dining room (2)	$ 2.70
Lunch (E. M.) club lunch, men's café	$ .60
Tip	$ .25
"Movies," magazines, soda water etc.	$ 1.30
Lunch to take with us	$ 1.80
Ice cream	$ .40

Motor

Omaha. Guy L. Smith Garage.
    Storage (2 days) $1.50
    20 gals. gas $4.40
    1 gal. oil $ .80

XVII

Next Stop, North Platte!

North Platte might really be called "City of Ishmael." For no reason that is discoverable except its mere existence, every man's tongue seems to be against it. Time and time again — in fact the repetition is becoming monotonous — people say to us, "It is all very well, of course, you have had fine hotels and good roads so far, but wait until you come to North Platte!"

Why, I wonder, does everyone pick out North Platte as a sort of third degree place of punishment? Why not one of the other names through which our road runs? Why always set up that same unfortunate town as a target? It began with Mrs. O. in New York, who declared it so dreadful a place that we could never live through it. Her point of view being extremely fastidious, her opinion does not alarm us as much as it otherwise might, but in Chicago, too, the mention of our going to North Platte seemed to be the signal for people to look sorry for us. Now a drummer downstairs has just added his mite to our growing apprehension.[1]

"Goin' t' th' coast?" he queried. "Hmm — I guess you won't like th' hotels at North Platte overmuch."

"Do you go there often?" I returned.

"Me?" he said indignantly. "Not on your life. No one ever gets off at North Platte except the railroad men — they *have* to!"[2] That is the one unexplained phase of the subject, no one of all those who have villified it has personally been there.

Just as I asked if he could perhaps tell me which of the hotels was least bad, a fellow drummer joined him. The usual expression of commiseration followed.

---

1. Apart from the preceding two paragraphs, the only part of this chapter that appeared in *Collier's* is the description of the "ocher-colored railway station" and the complaint about the low speed limit in Nebraska.

2. North Platte played and still plays an important role in the Union Pacific Railroad. The hotel was built in 1867.

"A bedroom in the Union Pacific Hotel, North Platte — not much of a hardship, is it?" This is the only bedroom that Emily Post included in her book.

"Well," said the second drummer, "it's this way. Whichever hotel you put up at, you'll wish you had put up at the other."

"Suppose it turns out to be the very worst we can think of — what *can* that worst be?" I asked rather shakily of Celia.

"Dirty rooms over a saloon with drunken 'bad men' shooting in it," she whispered with a shiver.

"Don't you think —" we suggested to E. M., "it would be a good idea to buy a pistol, in case —"

"In case —?" he asked with the completely indifferent tranquility of youth.

Celia prodded me. "Well, just in case —" I said lamely. I think Celia might have finished the sentence herself.

Of all the bogey stories, the one about North Platte is the most unfounded! Instead of a rip-roaring town, rioting in red and yellow ribaldry, it is a serious railroad thoroughfare, self-respecting and above reproach and the home of no less a celebrity than Mr. Cody — Buffalo Bill.[3]

---

3. North Platte, which boasted a population of 6,500 in 1917, had at that time nine churches, three hotels, three hospitals, three grain elevators, a theater and a library, as well as claiming the largest ice-house in the world. See *Nebraska State Business Directory and Gazetteer* Vol. XVI, (Omaha: Polk McAvoy, 1917). William Frederick Cody (1846–1917) was born in Iowa. An army scout and pony express rider, he earned his nickname after killing nearly five thousand buffalo in eighteen months as part of a contract to supply the Kansas Pacific Railroad with meat. After 1883 he toured with his Wild West show.

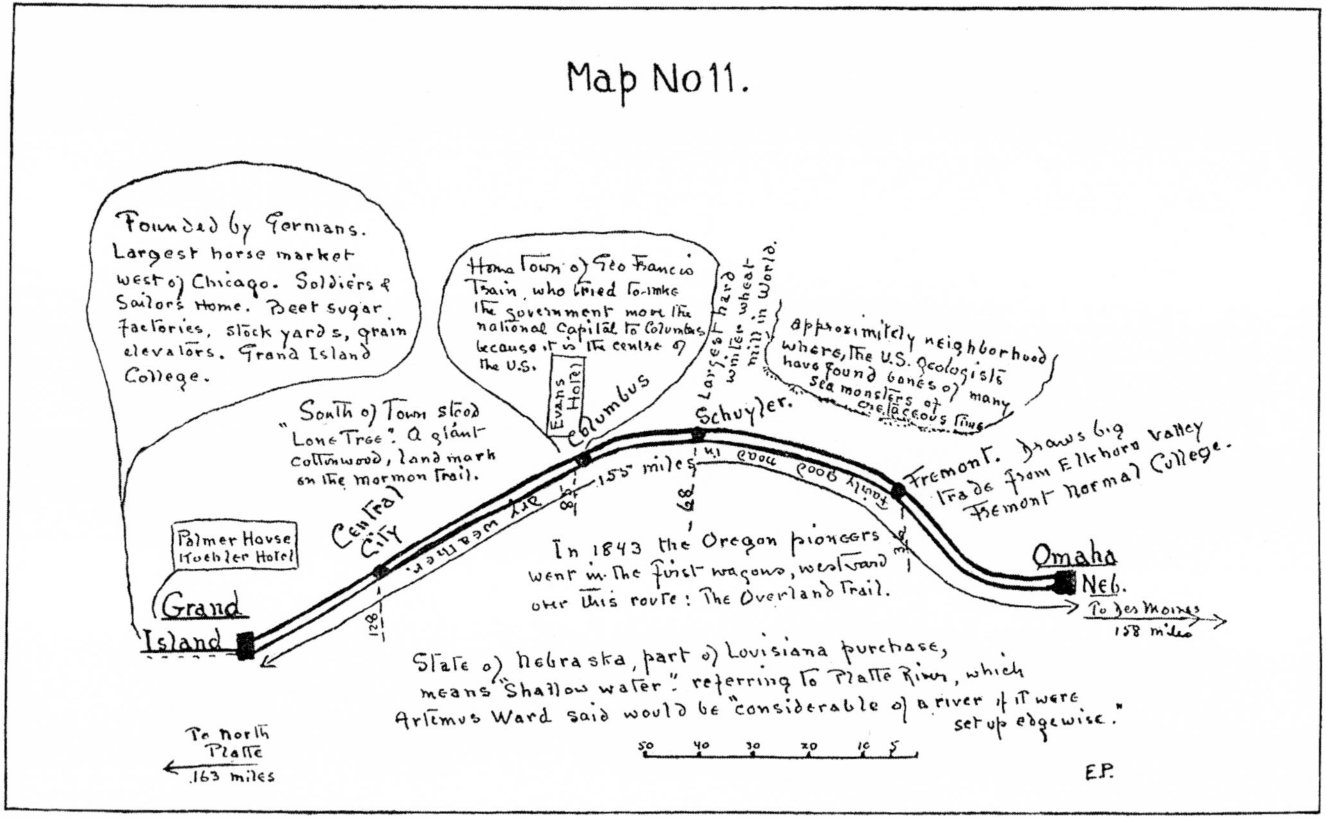

Map No 11.

Founded by Germans. Largest horse market west of Chicago. Soldiers & Sailors home. Beet sugar factories, stock yards, grain elevators. Grand Island College.

South of Town stood "Lone Tree." A giant cottonwood, landmark on the Mormon Trail.

Palmer House (Koehler Hotel)

Grand Island

Home Town of Geo Francis Train, who tried to make the government move the national Capital to Columbus because it's the centre of the U.S.

Evans Hotel

Columbus

Largest hard wheat mill in world.

Approximately neighborhood where, the U.S. Geologists have found bones of many Sea monsters of many cretaceous rivers.

Schuyler

Fremont draws 6,9 valley
Trade from Elkhorn College.
Fremont Normal College.

Omaha **Neb.**

To Des Moines
158 miles

In 1843 the Oregon pioneers went in the first wagons, (eastward) over this route: The Overland Trail.

State of Nebraska, part of Louisiana Purchase, means "Shallow water", referring to Platte River, which Artemus Ward said would be "considerable of a river if it were set up edgewise."

821

155 miles

60
89
90

Dry weather
Cherry City

To North Platte
163 miles

2006 above sea level

50 40 30 20 10 5

E.P.

Of course if you imagine you are going to find a Blackstone or a Fontanelle, you will be disappointed, but in comparison to some of the other hotels along the Lincoln Highway, the Union Pacific in North Platte is a model of delectability!

As a matter of fact, it is an ocher-colored wooden railroad station, a rather bare dining-room, and lunch counter, and perfectly good, clean bedrooms upstairs. You cannot get a suite with a private bath, and if you are more or less spoiled by the supercomforts of luxurious living, you may not care to stay for very long. But if in all your journeying around the world, you never have to put up with any greater hardship than spending a night at the Union Pacific in North Platte, you will certainly not have to stay at home on that account. There are no drunkards or toughs or even loafers hanging about; the food is cleanly served and good; the rooms, although close to the railroad tracks, are as spotless as brooms and scrubbing brushes can make them.[4]

Eleventh and Twelfth Days' Run, Omaha to North Platte Thursday May 13 and Friday May 14, 1915.

Personal

Lunch in car.
North Platte. Union Pacific Hotel.

3 rooms (no baths), supper and breakfast for three	$7.50
Tips, postcards, etc.	$1.35
Lunch to take with us	$1.60

Motor

Independent Garage, *Grand Island.*

15 gals. gas	$3.30

---

4. Since writing the above, the Union Pacific Hotel has unfortunately burned down — and still more unfortunately for tourists, the railroad is not building another, and will run a restaurant only. (Original Emily Post footnote). Emily Post was not quite right here, as a new hotel and depot was built in 1916. The North Platte Canteen in the depot served more than six million servicemen and women during World War II, when volunteers met every passing troop train and served home made cakes, coffee and sandwiches.

Opposite: "Map 11 Omaha to Grand Island, Thursday May 13 1915."

Map No 12.

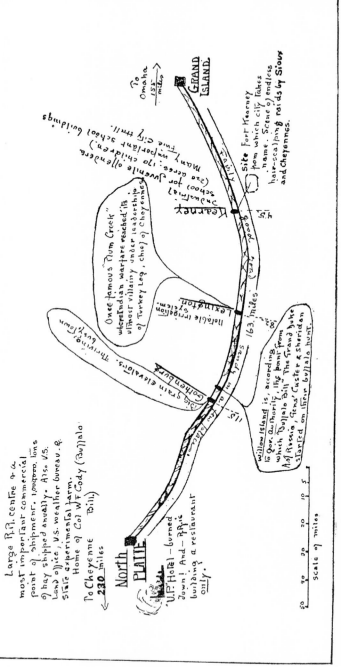

Large R.R. centre & a most important commercial point of shipment. 1,000,000 tons of hay shipped annually. Also U.S. Land office, U.S. weather bureau & State experimental farm.
Home of Col. W.F. Cody (Buffalo Bill)

To Cheyenne
230 miles

NORTH PLATTE

"U.P. Hotel" — burned down! And — R.R. is building a restaurant only.

Big grain elevators. Thriving, bustling town.

GOTHENBURG

113 miles

Once famous "Plum Creek" where Indian warfare reached its utmost villainy under leadership of Turkey Leg, chief of Cheyennes.

Natable irrigation system.

LEXINGTON

163 miles

Willow Island is, according to Gov. Authority, (Hg. bank from A. of Russia, Gen! Custer & Sheridan started on their buffalo hunt.

Industrial school for juvenile offenders (520 acres: 170 children.) Many important school buildings.

KEARNEY

Site Fort Kearney from which city takes name. Scene of endless hair-scalping raids by Sioux and Cheyennes.

GRAND ISLAND

To Omaha
155 miles

Scale of miles
50 40 30 20 10 5

North Platte. J. S. Davis Auto Co.[5]

Storage	$ .50
17 gals. gas (22c.)	$3.74
1 gal. oil	$ .60

There is a place, though, between the Missouri and the Rio Grande — there is no use in being more exact as to its locality — where, except in case of accident — ours was a broken spring — you are not likely to stay.[6] There our own particular horrors were pretty well realized: dirty rooms over a saloon and lounging toughs on the corner; uneatable hunks of food at a table in a barroom, our dinner put in front of us on a platter, and no plates used at all. And the bedrooms! I slept on top of my bed wrapped in an ulster with my head on the lining of my coat. And even so, I was seriously bitten by small but voracious prior inhabitants. The next day all the "bath" I had was a catlick with the corner of a handkerchief held reluctantly under a greasy spigot.

This experience was pretty unappetizing but also it was our only bad one, sent no doubt as a punishment for our lack of appreciation of one or two former stopping-places, which, as E. M. would say, "sounds fair enough." Also in order to live consistently up to that motor philosophy I wrote about, we will in time be glad of the color it will give to our memory book. But at present its color seems merely a grease spot on the page, and all the motor philosophy in the world doesn't seem potent enough to blot out the taste and smell, to say nothing of the stings.

By the way, I seem to have arrived at North Platte, and possibly farther, on a magic carpet — a little difficult for anyone taking this as a guide to follow! Therefore to go back, merely on the subject of the roads, almost as far as Des Moines. Taking the general average of luck in motoring, no matter how well things have gone for you, the chances are that you have had *some* delays. A day or two of rain that held you up, detours that made you lose your way, a run of tire trouble — something, no matter what it is, that has delayed you more than you expected. And whatever it is you find

---

5. According to their advertisement in the 1917 *Nebraska Business Directory*, the J.S. Davis Auto Company, which was distributor of Buick and Mitchell automobiles in Western Nebraska, also stocked Exide batteries and boasted oxy-acetylene welding equipment and 20,000 feet of floor space.

6. This unnamed place — Emily Post tactfully omits it from her list of expenses — was somewhere between North Platte, Nebraska and Cheyenne, Wyoming and by a process of elimination, was probably in Grand Island, Nebraska.

Opposite: "Map no. 12 Grand Island to North Platte," Friday May 14, 1915.

yourself thinking this does not matter very much because when we get to those Nebraska fast roads we can make up lost time easily.

The very sound "Nebraska" correlates "dragged roads" speed![7] While you are still running through the picturesque Sir Joshua Reynolds scenery of the River to River road in Iowa, you find that your mind is developing an anticipatory speed craze. So thoroughly imbued has your mind become with the "fast road" idea that the very ground has a speed gift on its dragged surface. What if your engine is barely capable of forty miles an hour, that miraculously fast stretch magically carries you at the easiest fifty. If you have a big powerful engine, you forget that ordinarily you dislike whizzing across the surface of the earth, and just for this once — even though you think of it more in terror than in joy, you are approaching the race-way of America, and you, too, are going to race!

"We must be sure that everything is in perfect running order," you exclaim excitedly as you picture your car leaping out of Omaha and shooting to Denver while scarcely turning over its engine. "Not many stopping places," you are told. What matter is that to you? You are not thinking of stopping at all. North Platte, perhaps, yes. Three hundred and thirty miles in a day is just a nice little fast road run.

"A nice little which?" says the head of a garage in Omaha.

"We'll leave early," you continue, unheeding, "and make a dash across the continental speedway —"

"See here, stranger," says the garage man, "what state of fast circuits d'y think y're in? This is Nebraska and the speed limit is twenty miles!"

"Twenty miles a minute!" you gasp, "that certainly *is* speed!"

The garage man half edges away from you. "Fr'm here t'Denver is about thutty-five hours straight travelin'. You gutta slow down t'eight miles through towns and y'can't go over twenty miles an hour nowheres!"[8]

When you manage to get a little breath into your collapsed lungs you say dazedly, "But we're going over the 'fast dragged' road."

"Road's fast enough! But the law'll have you if you drive over it faster'n twenty miles an hour."

If you can find the joke in all of this, you have a more humorous mental equipment and a sweeter disposition than we had.

Across Nebraska from the last good hotel in Omaha to the first comfortable one in Denver or Cheyenne is over five hundred miles. At the pre-

7. Before roads were surfaced with macadam or concrete, local farmers periodically flattened the ruts on the dirt roads by dragging logs, or other heavy objects. On sections of the Lincoln Highway teams were employed to drag the roads after heavy rains.
8. Omaha to Denver is 540 miles.

"Hours and hours, across land as flat and endless as the ocean."

scribed "speed" of about seventeen miles an hour average, it means literally a pleasant little run of between thirty and forty hours along a road dead level, wide, straight, and where often as far as the eye can see, there is not even a shack in the dimmest distance, and the only settlers to be seen are prairie dogs.

If between Omaha and Cheyenne there were three or four attractive little places to stop, or if the Nebraska speed laws were abolished or disregarded *and it didn't rain*, you could motor to the heart of the Rocky Mountains with the utmost ease and comfort.

In May, 1915, the road by way of Sterling to Denver was impassable; all automobiles were bogged between Big Spring and Julesburg, so on the advice of car owners that we met, we went by way of Chappell to Cheyenne. It is quite possible, of course, that we blindly passed comfortable stopping-paces, but to us that whole vast distance from Omaha to Cheyenne was one to be crossed with as little stop-over as possible. Aside from questions of accommodations and speed laws, the interminable distance was in itself an unforgettably wonderful experience. It gave us an impression of the lavish immensity of our own country as nothing else could. Think of driving on and on and on and yet the scene scarcely changing, the flat road stretching as endlessly in front of you as behind. The low yellow sand banks and flat sand islands scarcely vary on the Platte, which might as well be called

"A straight, wide road; not even a shack in sight — and a speed limit of twenty miles an hour."

the Flat, River.[9] The road does gradually rise several thousand feet but the distance is so immense your engine does not perceive a grade. Once in a while you pass great herds of cattle fenced in vast enclosures, and every now and then you come to a group of nesters' shanties, scattered over the gray-green plain as though some giant child had dropped its blocks, or as though some Titans, playing dominoes, had left a few lying on the table.

At greater intervals you come to towns and you drive between two closely fitted rows of oddly assorted domino-shaped stores and houses, and then on out upon the great flat table again. For scores and scores of miles the scene is unvarying, On and on you go over that endless road until at last far, far on the gray horizon you catch the first faint glint of the white-peaked Rocky Mountains.

You have long ago turned away from the river's yellow sand flats, and you watch that slowly rising snow-topped rim, until — it may be gradually, or it may be suddenly — your heart is thrilled by the sublimity of the amazing contrast of mountain upon plain.

Perhaps you may merely find dullness in the endlessly flat, unvarying monotonous land; perhaps you are unwilling to be enthralled by

9. The Platte River valley had been one of the main westward routes since the days of the California and Oregon wagon trains. Later it was the route for the pony express, the transcontinental telegraph, and the first transcontinental railroad. See Hokansen, *The Lincoln Highway*, 54.

Titanic cones of rock or snow. But steep your sight for days in flatness, until you think the whole width of the world has melted into a never-ending sea of land, and then see what the drawing close of those most sublime of mountains does to you!

And afterwards, when you have actually climbed to their knees or shoulders, and look back upon the endless plains, you forget the wearying journey and feel keenly the beauty of their very endlessness. The ever-changing effect of light and shadow over that boundless expanse weaves an enchanted spell upon your imagination that you can never quite recover from. Sometimes the prairies are a great sea of mist; sometimes they are a parched desert; sometimes they are blue like the waves of an enchanted sapphire sea; sometimes they melt into a plain of vaporous purple mystery, and then the clouds shift away from the sun and you see they are a width of the world, of land.

But however or whenever you look out upon them, you feel as though mean little thoughts, petty worries, or skulking gossip whispers, could never come into your wind-swept mind again. That if you could only live with such vastness of outlook before you, perhaps your own puny heat and mind and soul might grow into something bigger, simpler, worthier than is ever likely otherwise.

And now I am getting quite over my head, so better climb down the mountains again and go back to the motor, which may be supposed to have reached Cheyenne.

If you think Cheyenne is a Buffalo Bill Wild West town, as we did, you will be much disappointed, though it may be well not to show the progressive citizens of that up-to-date city that you hoped they were still galloping along wooden sidewalks howling like coyotes!

I thought that Celia and E. M. looked distinctly grieved at the sight of smooth laid asphalt, wide-paved sidewalks, imposing capitol and modern buildings. Even the brand-new Plains Hotel was accepted by both of them in much the same spirit as a child who thought it was going to the circus and found itself at a museum of art, would accept the compensation of a nice hot supper instead of peanuts and red lemonade.[10]

Unfortunately we had not friends in Cheyenne and therefore never got so far as even the threshold of society, but the following account taken

---

10. William Dubois, a prominent Wyoming architect, designed the luxurious Plains Hotel. According to Dazee Bristol, a local journalist who covered the hotel's grand opening in March 1911, "Nearly all rooms have baths and ALL have telephones." A major renovation and restoration completed in 2002 returned the Plains to its original exterior appearance.

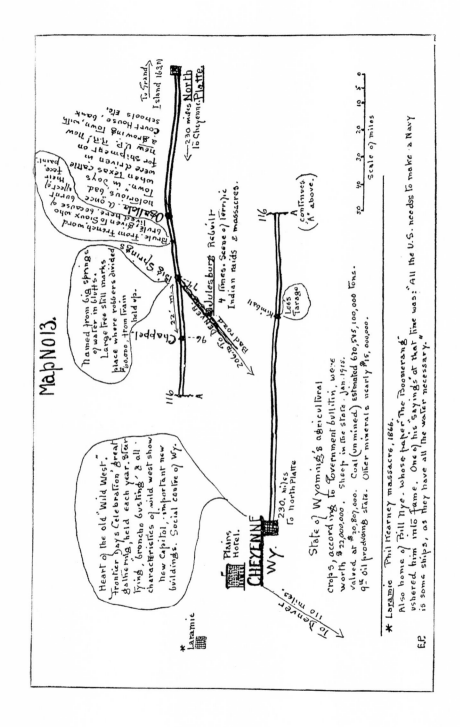

"Wyoming in the ranch country." Emily Post was rather disappointed to find Cheyenne an up-to-date city with paved sidewalks and asphalt streets.

from the morning paper is irrefutable evidence that Cheyenne, far from being a wild town of border outlawry, is a center of refined elegance and fashion:

"Governor and Mrs. K. tendered a beautiful courtesy to the Cheyenne and visiting cadets and their sponsors Sunday afternoon when they entertained them at an informal reception and luncheon at the executive mansion.[11]

"This brilliant social function was scarcely second in the estimation of the guests to the wall-scaling tournament Saturday evening, when world records were smashed by the invincible cadet squad from Casper.[12]

---

11. John B. Kendrick, governor of Wyoming from 1915 to 1917, went to Wyoming as a cowboy hired to drive a herd of cattle from Texas. Kendrick liked what he saw and stayed, marrying the seventeen year-old daughter of his employer. Though Kendrick had little education he became, with the help of his wife, a wealthy cattleman and politician. After serving in the Wyoming State Senate, he was elected governor in 1915, but resigned after two years to become the U.S. Senator for Wyoming. He died in office November 3, 1933 and was buried in Sheridan, Wyoming.

12. The "Cadets" were members of the Cheyenne Cadet Corps, a military training group composed of students at Cheyenne High School. The wall scaling involved moving the whole squad over a 14–foot wall. Those who made it to the top stood on a ledge on the far side and assisted their fellow-students. Images of this appear in the 1917 Cheyenne High School yearbook. My thanks to Carl Hallberg, Reference Archivist at the Wyoming State Archives for this information.

Opposite: "Map no. 13, North Platte to Cheyenne," Saturday May 15, 1915.

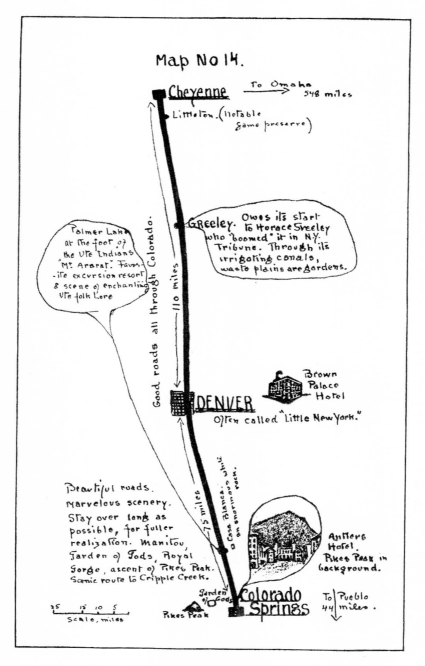

Cheyenne to Colorado Springs Sunday May 16, 1915.

"The Governor's mansion was exceedingly attractive with its luxurious furnishings, in artistic setting. One hundred and twenty voices mingled in chatter, laughter and song to the accompaniment of violin and piano. College songs and familiar popular airs in which everyone joined, made the 'welkin ring' as the exuberant spirits found vent in melody.

"To the hostess' understanding of the needs of boys and girls was due the satisfactory nature and quantities of the salads, sandwiches, ice cream and candies served so generously in the dining-room.

"The cadets outnumbered the pretty sponsors eight to one, and every girl was a queen at whose shrine a circle of admiring youths was in constant attendance."

In our ignorance we don't know what a "sponsor" is further than that the paper tells us she is a young girl who is a queen of despotic fascination, but what, or whom, or why or how she sponsors, is a mystery too deep for our solving. Cadet, of course, makes an instantaneous picture of a straight, square-shouldered young human being of an inflexibly rigid demeanor but with a quite susceptible young human heart beating underneath his rigid exterior.

The object in quoting all this is merely to show our fellow Easterners that the West of yesterday was no longer to be found in Cheyenne!

One day in the year, though, they have a Frontier Days Celebration — when, like in the midnight hour of the Puppen Fée, the West that was, comes back to life.[13] There are wonderful exhibits of "bronco busting" and rope throwing, and all the features of county fair, horse show, and wild west show in one.[14]

Thirteenth Day's Run, North Platte to Cheyenne (Saturday May 15, 1915)

Personal

Cheyenne, Wyo. Plains Hotel (brand new).

---

13. Literally, fairy puppet.

14. The first Cheyenne Frontier Days Rodeo took place in 1896 when a group of cowboys held an impromptu "cowboy contest." It soon became commercialized by the Union Pacific as a vehicle for promoting passenger traffic on the railroad. Promoter Frederick Angier thought of hosting a bronco show somewhere on the line, and approached Colonel E.A. Slack, editor of the Cheyenne *Sun-Leader* who jumped at the opportunity for promoting his and other Cheyenne businesses.

Tips, as usual	$1.75
Dinner and tip	$3.85
3 single rooms and baths	$9.00
Coffee and toast (in room, for two)	$ .90
Breakfast (E. M.)	$1.00

Motor

Cheyenne. Plains Hotel Garage.

Storage	$ .50
20 gals. gas	$4.40
2 gals. oil	$1.20

From Cheyenne to Denver, and from Denver to Colorado Springs, the road was uneventfully excellent all the way.

Denver, where we stopped merely for luncheon, is far too important a city to mention in a brief paragraph or two, and is for that reason left out altogether.

XVIII

The City of Recklessness

"For West is West, and East is East, and never twain shall meet"—except in Colorado Springs![1]

Mountains, plains, squatters' shanties, replicas of foreign palaces, cowboys, Indians, ranchers, New Yorkers, Londoners. The free open-air life and altitude of the plains, the sheltered luxurious manners and customs of the idle rich! Across the warp of Western characteristics is woven the woof of a cosmopolitan society.[2]

Before coming here I had imagined the place a sort of huge sanatorium.[3] I had expected long lines of invalid chairs on semi-enclosed verandas, even beds possibly, as in the outdoor wards of hospitals. I knew, of course, that there were good hotels and many private houses; and having friends who had come out here, I thought perhaps we might take luncheon or dinner with them in a quiet, semi-invalid sort of way — an early supper, and someone to tell us not to stay too long for fear of tiring Jim or Mary.

As a matter of fact Mary drove her own motor up to the hotel ten minutes after we arrived, and telling us of half a dozen engagements that

---

1. Colorado Springs was founded in 1871 by General William Jackson Palmer. Because of the scenery, (Pikes Peak is nearby) the elevation, (over 6,000 feet) and the mineral springs, it soon became a destination for both tourists and health-seekers, particularly people suffering from tuberculosis.

2. Warp comes from the Middle English wearp and denotes the series of yarns extended lengthwise in a loom; it is crossed by the woof, or weft. The phrase "warp and woof" to describe the basic structure of something dates from 1842.

3. See Robert E. Kravetz, M.D. and Alex Jay Kimmelman, *Healthseekers in Arizona* (Arizona: Academy of Medical Sciences of Maricopa Medical Society, 1998). I am grateful to Melissa Bingmann for bringing to my attention this and subsequent references to the open-air movement in the West. Physicians touted the advantages of Arizona, while the Santa Fe Railroad Company was one of the early promoters of Arizona health resorts. The company published pamphlets encouraging passengers to use their railroads to reach these resorts.

"Cripple Creek." Although Emily Post does not mention visiting Cripple Creek, she presumably went there to take this photograph.

she had made for us, including a dinner that she was giving that evening, wanted us to come out to polo then and there.

Hadn't she better rest? Not a bit of it!

Instead of the invalid regimen that we expected to fall into, we were kept going at a pace we could scarcely catch up with. We dined in extravagantly appointed houses, lunched on terraces overlooking gardens, danced into the first hours of the morning, and led the life typical of any fashionable pleasure resort. Of invalidism there was, *on the surface*, not a trace. Mary herself had come out a few years ago very ill, and Jim and L—, two men who had been sent away from home in an almost dying condition, seemed quite as unlike invalids as Mary. L— has a beautiful house, run exactly as his establishment in Newport used to be, and he leads much the same life as he used to lead there. Motoring takes the place of yachting; he plays poker, polo, and golf, and dines rather much, wines rather more, and has changed not at all.

Jim, not because he is different, but only because he is less rich, lives in a little bungalow in Broadmoor.[4] Instead of three or four footmen standing in the hall, as in L.'s house, Jim lives alone with a Jap boy who is cook,

4. Here Emily Post added in explanation "...the invalid village built expressly for "the members of the order of T.B." as Jim flippantly spoke of the colony and yet, even there, there was no effect of a sanitarium." *Collier's* September 11, 1915.

butler, valet, housemaid and nurse combined, but he gave us a delicious luncheon to which he had asked a few of his neighbors.

"They all have t.b.," he whispered, otherwise we should never have known it.[5]

After lunch he showed me his sleeping porch. Nothing unusual in that; everyone has a fad for sleeping out of doors nowadays. He did, however, happen to mention that his Jap boy was bully whenever he was ill, but it was only in his almost emotional gladness to see us, his wistful eagerness for every small detail of news from home that I caught a suspicion of what might once have been homesickness. Perhaps I only imagined that faint suspicion. Certainly he seemed cheerful and happy, and spoke of himself as a "busted lunger" as lightly as he might have said he was six feet two inches tall! As a matter of fact, his "busted lungs" are pretty well mended — for so long as he stays out here. Later we heard that there was likely to be a wedding between Jim and a young quite-lately widow who sat opposite him at lunch. She happily is not a member of the t.b. fraternity, but came out some years ago with a dying husband.

"What an old fox you are! Why didn't you tell me about her?" I said to him afterward. He grinned until he looked almost idiotically foolish; then he exclaimed:

"Isn't she wonderful?" and he squeezed my hand as though I and not he had made the remark.

Besides the conspicuous and palatial homes that one associates instinctively with Broadmoor, there are a few little bungalows, each with its sleeping-porch, a living-room, dining-room and a bedroom or two.[6]

---

5. The abbreviation "t.b." for the tubercle bacillus was of recent date; according to Merriam Webster, it was first used in 1912. On the other hand the Mycobacterium tuberculosis has infected humans for thousands of years; spines of some Egyptian mummies from 2400BC show signs of tubercular decay. Hermann Brehmer, who returned from a sojourn in the Himalayas apparently cured, built the first European sanatorium in the 1850s. German scientist Robert Koch first viewed tuberculosis bacterium in 1882 after developing a staining technique and by this time sanitoria were widely in use throughout Europe and the United States. They helped the healing process by providing rest, good nutrition, and a healthy environment, and also served to isolate the sick. In 1895 Wilhelm Konrad von Rontgen discovered an X-ray technique that made observation and monitoring of the disease possible. A further development was the BCG vaccine, which is still used widely today. In 1943 Selman A. Waksman, who had been working for decades to find an antibiotic that was effective against TB, was finally successful. Nevertheless, TB is still a problem in developing nations and the World Health Organization estimates that each year 3 million people die from TB, and eight million people are infected with the disease, 95% of whom live in developing countries. New Jersey Medical School National Tuberculosis Center. *Brief History of Tuberculosis.* (July 1996). www.umdnj.edu/~ntbcweb/history.htm.

6. As Julian Street pointed out, the architecture of Colorado Springs was nothing if not eclectic. He noted "half-timbered English houses, lived in by Englishmen and Scots; →

There are also, in Colorado Springs itself, many boarding-houses, and in both of these the people do live very simply and follow more or less the prescribed life of a health resort.[7] But in the general impression of Colorado Springs, one might imagine oneself in a second Newport, Monte Carlo, or Simla in India. Not that any of these places bear much physical resemblance to the heart of the Rocky Mountains, especially Simla, yet this last is suggested most of all.[8] The conditions are much the same in that the people are there because they have been ordered to be, rather than because it is a home they have themselves chosen. In India the people can't do very much because the climate is too enervating; in Colorado the people can't do very much because their health is too uncertain. In both places there is an underlying recklessness of attitude, of wanting to get all the fun out of their enforced extradition that they can; and the "fun" consists in both places in riding, driving, playing, or watching polo or tennis, flirting and gambling. The latter two are the favorites, as they afford the most diversion for the least physical effort. The Anglo-Indians plunge into whatever sort of amusement offers because the place would be deadly otherwise; the Coloradoites lead as gay a life as health will permit and ingenuity devise, because the deadliness may at any time be earnest. "Eat, drink and be merry, for tomorrow —" was never more thoroughly lived up to, even in the time of the ancients who originated the adage. Anything for excitement, anything for amusement, anything not to realize that life is not as gay as it seems!

Death is the one word never mentioned. If by chance they speak of one who has gone, they say he had "crossed the great divide." If someone leaves to go home hopelessly, the women say goodby as casually as they can; a few men at the club drink to him — once. That is all. They are peo-

---

Southern colonial houses built by people from the South Atlantic States; New England colonial houses built by people who have migrated from Boston and New York; one-story houses built by people from Hawaii, and a large assortment of other houses ranging from Queen Anne to Cape Cod cottages, and from Italian villas to Spanish palaces. There is even the Grand Trianon at Broadmoor, and an amazing Tudor castle at Glen Eyre." *At Home Abroad,* 418.

7. In the first decade of the twentieth century one in four deaths in Colorado Springs were attributable to tuberculosis, but by the time Emily Post arrived some local residents and landlords were afraid of catching the disease from the incomers, and many doctors were advising hospitalization nearer to the patients' homes, so there was a move to build sanitoria rather then rent properties to the consumptive.

8. Simla, a town in the Himalayan foothills, was the summer capital of India. It is not clear whether Emily Post had ever been there, or whether she was relying on Rudyard Kipling's tales of British life under the Raj, which include *Plain Tales from the Hills* (1888), and *Kim* (1901). Her son's biography refers to her extensive European travel, with no mention of India. See Post, *Truly Emily Post.*

ple facing the grim specter always, yet never allowing their eyes to see. Personally I should have had no inkling of the sadder side; I should have taken everything at its happy face value had it not been for one awakening incident.

I was sitting in the wide, cheerfully homelike hall of the Antlers Hotel when the people from an arriving train came in.[9] Among perhaps a dozen indiscriminate tourists one in particular attracted my attention and interest. He was little more than a boy — twenty-two perhaps, or twenty-three — good-looking, well-bred, and well off if one might judge of these things by his manner and appearance, and the pigskin bags, golf clubs, polo mallets and other paraphernalia that two porters were carrying in his wake.[10]

"There's a lucky young person," I thought, "evidently fond of sport and with the ability, wealth and leisure to gratify his taste. I saw him register and give a stack of extra baggage checks to the clerk, and then on his way to the elevator he passed close to me. He was moderately tall with a graceful, well-built frame, but his step lagged and his shoulders drooped, and in his drawn face I caught a lost, helpless, despairing expression that I recognized unmistakably. Near where I often go in the autumn is a boys' school and I have often seen little new boys on the first evening of their arrival look just so — livid and lost, poor little chaps — but you know that in a day or two they will be running about as happy as grigs in the excitement of school events and the exhilaration of football.[11] But the look in my "fortunate" youth's face went deeper and an illuminating word flashed to my mind: life termer! Homesick? He looked as though he would die of it.

A moment before the big splendidly kept hotel with its broad white hallways, wide verandas and sunny terrace under the very shoulder of

---

9. The original Antlers Hotel opened in 1883; it was built to cater for tourists traveling with the Boston company Raymond and Whitcomb. It was a mass of towers, turrets, balconies and porches and had seventy-five guestrooms, each completely different in design, and two bathrooms on each floor. In 1893 Wellesley professor Katherine Lee Bates (1859–1929), inspired by the view from Pikes Peak, returned to her room at the Antlers to write America's unofficial national anthem "America the Beautiful." The hotel was destroyed by fire in 1898, but a new and enlarged Antlers opened three years later. The lobby, which had a huge marble fireplace at one end, was decorated in gold, ivory and empire red. There were 230 guestrooms, a bowling alley, bicycle rooms, barbershop, a billiard room and a grand ballroom. This hotel was demolished in the 1960s, and a third Antlers opened in 1967.

10. Physicians touted the advantages of Arizona, while the Santa Fe Railroad Company published pamphlets encouraging passengers to use their railroads. One example is *Arizona Health Resorts*, Passenger Department, The Santa Fe, November 1902 (Chicago: Henry O. Shepard Co.)

11. According to the Merriam-Webster Dictionary, a grig (a word which dates from 1556) is a "lively lighthearted usually small or young person."

Pike's Peak, rising in snow-crowned glory above all the lesser glorious mountains, had seemed so beautiful. Suddenly, though, I saw it not merely with the eyes of one broken-hearted, homesick youth, but with some realization of the thousands of tearful eyes that have looked about its commonplace stations. What must it be like to be weak and ill when the strongest clings like a little child to the ones he loves best, and then to be sent far away to live always, or to die, perhaps, among strangers?[12]

After this I became more observing of the lives about us, and people told me many things— quite simply, as though it were all in the day's work. The greatest number who are sent out here are young, and strapping athletes are the most usual type. Sometimes they get well soon, and go back happily to their families; sometimes their families move out too, and in that way bring "home" with them, but the majority come and stay alone, and never leave again except for short annual furloughs. One of these latter lives here at the hotel. A friend of his told me that "Harry could never go home, poor chap," but the adverb "poor" scarcely seemed to qualify that young man from what I saw of him. He is always laughing, always shoving his shoulders through the atmosphere; inquisitive as *Ricki-ticki* and quite as full of life and vim; he seems ready to seize every opportunity of hazard or engagement that the moment offers.[13] He plays all games recklessly; the more dangerous as to stakes or excitement, the better. He drives a powerful motor-car and he is flirting outrageously with one of the prettiest women imaginable, whose invalid husband seems to care very little how much attention she accepts from her frivolous though ardent admirer.

But a little while ago I was in my window and he was on the terrace just below, close enough for me to see him without his seeing me. His face was turned toward the glory of the snow-capped mountains but his unseeing eyes too, had the exact look of the little homesick boys at school. I saw then why his friend had called him "poor chap" and I also a little better understood the exaggeration of his restlessness, the over-swagger of his shoulders, and the laugh and flippancy with which, like Jim, he speaks of "t.b." I wonder if anywhere in the world the moon looks down on more tear-stained pillows than here!

---

12. Many experts believed that it was best for whole families to move to Arizona, rather than exile the ailing member. See George G. Price, *Gaining Health in the West (Colorado, New Mexico, Arizona)* (New York: B.W. Huebsch, 1907) who wrote "the ideal way to live in a Western community, as anywhere else on earth, is for the married man or woman and the family to live regularly in their own comfortable home." Emily Post is meeting the very wealthy: families of other health seekers took jobs locally.

13. Rikki-Tikki-Tavi was a mongoose in Rudyard Kipling's *Just So Stories* (1902).

"Colorado. Pike's Peak in the distance."

And this is enough of the black side of the picture — the blackest side there is. For by no means all the people are homesick, unhappy or in any way ill. Families who have come out originally for the sake of a sick member have stayed because they loved the place and made it their home. And of the others, many who have been lonely and homesick at first have found the place an Eden because they have also found the "one in all the world."

In fact, meeting the "one" is the almost inevitable thing they do. Supposing the newcomers live in little bungalows in Broadmoor; opportunity need go no further. He, for instance, sits on his little porch in the sunshine, and she sits on her little porch across the way. Hours and hours and days and days, they sit on their little porches in the sunshine. Then by and by they sit together on the same little porch. It is quite simple.

Often the story ends as it should. They get well and marry and live happily ever afterward. Sometimes, of course, it ends sadly. But nearly always love brings its compensation of joy, and nearly all who have ever lived out here keep afterward in their hearts an unfading flower of romance.

Colorado Springs is a place unique in the world. Filled with people unhappy to come, deserted by people unwilling to go. And nearly always their coming and going is through no wish or will of their own. Sometimes their going is as sudden and tragic as their coming.

A friend of ours whom we had expected to find here had only the week before been obliged to pack up on a few hours' notice and go to California. She had just built a new house and had been in it hardly two months and now she has to begin in a new environment all over again. The great tragedy in this case is that the husband cannot stay long away from a high altitude and the wife must probably always live at a low one.

Of the fashionable element in the Springs a certain elderly lady told me with bated breath:

"It is the fastest society on earth! They just live for excitement, and they don't attend church half as regularly as they go to each other's houses to dance or gamble. If you see a woman out walking or driving with a man, it's more likely another woman's husband than her own. My dear, you may call such a state of affairs modern and up to date, but I call it shocking — that's what I call it!"

She, dear soul, is from Salem, Massachusetts, and I can well believe she thinks as she spoke. There is also a younger woman, the wife of a prosperous manufacturer whose home is in Omaha. The old lady from Salem I had known in York Harbor, Maine, but the Omaha lady we "picked up an acquaintance with" through the offices of E. M. in saving the life of an attenuated specimen of a dog from the grip of one whose looks were more flattering to the species.[14]

Apparently the old lady and the younger one sit and exchange opinions all day, a rather needless effort, as they share the same in the first place. At almost any hour that you pass them the old lady is saying:

"My dear, that *is* Mrs. Smith talking to Mr. Baldwin!"

And the younger, aghast, echoes, "Well, who'd have thot it!" ("Thot" is not a misprint, that is the way she pronounces it.) And then in unison they wonder where Mr. Smith can be and why Mrs. Baldwin is not out walking with her husband.

The point of view of the old lady and the younger one represent not unfairly the attitude of the majority of wives in the two thousand miles we had come through since leaving the corner of Fifty-ninth Street and Fifth Avenue, New York. An opposed attitude jumps from Central Park East to Colorado Springs. Central Park West is curiously like the gap between. On Fifth Avenue and South and East and again in Colorado Springs a wife does not believe the happiness of family life dependent upon her husband's never speaking to another woman but herself. More often is the shoe on the other foot. The husband generally goes from his office to his club, the wife more than likely goes with an agreeable young man to a dancing tea. Parlor Snake is the New York vernacular for this ideal type of a five-o-clock young man![15] Once west of Fifth Avenue and for two

---

14. Before she was married, Emily Price used to spend summers in York Harbor, Maine with her family.

15. Emily Post is very up-to-date with her slang — "parlor snake" is the 1915 version of "lounge lizard" with both phrases denoting, according to the American Heritage Dictionary, "an idle man who haunts establishments or gatherings frequented by the rich or fashionable; a social parasite."

thousand miles thereafter nothing like this at all! For Mr. X to cross the threshold of Mrs. B.'s house unless accompanied by Mrs. X.— and sometimes several little X.'s— would be just cause for storms and tears, if not for divorce. Even we as strangers could see wives trailing like veritable shadows behind their husbands. Let Mr. X. stop for a second to speak to any Mrs. W., Y. or Z. and Mrs X. sidles up and clings to her husband's sleeve as though a few sentences uttered apart from a general conversation were affronts upon the security and dignity of a wife.

In the small circle of Chicago's smart set this wifely attitude of "speak to him not; he is mine" is certainly not apparent. A very opposite attitude, however, is very noticeable in Colorado Springs where a perfectly adoring wife said to Celia, who is one of the most attractive women imaginable: "For Heaven's sake, do take Fred out on the veranda and talk to him; he has been here two years without seeing a new face, and scarcely anyone to talk to about home but me!"

Just how the pioneers and cowboys affect the place is hard to define, and yet they undoubtedly do. Colorado people love the very name "cowboy" with an almost personal sentiment, just as, in their love for them, they seem personally to appropriate the "mountains," and from both, in spite of the luxury which many have brought from Europe or the Atlantic coast, and in contrast to their mere recklessness, they have acquired directness of outlook, fearless, open-air customs of living, and an unhampered freedom from unimportant trifles. The spirit of going through with what you undertake and not being stopped by a little mud that we first met with in Rochelle is here much intensified. In Illinois they prided themselves on surmounting obstacles; out here they are so imbued with the attitude of the men who live out on the plains and through the mountains— the pioneers whose adventures the most frivolous social leader knows by heart — that they don't even recognize an obstacle when they see it.

Notwithstanding the luxury of his own house, L. goes off into the wilderness generally with one guide but sometimes entirely alone, sleeps on the ground, eats what he can kill and reverts to the primitive.[16] And you can sit in a room the interior of which might be in the Palace of Versailles and hear your hostess in a two-hundred-dollar simplicity of chiffon and

---

16. L.'s camping is a mixture of a (fashionable) return to the primitive and the contemporary craze for outdoor living. An outstanding example of the latter is Dr. John W. Flinn's tent camp near Prescott, Arizona, which opened in 1903 under the acronym PAMSETGAAF, which stood for the kinds of therapy he offered, namely Pure Air, Maximum Sunshine, Equitable Temperatures, Good Accommodations, And Food. See Kravetz and Kimmelman, *Healthseekers* 26, 45. See also Belasco, "Commercialized Nostalgia," in Lewis and Goldstein, eds., *The Automobile and American Culture* 107–111.

"In the Garden of the Gods"

lace repeat to you by the hour stories beginning: "Bill Simpson, who was punching cattle on the staked plains—" or "The Apaches were on the warpath and Kit Carson—" Possibly she may even tell you of a hold-up adventure of her own when as a child she was traveling in the Denver stage.[17]

One amusing anecdote told us one afternoon at tea was of a celebrated plainsman who, carrying a large amount of money and realizing that he was about to be held up, quickly stuffed his roll of money down his trouser leg, but craftily left two dollars in his waistcoat pocket. The outlaws finding him so ill-supplied with "grub money" made him a present of a dollar to show him that he had met with real gentlemen.[18]

Perhaps from habit, just as when someone says, "How are you?" you say, "Very well, thank you," though you may be feeling wretchedly, whenever anyone mentions the topic of motoring, I find myself saying:

"Can you tell me anything about the roads between here and—?" Why I keep on asking about the roads I really don't know! Hearing that they are good or bad is not going to help or hinder. I think I must do it for the sake of being sociable and making conversation. So, sitting next to

17. The first reference is probably to the cowboy poet Bill Simpson. His work includes "Like It or Not," and "The Glow." Christopher "Kit" Carson (1809–68) was an American trapper and hunter. He was guide to Fremont's expeditions in the 1840s and Indian agent in New Mexico in the 1850s, and became a legend in his lifetime.

18. Most of the rest of this chapter was added for the book version, and did not appear in the *Collier's* articles.

one of the prominent members of the Automobile Club, yesterday, I found myself quite parrotlike asking for details of the road to Albuquerque.[19]

"With good brakes, and an experienced chauffeur who won't get flustered or light-headed, you oughtn't to have much trouble. You will find teams nearly always available to pull you through dangerous fords," he said casually.

Having ourselves withstood the mud of Iowa without injury and survived the perils of the Platte River Valley without meeting any, we find ourselves as commonplace as anyone who had crossed Long Island would be to New Yorkers. These people out here talk about being hauled through quicksand streams, or of clinging along shelf roads at the edge of a thousand-foot drop as though it were pleasant afternoon driving. I don't like the sound of the word "shelf"—why not by calling them mountain view roads let us keep our tranquillity at least until we get to them? And beyond the precipices is the desert, where there is no place to stop over and Heaven alone knows what fate awaiting us should anything happen to the car.

My companion at luncheon volunteered further that he had unluckily never been further south than Pueblo himself, but he knew a drug clerk who was the highest authority on road information. Information and ice-cream soda at the same time was a combination too alluring to be resisted, and an hour later saw me thirsting at the fountain. The soda clerk called to another out of sight behind the drug screen:

"Say, Bill, there's a lady here wants to start for Albuquerque tomorrow. Do you know anybody that's gone over the Raton lately?"

A long, lanky, typical "Uncle Sam," sauntered in eating a stick of peppermint.[20]

"Why, yes," he drawled, "Bullard went down. I guess he went with a team though; it was about a month ago. But Tracey went last week and took his bride on their wedding-trip. Of course," he turned to me, "Tracey

---

19. The local automobile club had been interested in the good roads movement since 1905, but Emily Post was sensible to ask, as "... . auto touring in Colorado as late as 1915 was still a strenuous undertaking, safely attempted only in summer. One expert advised motorists driving east and north of Colorado Springs to equip themselves with crowbar, hatchet, shovel, pulleys, and 100 feet of rope; heading south and west they should add cans of oil, gas, and water, and 150 feet of chicken wire to lay over mudholes." Carl Abbot et al., *Colorado: A History of the Centennial State* 3rd edn., (Niwot, Colo., University of Colorado Press, 1994), 238.

20. Perhaps he was eating King Leo pure peppermint stick candy, which was developed and trademarked in 1901. The stick has been in continuous production since then and is still offered today in old-fashioned gift tins with the King Leo Lion motif by its current manufacturer, Quality Candy Company, Inc. See http://www.candyusa.org/History/timeline.shtml

is a big man. Used to work on the freight depot. He bought a good manila towline and he is as strong as an ox. He could haul his machine out of anything, I guess."

At this point an outsider entered; he was labeled from head to toe with prosperity, expensive clothes, diamond rings— one on the third finger of each hand — a diamond scarfpin, a breezy air of "here-I-am" self-confidence. He seemed to be a friend of the drug clerk's and he ordered a malted milk and sat on the stool next to me. Immediately the clerk who had been called "Bill" appealed to him.

"This lady is going down to New Mexico. Do you know anything about the Raton Pass?"

"Do I know anything about Raton? I was born there!" Then he laughed and turned to me: "You needn't tell anybody, though. Want to know about Raton? Well, I'll tell you, they have no streets, and they have no drainage, and when it rains the mud is so soft you can go out in a boat and sail from house to house! There's just a Santa Fé roundhouse and a bunch of cottages.[21] Oh, it's the road over the pass you want to know about?" He stirred his baby beverage. "Well, they say they have fixed the road up some since I was down there but I guess the best thing you can do is let your chauffeur take the automobile down, and you walk behind it with the wreath!"

But somehow these alarms no longer terrify! Are we, too, being imbued with the spirit of the West? Forgetting that our original intention was to motor as far as we could travel comfortably, we can now think of nothing but that we have arrived merely at the gateway of the land of adventure, where cowboys, prairie schooners, and Indians may possibly still be found!

The Honorable Geoffrey G., an Englishman whom we met in New York last year, says he is going with us as far as Santa Fé. He has just imported a brand-new little foreign car and is as proud as Punch over it. It is even lower hung than ours, and has a very delicate mechanism. He drives it apparently well, but from various remarks he has made I don't believe he knows the first thing about machinery.

---

21. The Santa Fe Trail passed through Raton, and merchants gathered to service the needs of travelers and ranchers. Starting in 1879 the Santa Fe Railroad used the Raton Pass, and built division headquarters, including offices, a roundhouse and machine shops in the town. With the simultaneous opening of a coalmine nearby, the population grew to nearly 3,000 within a decade. A typical frontier town, Raton had both an opera house and shootouts in the street.

Fourteenth Day's Run,
Cheyenne to Colorado Springs

They drove to Colorado Springs on Sunday May 16 and left on Wednesday May 19, 1915.

Personal

Lunch *Denver.*

Brown's Palace Hotel.	$3.60[22]

Colorado Springs, Antlers Hotel.

Usual tips	$1.75
An average dinner (3)	$4.80
Drive over "high drive" (motors not allowed) (for 3)	$6.00[23]
Tip to driver	$ .50
Enormous double room with dressing room, bath	$6.00
Single room and bath	$3.50
Coffee and toast (in room)	$ .70
Tip	$ .25
(Especially attractively served)	
Breakfast (E. M.) (averaged)	$ .95
Tip	$ .25
Valet (pressing all our clothes)	$8.00
Laundry	$6.20

Motor

Colorado Springs. Mark Sheffel Motor Co. (highest class garage.)

Take off pan, stop leak, crank case and gaskets	$8.80
Vulc. case	$4.50
Greasing and tightening bolts.	
7 cups grease	$1.40

---

22. Henry C. Brown's grand hotel opened in 1892 when it cost an extraordinary $1.6 million. Designed by Frank E. Edbrooke, it had (and still has) an eight-story atrium lobby decorated with pale gold Mexican onyx and a stained glass skylight. Afternoon tea is still served there to the sound of harp and piano. An original 720-foot well continues to supply Rocky Mountain spring water to every room. The Brown Palace Hotel served as President Dwight D. Eisenhower's summer White House in the 1950s.

23. Spencer Penrose, a member of an old Philadelphia family, made a fortune in mining after moving to Colorado Springs in 1892. In 1915 he decided to build a new tourist attraction for the town, and invested $250,000 into building an auto road to Pikes Peak. Emily Post must have been part of one of the last group of tourists to travel this road before it was opened to individual motorists.

1 pt. kerosene	$ .05
1 pt. cylinder oil	$ .05
3 days' storage	$1.50
35x4 B.L. Republic red tube	$7.35
4½ B.O. patch	$ .90
22 gals. gas	$3.30
3 gals. oil	$2.40

XIX

A Glimpse of the West That Was

We might have been taking an unconscious part in some vast moving picture production, or, more easily still, if we overlooked the fact of our own motor car, we could have supposed ourselves crossing the plains in the days of the caravans and stage coaches, when roads were trails, and bridges were not!

To Pueblo by way of Canyon City and over the Royal Gorge loop, you go through great defiles between gigantic mountains, then out on a shelf road overlooking now vistas of mountains, now endless plains, now hanging over chasms two or three thousand feet deep, now dipping down, down to the brink of the river tearing along the base of the canyon walls.[1] All of the mountain roads of Colorado are splendidly built — even though some of their railless edges are terrifying to anyone light of head, and by no means to be recommended to an inexpert driver. One famously beautiful drive has a turntable built at an otherwise impossibly sharp bend.

After Pueblo — which by the way is not in the least quaint or Indian

---

1. In the *Collier's* version Emily Post abdicated the responsibility to describe the scenery, saying it was "far beyond any power of mine to describe." Julian Street was equally speechless: he wrote "though I saw the Royal Gorge, though I rode through it in the cab of a locomotive, with my hair standing on end, and though I found it 'as advertised,' I have no idea of trying to describe it, more than to say that it is a great cleft in the pink rocks through which run a river and a railroad, and that how the latter managed to keep out of the former was a constant source of wonder to me." *At Home Abroad*, 426. Emily Post presumably took the train, and was certainly taking the scenic route: instead of going south along the Fountain River valley to Pueblo, she took a southwesterly route' which involved the Royal Gorge loop of the Arkansas River, a dramatic thousand-foot gorge through igneous rock. Construction of the railroad led to legal conflicts in the 1870s between the Santa Fe and the Denver and Rio Grande railroads. The Santa Fe group constructed a hanging bridge at a place where the gorge is only thirty feet wide, and suspended the track from the north side of the gorge. The bridge cost $11,759 in 1879; it is still in use.

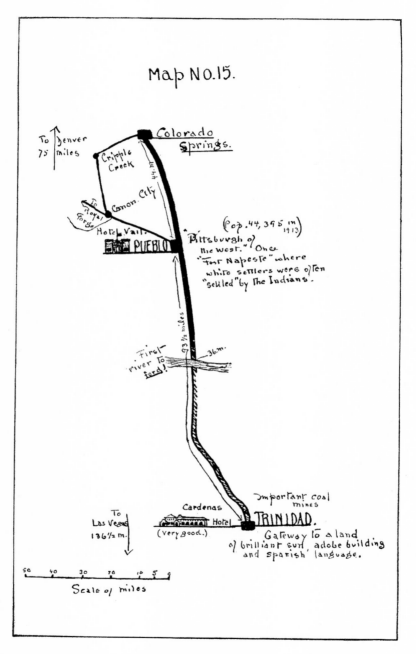

Map No. 15.

To Denver 75 miles

Colorado Springs.

Cripple Creek

14.44

To Royal Gorge

Canon City

Hotel Vail.

PUEBLO

(Pop. 44, 395 in 1913)

Pittsburgh of the west." Once "Fort Napeste" where white settlers were often "settled" by the Indians.

93½ miles

"First river to ford."

36. m.

Important coal mines

To Las Vegas 136½ m.

Cardenas Hotel (very good.)

TRINIDAD.

Gateway to a land of brilliant sun, adobe building and spanish language.

50 40 30 20 10 5 0

Scale of miles

"Map no. 15 From Colorado Springs to Trinidad" via the Royal Gorge, Wednesday May 19, 1915.

"A glimpse of the West of yesterday." Note the telegraph poles, and the truck coming towards the horse-drawn covered wagon.

as its name promised, but a smoky and smeltering industrious little Pittsburgh — you come out upon the plains, plains that look as you imagined them, on which cattle and cowboys ranged and prairie schooners came slowly over the horizon.[2] A few miles beyond Pueblo, exactly like a scene in the moving pictures, we passed three of the white-topped wagons, their hood rocking and gleaming in the sun and little burros with saddles on them trotting either side. A man walked at the head of the caravan and two others walked behind. One wagon was driven by a woman, while a man slept, and two children peered out at us from within. A young man drove the second wagon; by his side was a young woman holding a baby. All that was needed to make a frontier drama was a band of befeathered Indians on the warpath.

A little way farther we saw a cowboy galloping over the plains swinging a lariat. He laughed when we came up to him, as though he had been caught doing something foolish. In the next few miles we passed another caravan and through a herd of cattle driven by three cowboys, but not a sign of our friend, the Englishman, with whom we had planned to lunch. He, having taken the direct road, which was about sixty miles or so shorter

---

2. Pueblo (Spanish for town) developed in the mid 19th century as a fur trading post. Its real growth began when large iron and coal deposits were found nearby, and by the 1880s it was the largest industrial center in Colorado. This explains Emily Post's reference to Pittsburgh.

"Halfway across a thrilling ford, wide and deep, on the Huerfano River." This crossing would have been a few miles north of the town of Walsenburg.

than ours, had agreed to select an attractive spot and wait for us. We had
about decided that he had either been lost or overlooked, when we saw a
team coming toward us and behind it, being towed, his nice, new, little
car. He had come to a ford through a wide, swift river which he so mis-
trusted from the start that he made his valet wade across it first. But as the
water came up only to the man's knees, and the bottom was reported to
be firm and pebbly, the Honorable Geoffrey plunged in — and bang! she
blew up! The water flooding his carburetor sucked into the hot cylinders
and was changed so violently into steam that it blew off the cylinder heads![3]

Mixed with our very real sympathy with the Englishman was not a
little doubt as to whether we had better risk a like fate. The driver of the
team, seeing our doubt, explained: "The river's a mite high just now, but
when you come to the bank, just go in slow and steady, and if the water
comes up too high, stop your engine quick and fire a revolver! See! I'll hear
you and send someone to pull you through!"

The thought of luncheon had vanished. We parted with our unfortunate friend and approached with not a little trepidation the rushing
waters that had wrecked him. The river looked formidable enough; wide,
swift, bubbling, and opaque — like coffee with cream, exactly. We remembered that it had a gravel bottom, and that its greatest depth was very little over the drenched valet's knees.

We went in very cautiously, very slowly, the water came up and up,

---

3. The Honorable Geoffrey G — was presumably fording the Fountain River.

"First cowboys and cattle." Emily Post was traveling at a time when the open range had practically disappeared.

almost to the floor boards. The rest of the story is perfectly tame and flat; our car went through it like a duck!

Further on, we came to several fords, all small and shallow, and we splashed through them gleefully. We passed great herds of cattle and any number of cowboys.[4] We saw hundreds of gophers, ran our wheels over two rattlesnakes, and escaped — one skunk.

FIFTEENTH DAY'S RUN, COLORADO SPRINGS TO TRINIDAD WEDNESDAY MAY 19, 1915

Personal
Lunched, *Pueblo.*
    Vail Hotel $ 3.00[5]

---

4. An interesting sentence in the *Collier's* version was omitted in the book; the original read: "...cowboys, all friendly. I snapped a kodak and one of them grinned: 'Say friend, d'you think you've got a good likeness?'" George Eastman trademarked the name Kodak in 1887 and it was soon being used as a noun, verb and adjective.

5. The Vail Hotel, which claimed to be the most magnificent hotel in the West, was opened in September 1911 in time for the Colorado State Fair. Although it is on the National Register of Historic Places, it deteriorated over time, and in 1981 was remodeled to provide accommodation for senior citizens.

Trinidad. Hotel Cardenas (our first of the
    Harvard chain of hotels)[6]
    Am. plan, 3 good rooms with 3 baths and good
        "American cooking" meals ($4.50) $13.50
    $1.50 deducted for lunch we were not to have.
    Tips $ 1.75
    Incidentals, movies, etc. $ 1.30
    Lunch to take with us $ 1.60
Las Vegas. The Castenada.[7]
    (Did not telegraph ahead, so could not get baths)
    3 rooms ($3.25) $ 9.75
    American plan (lunch deducted)
    Lunch to take with us $ 1.50
    Tips $ 1.75
    Telegrams, sundries $ 2.50

Motor

Trinidad Novelty Works Co.
    Storage $ .50
    14 gals. gas (15c.) $ 2.10
    2 qts. oil $ .40
Las Vegas, 145 miles.
Las Vegas Auto Co.
    Storage $ .50
    15 gals. gas $ 2.50

    In Trinidad we ran across our first companion motor tourists. "Kansas City to Los Angeles" was written in letters six inches high with an American pennant on one side, and the name of a popular machine on the other. Another car, a Ford, announcing that it was bound from Lincoln,

---

6. This is a misprint in the original book. The Hotel Cardenas was part of the Harvey chain. It was opened in 1904, and after its demolition the site became a small park. English immigrant Fred Harvey opened his first hotel in Topeka, Kansas in 1876, and by the end of the century had numerous hotels and restaurants along the Santa Fe railroad. He specialized in good food and fast, efficient service. He hired well-groomed and well-trained young women as waitresses— they wore black dresses with crisp white aprons and soon became famous as "Harvey Girls" adding to the attraction of his establishments. MGM even made a movie about them in 1946. See Lesley Poling-Kempes, *The Harvey Girls: Women Who Opened the West* (New York: Marlow Co., 1991).

7. Originally part of the Harvey chain, the 25,000 square foot hotel was built in 1898. It served as the social center of Las Vegas for many years, and was the site of numerous reunions of Theodore Roosevelt's Rough Riders, twenty-one of whom came from Las Vegas. It is now on the endangered list of the New Mexico Heritage Preservation Alliance.

Nebraska, to San Francisco, had enough banners to decorate the room of a schoolboy.[8] The owners of these two talked volubly on touring in general and the roads ahead in particular. The owner of the Ford, adjusting the vizor of his yachting cap and pulling on his gauntlets, looked at us doubtfully.[9]

"Well," said he, "everyone to his own liking! I myself prefer a shorter, lighter car!"

"Are you going to try to take that machine down the Bajada?" asked the other. "I'm glad I haven't the job of driving her even over the Ratton!"[10]

"My, but she's a peach!" exclaimed an enthusiastic mechanic. "Don't you have no fear, mister!" he whispered to E. M. "The stage coaches they used to go over this road to Santa Fé; if they could get over it, I guess *you* can!"

It had never occurred to us that we couldn't, but the reminder of the lumbering caravans was comforting, and we started tranquilly to climb the Colorado side of the Raton divide. We passed first one, and then the other of the two cars, whose owners had little opinion of ours. Did they believe their ugly snub-nosed tin kettles, panting and puffing and chug-chugging up the grade, like asthmatic King Charles spaniels, better hill-climbers than our beautiful, big, long engine, that took the ascent without the slightest loss of breath even in the almost nine thousand feet of altitude? We had looked at the two machines in much the same way that passengers in the cab of a locomotive might look at a country cart trundling along the road, for we had pulled smoothly by them in much the same way that the locomotive passes the cart.

We have all heard the story of the hare and the tortoise, and the old adage, "He who laughs last —" It was all very well as long as we remained in the state of Colorado! But the instant we crossed the Divide, our beautiful, great, long, wonderful machine lay down perfectly flat on its stomach and could not budge until one of these despised snub-nosed spaniels heaped coals of fire on our heads by kindly pulling us out.

Because of their highness— one of the chief attributes of their ugliness— the other two cars could under the present conditions travel along without hindrance, whereas we discovered to our chagrin that we had far too little clearance, and the first venturing into New Mexico ruts held us fast.

---

8. Emily Post was not alone in her long-distance quest, so it is interesting that this is the first time she mentions meeting some of her fellow travelers.

9. This anecdote was missing from the *Collier's* version, as was any mention of Ford cars.

10. Bajada Hill was so steep that many cars of the Post era had to climb it backwards, as reverse was their strongest gear. See below for an account of the Raton Pass.

"Sometimes we struck a bad road." Note the Massachusetts plates on the car; Ned must have been using it at Harvard.

The road over the Raton Pass, by the way, was originally built by a famous character known as "Uncle" Dick Wooten. Having defrayed all of the expenses out of his own pocket he established a tollgate so he might somewhat reimburse himself. The American traders paid the toll without a murmur; the Mexicans paid only through the persuasion of a revolver, and the Indians would not pay at all. After going over the road we agreed with the Indians.[11]

The rest of our story all the way to Santa Fé is one long wail. But in justice to the roads of New Mexico, it is necessary to go into some explanation of the wherefore of our particular difficulties. In the first place we went out there in the very early spring after the worse of the thaw, but

---

11. The toll was $1.50. Richens Lacy Wooten, scout and frontiersman, was born in Virginia in 1816. When he was seven years old his parents removed to Kentucky, and in 1836 he went to Independence, Missouri, where he became a teamster in the Santa Fe trade. In childhood he had the misfortune to lose two fingers on his left hand, which led to Arapahoe Indians dubbing him "Cut Hand." To the white men of the West he was familiarly known as "Uncle Dick." In 1866 he received authority from the legislature of Colorado and New Mexico to construct a road through the Raton Pass. He lived in the pass, and died there in his 90th year, having otulived all of his five wives and 17 of his 20 children. It is said that he sometimes collected toll at the muzzle of his rifle from travelers over his road. The Atchison, Topeka & Santa Fe Railroad Company named one of its locomotives "Uncle Dick" in his honor. Frank W. Blackmar, ed., *Kansas: a cyclopedia of state history, embracing events, institutions, industries, counties, cities, towns, prominent persons, etc.* Vol. II (Chicago: Standard Pub. Co., 1912).

"In order to cross here, E.M. built a bridge with the logs at the right."

before any repairs, which might have been made for the summer season, had been begun. As for equipment, ours could not by any possibility have been worse.

With a wheelbase of one hundred and forty-four inches, our car has a center clearance of only *eight* inches![12] Furthermore, we have a big steel exhaust pipe that slants from ten inches above the ground to eight and one-half inches above the ground where it protrudes behind the left rear wheel. Therefore, where shorter, higher cars can go with perfect ease, it requires great skill and no little ingenuity for a very low and long one to keep clear of trouble. For instance, over deep-rutted roads we have to stay balanced on the ridges on either side, like walking a sort of double tight rope; if we slide down into the rut, we have to be jacked up and a bridge of stones put under to lift us out again. On many of the sharp corners of the mountain passes we have to back and fill two and often four times, but our real difficulties are all because of that troublesome exhaust pipe.

Out on the cattle ranches they build a great many queer little ditch crossings; two planks of wood with edges like troughs, and a wheel-width apart. They are our particular horror. Again, right wheels went over perfectly, but the only way we can get the left ones over is to build up the

---

12. The standard United States specification for a 2004 four-door sedan is that it has a minimum wheelbase of 110.5 inches. A Buick LeSabre, for example, has a wheelbase of 112.2 inches.

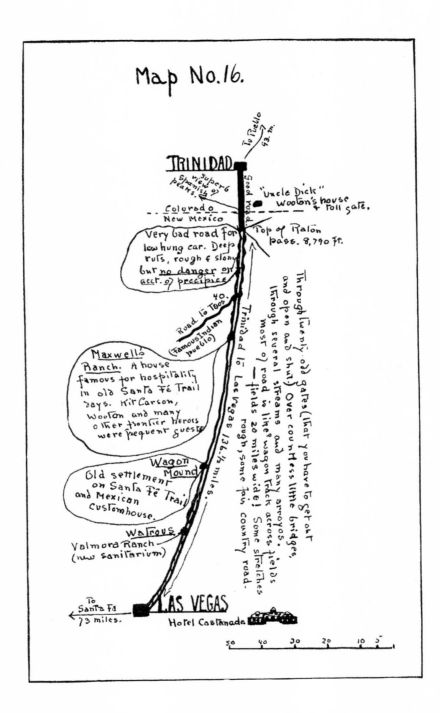

Map No.16.

To Pueblo 93. m.

TRINIDAD

superb view of Spanish peaks.

Good road

"Uncle Dick" Wooton's house & toll gate.

Colorado ──── New Mexico

Top of Raton Pass. 8,790 ft.

Very bad road for low hung car. Deep ruts, rough & stony but **no danger** on acct. of precipice

40. Road to Taos (Famous Indian pueblo)

Trinidad to Las Vegas 136.½ miles.

Through twenty old gates (that you have to get out and open and shut.) Over countless little bridges, through several streams and many arroyos. Most of road is like wagon track across fields — fields 20 miles wide! Some stretches rough, some fair country road.

Maxwell's Ranch. A house famous for hospitality in old Santa Fé Trail days. Kit Carson, Wooton and many other frontier heroes were frequent guests

Wagon Mound

Old settlement on Santa Fé Trail and Mexican Customhouse.

Watrous

Valmora Ranch (new sanitarium)

To Santa Fé 73 miles.

LAS VEGAS

Hotel Castanada

50   40   30   20   10 5

"Map no. 16, Trinidad to Las Vegas," Thursday May 20, 1915.

hollows with pieces of wood — some barrel staves we found by luck and that we now always carry with us.

Another particular joy to us is sliding down into and clambering out of arroyos, on the edge of which the car loves to make believe it is a see-saw.[13] Our only good fortune seems to be in having plenty of power, and the carburetor high enough not to be flooded — as yet — by any streams we have gone through. Once, in order to find a bank that we could crawl up on, we had to wade up the stream, with the possibility of quicksand, for nearly half a mile.

After three days of this sort of experience, you can't help wincing at the very sight of ruts or rocks or river beds, in exactly the same way that you wince at the close approach of dentist's instruments.

Between Trinidad and Las Vegas we were overtaken by a blizzard.[14] It rained, hailed, and finally snowed, and it all passed by us in less than an hour. But in the midst of it we lost our way and wandered for miles across the prairie. Finally, at the end of about twenty miles, we saw an open wagon and two men resting under it, but they spoke only Spanish and we understood their directions so vaguely that when our road disappeared into hilly, roadless prairie, and we came to a new bridge without any tracks leading to it, and apparently uncrossable between it and us, it was snowing again, there were no shadows to tell the points of the compass by. As E. M. drove at a snail's pace, wondering which direction to turn, two Indians on ponies appeared over the edge of a nearby hill.

Again we had no language in common. But we repeated "Las Vegas," and they, gravely motioning us to follow, led us through a labyrinthian path between the hillocks to the mesa from which the bridge started. Although they helped us with greatest willingness, and accepted a coin with grave courtesy, their faces were as expressionless as wood-carvings and neither uttered a sound or smiled.

Finally, because we were hungry and not by reason of any inviting charm at that particular point of the earth's most dreary surface, we stopped for luncheon. We had just about spread out our food paraphernalia when, turning at the sound of a galloping hoofed animal, we saw a horseman tearing across the plains toward us. He rode as a brigand might, and only a Westerner can. Standing in his stirrups rather than sitting in

---

13. An arroyo is a deep gully cut by flooding of a usually dry stream.

14. Here, according to the *Collier's* article, Ned Post drove "nine hours without taking his hands off the wheel." His mother "fed him hardboiled eggs and sandwiches as he drove."

his saddle, and seemingly unaffected by the rocking motion of his mount, his body was poised level with the horizon.[15]

Was he a highwayman, one of those notorious bad men that the Southwest is said to be infested with, or was he just a cowboy? His outline fitted into any sort of a part your fear or delight might imagine. The wide-brimmed hat, bandanna handkerchief around his neck, leather cuffs on his shirt and murderous-looking cartridge belt and revolver, suited equally a make-up for good or bad.[16]

My heart thumped with the excitement of a possible hold up, and yet I was far too fascinated to feel either fear or inclination to escape. As he came nearer, he came slower, and when quite close he brought his horse to a leisurely walk that had no longer any hold-up suggestion in it and I took a bite out of my hitherto untouched sandwich. When almost beside us, he leaned a little sideways in his saddle and glanced at our State license number, and then at us, with a manner as casual and unconcerned as though we might have been an inanimate hillock of the landscape.

Then, "Howdy, strangers!" he said. The tone of his voice was friendly enough, in spite of his taciturn and utterly unsmiling expression. It has struck us all through the West how seldom anyone has smiled.

"How are you!" echoed E. M., matching manner for manner. His tone, too, had a friendly ring, but he went on opening a tin of potted meat as though no one else were present.

"Come all the way from back East in that machine?" the Westerner asked, with a little more interest. "How long you been comin?"

E. M. glanced up from his tin-opening and the two exchanged a few remarks on the subject of roads and horses and motors and then, as nearly as I can remember, the Westerner said:

"It'd be a mighty long ride on a cayuse![17] Which them machines shorely disregards distance a whole lot."

E. M. asked the Westerner, "Won't you have some lunch with us? Awfully glad if you will!"

"Thank *you*," but he moved a little away from us, as though for the first time embarrassed. "Thank YOU!" he said again. "I et dinner 'bout an hour ago!"

---

15. The long and vivid account of Emily Post's encounter with the cowboy from Boston was not in the original *Collier's* article.

16. As historian John A. Jakle has noted, "Diligent tourists cultivate chance encounters.... Surprise discoveries and their reaction to these discoveries stand as travel highlights." Jakle, *The Tourist*, 36.

17. A cayuse is an Indian pony, or more generally a term used to describe a horse of poor quality.

"We have only cold things," I explained, not only thrilled at an encounter with a real life cowboy but attracted by his distinctly pleasing personality. He had no manner at all and yet in his absence of self-consciousness there was very real dignity. And in contrast to the copper-brown of his face his unsmiling eyes were so blue that their color was startling. I had been wrapped in admiration of E. M.'s color, which I thought as brown as the sun could make a man, but beside this other of the plains, E. M. looked almost pallid.

"I don't aim to have you deny yourself nothin' for me!" he hesitated.

"Oh, we have *lots* of food!" said Celia. "Cold food, though, you know; nothing hot."

For the first time his eyes crinkled into a half smile:

"The grub we get is *hot*, which is most of the virchoos you can claim for it."

Meanwhile E. M. had proffered an open box of eggs and sandwiches. The other dismounted, threw the reins forward over his horse's neck, and accepted our hospitality. He turned a paper plate and a thin tin spoon in his hands as though dubious of such flimsy utility until he discovered it was to be used for ice cream. Hard frozen ice cream under the midday sun and fifty miles from where it could be bought, interested him.

"I've seen bottles for liquids, but I've never seen one like that for solids. It sure is cold!" he said. And with its coldness, he quite thawed. He did not look more than thirty, yet talked quite a while about the old times that he himself remembered, generalities for the most part, but with a lingering keenness in describing the qualifications that men on the range used to have.

Also he told us a string of yarns — that may have been true — or they may have been merely the type of divertissement whereby Westerners love to entertain themselves at the expense of Eastern credulity. One amusing story, at any rate, was of the hold-up of a passenger stage by a single masked man. Afterwards when the sheriff and his men followed his horse's tracks, they suddenly disappeared as though the earth had swallowed them. It had. They found the thief's buried boots with horseshoes nailed to them on a path that had too many footprints to single out one to follow.

He added quite regretfully that cow-punching was not what it used to be. Cattle were getting tame and the ranches were enclosed in wire fences and life was so soft and easy, that cattle raising was no more exciting than raising sheep. Finally he volunteered:

"I've got folks in Massachusetts; my brother Sam's in Boston."

When E. M. told him that he had come from Boston, as he was still a student at Harvard, the Westerner could neither understand how it was that E. M. did not know his brother, nor that a man of such an age and size could still be getting an education.

"Book learning" was a good thing, he thought, but twenty years of age was too late in his opinion to be still acquiring it. He himself had run away from home at the age of eleven. Not because of ill-treatment, but merely that it seemed the manly thing to do. In his opinion a boy was a no-account specimen who would stay past his twelfth year "hangin' round his womenfolks."

To run away and never send a word home seems to be the common-place behavior of Western boys. "I don't know how your mothers stand the anxiety," I said aloud, "not to know whether their sons are even alive."

"I reckon that's so. I never showed up nor wrote for six years. One evening I walks in on the old folks, and they didn't recognize me; the old woman went plum' over backwards when she saveys it was me. That was some years ago and I haven't been back since."

Having finished luncheon E. M. cranked the car, and our guest gathered up the trailing reins of his patiently standing horse. Once his rider was in the saddle, however, the bronco, as though to show what he could do, gave quite a gallery display of bucking, while his rider gave no less an exhibition of Western horsemanship, rolling a cigarette in tranquil disregard of his pony's hump-backed leaps, which, however, soon settled down to a steady gallop that carried our friend across the plains. On the top of a nubble he waved to us and we waved back as we continued, on our side regretfully, our separate ways.

We have passed any number of little Mexican, or Indian, adobe villages. One house was surrounded by a picket fence painted bright laundry blue. Several had blue door and window frames. The houses were all one-storied and the people looked more Mexican than Indian.

When we finally arrived, without further difficulty, at Las Vegas, it seemed rather questionable whether we would be able to go on next day or not. The barometer was down, several other motorists doleful, and the outlook very glum.

"What did you start so early in the season for?" we heard one driver ask another.

"Well," said the second, "I don't mind a little speculation as to what you're going to run into. If you know the road ahead is all fine and dandy, what's to keep your interest up?"

Leaving Las Vegas early the next morning, we encountered the same erratic weather that we ran through the day before. When we happened to be under an unclouded area, we could see that all about us were separate storm clouds, black smudges against an otherwise clear sky. As we drove

Top: "Your route leads through many Mexican and Indian villages." *Bottom:* "The Indian pueblo of Taos."

beneath one of the black areas we were deluged with rain, or hail, or snow, and through it came into sunny weather again. It was the most curious sensation to run into a blinding storm, and being able to gauge beforehand how long it would take us to pass through it.

As we approached a ford some Mexicans standing beside it motioned us to make a wide sweep; it landed us in deep soft sand up to our hubs. Whereupon they attached their horses to us and pulled us through.

"To see the sleeping beauty of the Southwest, the path is by no means a smooth one to the motorist."

"Do many motors have to be helped?" I asked.

"Every one, all same!" they replied.

We had passed two cars, so I held up my fingers. "Two more are coming!" I said.

They immediately broke into a broad grin.

I rather wonder do they make all cars drive in that large circle to *avoid* the sand pile!

Between Las Vegas and Santa Fe, the going was the worst yet.

Washed-out roads, arroyos, rocky stretches, and nubbly hills. We just about smashed everything, cracked and broke the exhaust, lost bolts and screws, and scraped along on the pan all of the way.

And yet the dread Bajada Hill, in which we are to drop nine hundred feet in one mile and long cars are warned in every guidebook of the sharp and precipitous turns, is still ahead of us. One thing, if it is worse than from the top of the Raton we might as well be prepared to leave all that is left of us scattered in odd pieces along the road.

The next time we motor the trail to Santa Fé we are unanimously agreed that it is going to be in a very different kind of car — or best of all, on the backs of little sure-footed burros!

XX

Our Little Sister of Yesterday

With straight black Indian hair piled high under a lace mantilla, with necklaces of gold and silver and coral and turquoise as big as hens' eggs, with her modern American dress barely showing under her Indian blanket of holiest red, her head pillowed against the mountains of the North, and her little pueblo feet in the high-heeled Spanish slippers stretched out upon the plains of the South, Santa Fé sits dreaming in the golden sunlight.[1]

Sometimes she dreams idly of her childhood when she ran about the mountains barefooted, her hair done in two squash-blossom whorls on either side of her dusky head, so long ago that no white man had ever set foot on the western continent. Or perhaps, half shutting her unfathomable eyes, she remembers the heroes who fought and died for her, or the pomp of her marriage with her Spanish first lord, Don Juan d'Onate — noble in estates rather than character, though he brought her a wedding-gift of white wooly animals, afterward called sheep, and furthermore dressed her in fine clothes, put her in a palace, and made a lady of her.[2] Her little bare

---

1. Emily Post was not the only traveler bewitched by Santa Fe; to many upper-class tourists, concerned about the changes taking place in America, it seemed to be a vision of a purer, preindustrial world. The irony, of course, lay in the dependence on the wealth created in industrial America that permitted tourists to visit and experience Santa Fe. See Hal K. Rothman, *Devil's Bargains: Tourism in the Twentieth-Century American West* (Lawrence: University Press of Kansas, 1998), 90, 111–12.

2. Don Juan de Oñate was the first successful European colonizer of the American Southwest. He was very well-connected, as his wife was granddaughter of Hernán Cortéz and great granddaughter of Moctezuma. In January 1598, he led a four-mile procession comprising six hundred colonists, plus soldiers, priests, families, Indians and Africans, 83 wagons and over 7,000 animals. Friendly Manso Indians from the El Paso region guided them across the desert to the river crossing. The Spanish took possession of the land for their king on April 30, 1598, and celebrated with a mass and a great feast, believed by some to be the first Thanksgiving in the nation.

feet were shod in scarlet slippers, and she had many skirts of silk and velvet, though never a bodice to one of them, but her breast was strung with
necklaces and her arms with bracelets, and she had shawls of silk and man-
tillas of lace to wrap most of her face and all of her bare brown shoulders
in. The palace had walls six feet thick; some say the thick walls were to
hide the true palace already built by her own Indian forefathers. All the
same, nobles in broadcloth embroidered in silver and gold crowded her
audience room when the Island of Manhattan was a wilderness, and the
wood of which the *Mayflower* was to be built was still growing in the forest of England.

But then the dream becomes a sad one of injustice and cruelty; of long,
long miserable years under the oppression of a dissipated gambling tyrant
who put her family to the sword or made them slaves. Then came revolt
and savage warfare; massacres that made her palace steps run red, vivid
days of flame, black ones of darkness until—And this is her dream of
dreams! She forgets it all happened in the long ago. The quick blood leaps
in her veins, her heart bears fast, her pulses quiver at the magic name of
her hero, her conqueror, her lover, Don Diego de Vargas! Again she sees
him, surrounded by his panoplied soldiers, lances flashing, banners waving, marching victorious across the plaza, and planting his cross at her
palace door in the name of the Virgin, demanding her glad surrender![3]

"Ah, to love was to live!" says Santa Fé. "Yet in all the world there was
only one De Vargas—and he has passed!" And she wraps herself in her
Indian blanket and falls again to dreaming.

Her alliance with the American Republic is what one might call a

---

3. Emily Post is making an oblique and sympathetic reference to the reconquest of New
Mexico in 1692–96 after the Pueblo rebellion of 1680. In 1690, Diego de Vargas Zapata Luján
Ponce de León was appointed Governor of New Mexico, and instructed to subdue the rebel-
lious Pueblos. He left El Paso in August 1692 with fewer than fifty soldiers and three friars, arriving at Santa Fe to find the former Spanish capital fortified and its inhabitants
defiant. Mixing diplomacy and threat of a siege, he soon obtained their surrender, and by
the end of 1692 most of New Mexico's Pueblos had been officially restored to the Spanish
empire without a shot being fired or any blood shed. His success is observed every September at the famous Fiesta de Santa Fe (see below). The second portion of the reconquest
was, however, far from peaceful. In late 1693, de Vargas returned to Santa Fe with seventy
families, eighteen Franciscan friars, and a number of Tlaxlacan allies to begin the recolo-
nization of New Mexico. Some of the Pueblos had second thoughts about the Spanish intentions and refortified Santa Fe. After two weeks' negotiation, de Vargas decided to take it by
force. After a fierce battle seventy Pueblo defenders were executed and several hundred
captured men, women, and children sentenced to ten years' servitude. By the summer of
1696, the situation deteriorated into a general rebellion known as the Second Pueblo Revolt.
Many Pueblos were abandoned and their population dispersed as their inhabitants sought
refuge in the mountains and among the Navajo and Apache, but the Pueblos were weak-
ened and unable to resist effectively. Soon, more Spanish families arrived in Santa Fe, the
missions were reestablished, and Spanish settlements grew.

marriage of arrangement. Foreign in race, in sentiment, in understanding, she has never adopted the customs or manners of her new lord, but lives tranquilly, uneventfully, dreaming always of the long ago.[4]

And even though Don Diego de Vargas has lain for two centuries in the grave of his forefathers, though Indians no longer go on the warpath, though the eight-horse wagon mile-long caravans of the traders and travelers from the far East beyond the Mississippi no longer come clattering down over the mountains, to the excited and welcoming shouts of the populace of, "*Los Americanos! La Caravana!*" crowding into the Plaza to receive them, if the streets of Santa Fé no longer riot in tumult and bloodshed, they at least still riot in color and picturesqueness, kaleidoscopic enough to vie with anything in Constantinople or Cairo. You might think yourself in the Orient or in a city of old Spain transported upon a magic carpet, but nothing less like the United States can be imagined. Along the narrow crooked streets, dwellings hundreds of years old stand shoulder to shoulder with modern houses that have wedged themselves between.[5] Down a zigzag lane you may see an Indian woman hooded in a white cotton shawl, and balancing a jar of water on her head as in the Biblical pictures of Rebecca.

Besides big modern automobiles are Indians leading little burros so loaded down with firewood that their meek little faces are all there is to be seen protruding in front, little switching tails or kicking heels in the back, and the whole bundle supported by spindly tiny-footed legs. On a corner is an Indian wrapped in his bright blanket. Two Mexicans in high-crowned wide-brimmed sombreros lean against a door frame and smoke cigarettes. Cowboys in flannel shirts have vivid bandanas around their throats, and there is more color yet in women's dresses, in flowers, in fruits, in awnings—color, color rioting everywhere. Over everything the sun bakes just as it does in Spain or Northern Africa, and the people all look as silent and dreamy as the town.

Only a few hundred miles away are typical striving American cities shouting to anyone who will hear, and assailing the ears of those who won't, "Watch me grow — just watch me!" The big ones boom it, the little ones pipe it, but each and every one shouts to the earth at large, "Yesterday I was a community of nesters' shanties; today I'm an up-to-date thriving town. Tomorrow — wait, and you shall see!"

---

4. In 1846 Stephen Watts Kearney annexed New Mexico to the United States during the Mexican-American War; New Mexico was admitted to the Union as the 47th state in 1912.

5. In the *Collier's* article, Emily Post wrote: "On the Plaza are little bazaars where the Indian silversmiths hammers out his wares, or strings of turquoises."

Yet their little Indian and Spanish sister in the center of a vast domain of buried cities, of unmined treasures, dozes in the sun and cares not a bit how much the world outside may strive, or teem or grow. Can anyone fancy her waking from her reverie, dropping her indolent soft Spanish accent and shouting in strident tones that she, too, will be a bustling growing town?[6] Sooner fancy the Sphinx on the African desert urging, "Votes for women!"[7]

6. Santa Fe was, in fact, a modern town with a deliberately "old" look. As historian Hal Rothman has suggested, the appearance of the town was the brainchild of an Anglo newcomer, Edgar L. Hewett, who, after he was fired from the presidency of the New Mexico Normal School became an amateur archaeologist (though he gained professional respectability with his Ph.D. in 1908). He established the School of American Archaeology in Santa Fe in 1905, and went on to found other nostalgic cultural institutions. One of them, the Santa Fe Fiesta, included a bullfight as well as a reenactment of De Vargas's return to Santa Fe. Most importantly for the appearance of the city, he helped create the building code that merged Spanish and Native American styles "and fashioned Santa Fe into a town where the mythic and real were purposely indistinguishable." K. Rothman, *Devil's Bargains*, 81–86.
7. Even if Egyptian women were to wait until 1956 for suffrage, by 1915 eleven American states—Wyoming, Utah, Colorado, Idaho, Washington, California, Oregon, Montana, Kansas, Arizona, and Nevada had given women the vote. The women of New Mexico had to wait for the ratification of the 19th Amendment to the U.S. Constitution in 1920.

XXI

Ignorance with a Capital I

Imagine people living all their lives in Cairo never having seen the Pyramids. Imagine anyone living in Italy never having been to Pompeii. Yet we, ourselves, to whom the antiquities and wonders of far countries are perfectly familiar, did not even know that the wonders of the Southwest existed! We thought that Pueblo had a nice Indian sound, that Santa Fé must be an important railroad terminal. Arizona we pictured as a wide desert like the Sahara, with the Grand Canyon at the top of it, and a place called Phoenix, appropriately named as the only thing that could survive the heat, and another place called Tombstone, also fittingly named, in the middle of a vast area of sizzling sand.

Was there ever any place less like a railroad center than Santa Fe? The main line of the railroad which has taken its name does not even go there.[1] A little branch runs to the terminal city from a junction called Lamy, where, by the way, there is a Harvey hotel, which means, of course, a good one.[2] This is a word of advice to the tourist who finds the one in Santa Fe poor. Still, in a city that is old and colorful, and quaint, one hardly expects won-

---

1. Although there was a small branch line to Santa Fe, the effect of the railroad's by-passing the town was almost fatal; by 1910 more than 20 per cent of its 1880 population had left, and Santa Fe was smaller than it had been in 1817. On the other hand, the fifteen-mile ride by wagon or automobile along the bumpy track marked for some tourists a crucial division between the modern bustling world and a more romantic past. See Rothman, *Devil's Bargain*, 82, 93.

2. Collaboration between the Harvey Company and the AT&SF was instrumental in "inventing the west" as a tourist attraction. See Leah Dilworth, *Imagining Indians in the Southwest: Persistent Visions of a Primitive Past* (Washington: Smithsonian Institution, 1996) especially chapter 2, which deals perceptively with the role of the Fred Harvey hotel chain in the development of both the Indian as spectacle and the promotion of Indian crafts.

derful accommodations. The hotel in Biskra, Africa, did not use to be much to boast about, either.[3]

As for our ignorance about the country, we came across a woman today who was certainly, at least to us, a new type. She was traveling on mule-back and absolutely alone![4] At first it seemed the most dangerous and daring thing I had ever heard of, but a few minutes of her conversation convinced me that *she* was quite safe. Never did I believe a human being could so closely resemble a hornet. She looked us over as though we might have been figures in the Eden Musée.[5] Then she asserted:

"Humph! You're the English people! I saw a British emblem on a car outside, and it's easy to see that you are the ones it belongs to!"

We denied the nationality but claimed the car.

She shrugged her shoulders:

"Well, if you aren't English, you're either from New York or Boston — it amounts to the same thing! Ever been to Europe?"

We had.

"Ever been out here before?"

We hadn't.

"I knew it! I knew it the very first moment I clapped eyes on you!"

Like a phonograph she recited a long tirade on the topic of the "Americans who go spend money in Europe and neglect their own country." She asserted the superiority of our own land over that of every other in generalities and in detail, ending with a final thrust: "What can you get over there, I'd like to know, that you can't get here?"

She asserted that a two-hundred-thousand-dollar collection of modern paintings was far more worth seeing than the incomparable masterpieces of Italy; she declared that Egypt and Pompeii held no treasures comparable with the New Mexican cliff-dwellings.[6]

---

3. Biskra is a town in Northeastern Algeria known for its date palms and thermal springs. It is not clear whether Emily Post had ever been there.

4. Although this anecdote did not appear in *Collier's*, this unidentified woman is an excellent example of both the camping craze and the "See America First" movement. Although the slogan had been promulgated since 1906, it gained momentum when the activities of German U-Boats made transatlantic travel risky. It was also intertwined with patriotism. See Shaffer, *See America First*, 26–39. Promoters of the Panama-Pacific International Exposition were particularly active in encouraging tourists to "See America First."

5. The Eden Musée, which operated at 53 West 23rd Street in New York from 1884–1916, included the "usual retinue of freaks, midgets, fire-eaters, sword-swallowers, waxworks, a Chamber of Horrors, and 'Ajeen the Chess Mystery,'…a hollow figure inhabited by a child dwarf." (Luc Sante, *Low Life: Lures and Snares of Old New York* (New York: Vintage, 1992). It was, apparently, so popular it had its own streetcar stop.

6. The Gila cliff-dwellings in New Mexico are thought by archaeologists to have been occupied by the Mogollon people from about 1000 AD. They are now a national monument.

Our cliff-dwellings like little bird holes along the face of solid rock in which cave men lived hundreds— maybe thousands of years ago, are marvelously interesting, but to the spoiled globe-trotter, looking for profuse evidence of bygone manners and customs and beauty, such as you find in Alexandria or Pompeii, there are none.

There is, however, we had been told, an Arizona cave-dwelling that has a mural that can rival in interest the frescoes in Italy or the hieroglyphics of Egypt. It is merely the imprint of a cave baby's hand pressed thousands of years ago when the adobe was soft. You can also see cave-dwellings of a pigmy people that lived in the Stone Age and wore feather ruching around their necks; enchanted pools that have no bottoms; a lava river with a surface so sharp, brittle, like splintered glass, that nothing living can cross it and not be footless, actually, in the end. You can also find, to this day they say, a religious sect of Penitents who, in Holy Week, practice every sort of flesh mortification, carry crosses, lie down on cactus needles flay themselves with cat-o'-nine-tails, and they used, a few years ago, to crucify especially fervent members.[7]

But why try to convince people that traveling in the byways of the Southwest is not a strenuous thing to do? Our hornet inquisitor told us, "What do you want better than a cave to sleep in? It's as good as your European hotels any day!" We forgot to ask her how she got up the face of the cliffs to get into the caves— a feat far above any ability of Celia's or mine. She also said she liked taking potluck with the Indians. I wonder does she like, as they do, the taste of prairie dogs, and they say, occasionally, mice and snakes?[8]

Although she did her best to spoil it all for us, we took away an unforgettable picture of an enchanted land. Why, though, I wonder, did she want to speak of it or think of it as different from what it really is? Vast, rugged, splendidly desolate, big in size, big in thought, big in ideals, with a few threads of enchanting history like that of Santa Fé, or vividly colored romances of frontier life and Indian legends that vie with Kipling's jungle books.

---

7. A slightly later woman traveler, who was in New Mexico in 1920, went "Penitente Hunting" in Alcade, near Santa Fe. She was warned not to take photographs as she watched a small group of men and boys stumble past, bearing the bloody marks of their self-inflicted wounds. See Winifred Dixon, *Westward Hoboes* (New York: Scribner's, 1921), 168.

8. Emily Post was far from convinced of the cultural value of many of these sights and practices.

XXII

Some Indians and Mr. X.

The best commentary on the road between Santa Fé and Albuquerque
is that it took us less than three hours to make the sixty-six miles, whereas
the seventy-three from Las Vegas to Santa Fé took us nearly *six*. The Bajada
Hill, which for days Celia and I dreaded so much that we did not dare speak
of it for fear of making E. M. nervous, was magnificently built. There is
no difficulty in going down it, even in a very long car that has to back and
fill at corners; there are low stone curbs at bad elbows, and the turns are
all well banked so that you feel no tendency to plunge off. A medium length
car with a good wheel cut-under would run down the dread Bajada as easily as through the driveways of a park!¹ And the entire distance across San-
doval County, although a tract of desert desolation or bleak sand and hills
and cactus, is an easy drive over a smooth road.² In one place you can go
through a great cleft cut through an impeding ridge, but most of the way
you can imagine yourself in a land of the earth's beginning and where

---

1. Emily Post was more sanguine about this road than A.L. Westgard, vice president and
director of the Transcontinental Highway, and probably the A.A.A. expert she consulted
before setting off from New York. He published an article entitled "Motor Routes to the
California Expositions" in the March 1915 issue of *Motor* magazine. He wrote "Regretfully
leaving Santa Fe, the tourist goes south over a good road. Nineteen miles out one almost
jerks his car to a stop, and, if I am a judge of human nature, spends a half-hour in admiring contemplation from the rim of La Bajada Hill. In the far distance across the desert towers Sandia Mountain, while to the west one looks across the Valley of the Rio Grande. It is
truly a marvelous view. After taking several photographs the traveler leaves the rim of the
precipitous lava hill and gingerly proceeds down a very winding road, where three or four
turns are so sharp that with a long wheelbase he will be compelled to back up to make it.
Though the road is good, one had better go slow and use extreme caution, with the hand
on the brake, because a couple of the sharpest turns, where he may probably have to back
up, simply lead into nothing more substantial than atmosphere, and mighty thin atmosphere at that, should the car refuse to stop at the exact spot on an inch ruler where it is necessary to manipulate for the turn."
2. Emily Post has now joined what was to become the famous Route 66.

white man never was. Two Indian shepherds in fact were the only human beings we saw until our road ran into the surprisingly modern city of Albuquerque.

Stopping at the various Harvey hotels of the Santa Fé system, yet not being travelers on the railroad, is very like being behind the scenes at a theater. The hotel people, curio-sellers, and Indians are the actors, the travelers on the incoming trains are the audience. Other people don't count.[3]

For instance, you enter a tranquilly ordered dining-room. The head waitress attentively seats you, your own waitress quickly fetches your first course, and starts towards the pantry for the second, when suddenly a clerk appears and says, "Twenty-six!" With the uniformity of a trained chorus every face turns towards the clock, and the whole scene becomes a flurry of white-starched dresses running back and forth. Back with empty trays and forth with buttered rolls, radishes, cups of soup, like a ballet of abundance. You wonder if no one is going to bring your second course, but you might as well try to attract the attention of a hive of bees when they are swarming. Having nothing else to do you discover the mystic words twenty-six to be twenty-six places to set. Finally you descry your own waitress dealing slices of toast to imaginary diners at a far table. Then you hear the rumble of the train, the door leading to the platform opens and in come the passengers. And you, having no prospect of anything further to eat, watch the way the train supper is managed. Slices of toast and soup in cups are already at their places, then in files the white-aproned chorus carrying enormous platters of freshly-grilled beefsteak, and such savory broiled chicken that you, who are so hungry, can scarcely wait a moment patiently for your own waitress to appear. You notice also the gigantic pots of aromatically steaming coffee, tea and chocolate being poured into everyone's cup but your own, and ravenously watch the pantry door for that long tarrying one who went once upon a time to get some of these delectable viands for you.

"Will you have broiled chicken?" asks the faithless She you have been watching for, bending solicitously over a group of strange tourists at the next table. At last when the train people are quite supplied, your speeding Hebe returns and apologizes sweetly, "I am sorry but I had to help get

---

3. Emily Post, being a motorist rather than a train traveler, was in a good position to see this as performance. Leah Dilworth notes that her remarks are unusual for the period, and furthermore "reveals the degree to which the encounter between Native Americans and tourists was mediated by the Santa Fe and the Harvey Company and the centrality of market relations in the encounter." Dilworth, *Imagining Indians*, 109.

train Number Seven's supper. They've eaten all the broiled chicken that was cooked, but I'll order you some more if you don't mind waiting twenty minutes."[4]

By and by the train people leave, your chicken arrives and you finish your supper in common-place tranquility. But let us look at another comedy, for which the scene shifts to the railroad station at Albuquerque where the long stone platform is colorless and deserted. You have always on picture postcards seen it filled with Indians.[5] There is not one in sight. Wait though until ten minutes before the California limited is due. Out of nowhere appear dozens of vividly costumed Navajos and Hopis; their blankets and long braids woven with red cloth, their headbands and beads and silver ornaments fill the platform with color like a flower display. Old squaws and a few young squat themselves in two rows, forming an aisle between the train and the station salesroom. Although you walk up and down between their forming aisles watching them display their baskets and pottery, they are silent until the first passenger alights, and then unendingly they chorus two words:

"Tain cent!" "Tain cent!" The words sometimes sound like a question, sometimes a statement, but generally a monotonous drone. There is a nice old squaw—although I believe the Hopis don't call their women squaws—sitting at the end. I tripped and almost fell into her lap. She looked up, smiled, and by her inflection, conveyed, "Oh, my *dear,* did you hurt yourself?" but what she said was, "Tain cent!"[6]

The third Harvey scene is frankly a vaudeville performance of Indian dancing and singing. The stage the adobe floor of the Indian exhibit room, the walls of which are hung to the ceiling with blankets, beadwork, baskets, clay gods, leather costumes—everything conceivable in the way of Indian crafts. Immediately after supper the tourists take their places on benches ranged against three sides of the apartment. Generally there is a big open fire on the fourth side, adding its flickering light as the last note to a setting worthy of Belasco.[7]

4. In Greek mythology, Hebe, daughter of Zeus and Hera, was the goddess of youth. On Mount Olympus she poured the nectar of the gods.

5. The Harvey Company was a major producer of postcards. They displayed a mythologized version of the West, featuring dramatic scenery and Native American craftsmen and women in order to attract new visitors.

6. The material from here to the end of the chapter did not appear in the *Collier's* article.

7. David Belasco (1853–1931) San Francisco-born theatrical producer, director, playwright, paid his theatrical dues in the mining camps of the West, playing everything from Hamlet (and Gertrude) to Fagin in *Oliver Twist* and Topsy in *Uncle Tom's Cabin.* He was mentor to Cecil B. DeMille. By 1907 he ran the two most lavish theaters in New York; one

The Indians dance most often in pairs but occasionally there are as many as eight or nine in a row or a circle, with an additional background of others beating time. The typical step is a sort of shuffling hop; a little like the first step or two of a clog dancer before he gets going, or else just a bent kneed limp and stamp accompanied either by a droning chant or merely a series of sounds not unlike grunts. To our Anglo-Saxon ears and eyes it seemed very monotonous even after a little sample. Yet we are told they keep it up for eight or ten or twelve hours at a stretch, when they are dancing seriously and at home. Dancing to them is a religious ceremony, not merely an informal expression of gayety.

The women we saw wore heavy black American shoes and calico mother hubbards with a ruffle at the bottom, and generally a shawl or blanket around their shoulders.[8] Only one wore the blanket costume as it is supposed to be worn: around her body and fastened on one shoulder leaving the other arm and shoulder bare and also bare feet.

The men were much more picturesque, in dark-colored velvet shirts, silver belts, necklaces of bright beads and white cross-bars that looked like teeth, huge turquoise square-cut earrings and red head-bands. The "Castle cut" head-dress that has been the rage in New York for the last year or two is simply that of the Navajo Indians. Their head-band is a little wider and invariably of red, and the black straight hair ends as stiffly as a tassel.[9]

In some places as at the Grand Canyon, there are Navajo huts and a Hopi communal house where the tourist can see something of the way the Indians live; the way they weave blankets or baskets, beat silver or make and paint pottery.[10]

---

of them, the Stuyvesant (now the Belasco) had a sophisticated lighting system, and was the most technically advanced theater of its day.

8. A Mother Hubbard was a floor-length loose-fitting dress.

9. Irene Foote Castle (1893–1969) dancer, together with her husband Vernon Castle Blythe (1887–1918), were perhaps the biggest celebrities in America just before the outbreak of the war in Europe. Irene Castle cut her hair in 1914 before entering the hospital for an appendectomy; as she explained later, "I tried to cover up my clipped head by wearing, whenever I appeared in public, a tight turban or toque under which I tucked every spear of hair except some little square sideburns. Those of my friends who saw me in the country without a hat begged me to wear my short hair in public, and so one night when we were going to town to dinner I wore it down, and in order to keep it in place wrapped a flat seed-pearl necklace around my forehead — which was, I think, the beginning of what they afterwards called the "Castle Band." (*Ladies' Home Journal*, October 1921): 124.

10. The Hopi House at the Grand Canyon was the first project undertaken by architect Mary Elizabeth Jane Colter (1869–1958) for the Harvey Company. Completed in 1905, it amalgamated the pueblo style of Santa Fe and the Hopi mesas of New Mexico, (though it ignored the mud and stick structures of the Havasupai people who actually lived in and near the Grand Canyon) and was designed to showcase crafts made by Hopi weavers, potters and silversmiths who lived and worked in the house.

But to go back to Albuquerque, where although we saw less of the Indians than later in other places, we were lucky enough to hear a great deal about them. After dinner — there was no dancing — we were in the Indian Exhibit room — probably the most wonderful collection of their crafts that there is. As we were admiring an exceptionally beautiful blanket of red, black and white and closely woven as a fine Panama hat, a man — we took him to be the proprietor at first — said:

"It took three years' bargaining to get that blanket from a Navajo chief. You can't get them made of that quality any more. They'd rather get ten or twelve dollars for a blanket they spend a few weeks on and get paid often, than work a year on a single blanket that they can sell for a hundred."[11]

He picked out various examples of pattern and weaving and explained relative values. The amount of red, for instance, in the one we had been looking at added greatly to its price. We found out later that although not stationed at Albuquerque, he was one of the Harvey staff, and as we spent the whole evening talking to him, and he might not care to have his name taken in vain, I'll call him Mr. X. He has lived for years among the Indians. We could have listened to his stories about them forever, but to remember the greater part would be a different matter.[12]

On the subject of business dealings, an Indian, he said, has no idea of credit. No matter how well he knows and trusts you, he wants to be paid cash the moment he brings in his wares. To wait even an hour for his

11. The criticism of the Navaho response to commercial pressure is an echo of the words of a noted rug collector who wrote in 1914: "There are still Navahos (20,000 of them), and there is still vayeta [vayeta was a woolen cloth, imported from Turkey and unraveled by the Navaho weavers then rewoven into blankets etc]; and as there are people who would give $500 for an absolutely first-class vayeta blanket, you might think that the three things would pool. But that is to forget the Navaho. He is a barbarian, to whom enough is an excellent sufficiency. By weaving the cheap and wretched blankets of today — wretched, that is, as works of art — he can get all the money he desires. Why then toil twelve month over a blanket for $500 (which is more coin than he can imagine anyhow) when a week's work will bring $5?" George Wharton Jones, *Indian Blankets and Their Makers* (Chicago: A.C. McClure, 1920), chapter 4.

12. Emily Post's informant Mr. X may have been Herman Schweitzer, who managed the Albuquerque part of the Harvey operation; he was responsible for buying and selling Indian artifacts from 1901 until his death in 1943. He dealt with the Native Americans themselves, other traders and collectors, and sold to tourists, collectors (including William Randolph Hearst) and museums. He bought old artifacts and commissioned new ones, and because of the Harvey Company's connections with the Atchison, Topeka, and Santa Fe Railroad his goods were shipped east at favorable rates. Schweitzer also created the Harvey Company's collection of Indian material culture, and the two most important sites for display of this collection were the Indian Building at Albuquerque, which opened in 1902, and the Hopi House next to Harvey's El Tovar Hotel at the Grand Canyon, which opened in 1905. See also Dilworth, *Imagining Indians*, 82–84.

money will not satisfy him. A puzzling thing had happened on the platform that afternoon. I heard a lady say to an old squaw, "I'll take these three baskets." Whereupon instead of selling the baskets, the Indian hastily covered all of them with a blanket, got up and went away!

I told this to Mr. X. He considered a minute, then asked:

"Did the lady by chance wear violet?"

"She did!" interposed Celia. "She had on a violet shirtwaist and —"

"That explains it!" Mr. X. broke in. "No wonder she ran away. To an Indian violet is the color of evil. None but a witch would wear it. Red is holy; they love red above all colors. Also they love yellow, orange and turquoise."

As we were talking a young Navajo who was standing near us, suddenly covering his eyes with his arm, rushed from the room. Naturally we looked at our clothes for an evidence of violet, but Mr. X. laughed.

"It wasn't a case of color this time! Do you see that old squaw that just came in? She is his mother-in-law. Navajos won't look at their wife's mother; they think they will be bewitched if they do. He's going back to the Reservation tomorrow, because the old woman came down today. He is an intelligent Indian, too, but if he spies a stray cat or dog around tonight, he will probably think it is his mother-in-law having taken that shape. Their belief in witchcraft is impossible to break. At the same time they have an undeniable gift for necromancy, second sight or whatever it may be called, scarcely less wonderful than that of the Hindoos of India. The boy in the basket trick and the rope-climbing trick of Asia are not to be compared with things I have seen with my own eyes in New Mexico.

"I have seen a Shaman, or priest, sing over a bare adobe floor, and the floor slowly burst in one little place and a new shoot of corn appear. I have seen this grow before my eyes until it became a full-sized stalk with ripened corn. Instead of waving a wand, as European magicians do, the priest sings continually and as long as he sings the corn grows, when he stops the corn-stalk stops.

"The same Shaman can pour seeds and kernels of corn out of a hollow stalk until all about him are heaping piles of grain that could not be crowded into a thousand hollowed cornstalks. Medicine men of all tribes can cure the sick, heal the injured, get messages out of the air and do many seemingly impossible things.

"Navajos abhor snakes as much as we do, but Moquis hold them sacred. Before their famous snake dance, during which they hold live rattlesnakes in their mouths and bunches of them wriggling in each hand, they anoint their bodies with the juice of an herb, and drink an herb tea;

both said to be medicine against snakebite. At all events they don't seem
to suffer more than a trifling indisposition even when they are bitten in
the face. One theory is—and it certainly sounds reasonable—that from
early childhood the snake priests are given infinitesimal doses of rattlesnake poison until by the time they reach manhood they are immune
to any ill effects."[13]

We had by this time wandered out of the Indian room and seated ourselves in the big rocking chairs on the veranda of the Alvarado, Mr. X.
with us.[14] Every now and then he stopped and said he though he had talked
about enough, but we were insatiable and always begged him to tell us some
more. Of the many things he told us, the most interesting of all were the
stories of the medicine men and the combination of articles that consti-
tutes each individual's own fetich or "medicine." To this day not only
medicine men, but chiefs, would as soon be parted from their own scalp-
locks, as from this talisman. Each has his own medicine that can never be
changed, though upon occasion it may have a lucky article added to it.
Most commonly the fetich is composed of a little bag made of the pelt
of a small animal and filled with a curious assortment of articles such
as bear's claws, wolf's teeth, things that are associated with the wearer's
early prowess in the world, or more likely a former existence. At all events,
an Indian's standing and power in his tribe is dependent upon this fetich,
and to lose it is to lose not only power but caste—much more than life
itself.

In the days past of the Redman's war prowess, this sort of "medicine"
worn by warriors most especially, was supposed to grant them supernat-
ural powers to kill enemies and preserve their own life. If they were
wounded or killed, it meant that the enemy's medicine was even more
powerful. But using the word "medicine" in our sense, their "medicine

---

13. Between 1880 and 1920 the Hopi Snake dance was one of the most photographed and
described Indian rituals. The dance was the last event of a nine-day ceremony usually per-
formed in August in the hope of ensuring rain for the autumn corn crop. It was described
by serious ethnographers and by the popular press, and tourists including Theodore Roosevelt flocked to see the Snake Priests carry live snakes, including rattlesnakes, in their
mouths. In the early 1920s the Hopi closed the ceremony to outsiders. One of the earliest
accounts was John G. Burke's *The Snake-Dance of the Moquis of Arizona* (London, Samp-
son Low, 1884). Part of its long subtitle suggests his approach: "*A description of the manners and Customs of This Peculiar people, and Especially of the Revolting Religious Rite, THE
SNAKE-DANCE.*"

14. Emily Post was staying at the Harvey Company's Alvarado Hotel in Albuquerque. It
was built in 1902 and demolished in 1970. Huge and red, its colonnades faced the railroad
track, and its lunchroom featured refrigerated food display cabinets. Images (undated) of
the display cabinets and the Indian storeroom at the hotel can be found on the University
of Arizona's website.

men"— healers—certainly know of mysterious potent cures, the secrets of which no white man understands.

Their most usual way of effecting a cure is, apparently, to dance all night in a circle around the afflicted person, with curative results that are too uncannily like magic to be believable. One case that Mr. X. vouched for personally was that of a child dying of blood poison. Two white surgeons of high repute said that the child had scarcely a chance of living even by amputating an arm that had mortified beyond any hope of saving; and that without the operation, its death was merely a matter of hours. The Indian parents refused to have it done, and insisted on taking the child to the Reservation. The white doctors declared the child could not possibly survive such a journey but as, in their opinion, it could not live long anyway, the parents might as well take it where they pleased. They started for the Reservation. It was a Sunday. "Four sleeps we come back, all right. On Thursday, the fourth day, exactly, back they came again with the child well, and its arm absolutely sound. That a mortified arm should get well, comes close to the unbelievable — even though vouched for, as in this case, by several reputable witnesses.

As a case of mental telepathy, Mr. X. told us that time and time again he had known Indians to get news out of the air. An old Navajo one day cried out suddenly that his squaw was "heap sick." He was so excited that he would not wait for Mr. X. to telegraph and find out if there was any truth in his fear, nor would he wait for a train, but started on a pony ride to the Reservation. After he had gone a telegram came saying that the squaw had been bitten by a rattlesnake and was dying.

After a while the topic turned upon our own trip. We had intended to ship the car at Albuquerque, but the road from Santa Fé had been so good we were encouraged to go further and Mr. X's enthusiasm settled it.

"Having come down into this part of the country," he said, "you really ought not to miss seeing some of the wonders of our Southwest. The Pueblo of Acoma is a little out of the way, but there is nothing like it anywhere. 'The city of the sky' they call it — I won't tell you any more about it — you just go and look at it for yourselves.[15] Isleta, a short distance south from here, is a pueblo that lots of tourists go to see, and Laguna is fairly

---

15. The Pueblo of Acoma, or "Sky City," is situated on a 367 feet high sandstone rock and is said to be the oldest continuously inhabited village in the United States. It was nearly destroyed in 1598 by Governor Juan de Onate in retaliation for the killing of thirteen Spanish soldiers who had tried to steal grain from the pueblo storehouses. The Acoma people are now famous for their thin-walled pottery.

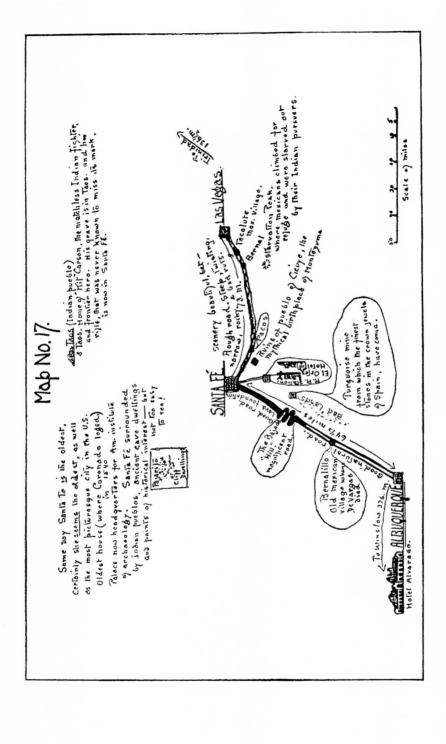

well known, too.[16] They are both on your road if you go to Gallup. Acoma is off the beaten track but you wait and send me a postcard if it is not worth considerable exertion, even to behold it from the desert. The Enchanted Mesa, the higher one that you come to first, is interesting chiefly because of its story. The truth of it I can't vouch for, but it is said to have been inhabited once by people who reached its dizzy summit by a great ladder or rock that leaned against its sides. One day in a teriffic storm while the men were all plowing in the valley below, the rock ladder was blown down and the women and children were left on this unscalable height to perish.[17] Laguna is about half way between here and the continental divide, or about one-third of the distance to Gallup. Acoma is perhaps eighteen miles south of Laguna where you can get a guide and also more definite information. Or you can just go south across the plain by yourselves, fairly near the petrified forest later — no, that not until you are on the way to Holbrook. You also skirt the edge of the lava river — I don't think you'd know it was anything to look at unless you were told. At the time of the eruption, the lava on the surface cooled while that underneath was still boiling, and the steam of the boiling mass burst through the hardened surface and splintered it like broken glass. Glass is in fact the substance it most resembles. The country is full of stories of men and animals that have tried to cross it, but neither hoofs nor cowhide boots have ever been made that can stay intact on its gashing surface.

"And of course you must get a glimpse of the painted forest.[18] After that you can take a train when you please" — then with a laugh he corrected — "when you get where a train goes."

"Where could we sleep?" asked Celia.

"Well, you can sleep at the hotel in Gallup — it isn't an Alvarado but it'll shelter you. For my own part, if you have a fine night, I'd sleep out!"

---

16. Pueblo Isleta, which is only seven miles from Albuquerque, now claims to have New Mexico's grandest resort and casino. Pueblo Laguna, some forty miles from Albuquerque, sits on rich uranium fields. Although the Laguna people benefited in the short term from the Anaconda Company's strip mining operations, which lasted from 1952 to 1981, since the company pulled out, they have faced widespread unemployment, not to mention an environmental disaster.

17. The Enchanted Mesa is a 430–foot high sandstone butte. Most modern sources say there is no evidence to support the legend that a storm or an earthquake destroyed the only approach to the dwelling atop the cliff.

18. Emily Post is conflating the Petrified Forest and the Painted Desert; the latter is named for the multi-colored mineral stratifications on its steep hills. Had she been traveling on the Santa Fe railroad, she would have seen it from the train.

Opposite: "Map no. 17. Las Vegas to Albuquerque," Friday May 21, 1915.

Seventeenth Day's Run,
Las Vegas to Albuquerque
Friday May 21, 1915

Personal

Lunched *Santa Fé.*
  (own lunch.)
Albuquerque. Hotel Alvarado.

Usual tips	$ 1.75
Telegrams and sundries	$ 2.80
3 delightful rooms, supper and breakfast ($4.25 each)	$12.75
Extra amount of food to take:	
Eggs	$ .60
Cake	$ .80
Sandwiches	$ 2.10
Cocoa	$ .20
Ice cream	$ .30

Motor

Santa Fé Transcontinental Garage.
  2 men, 1½ hours, patching muffler and exhaust
  and tightening bolts, etc. $ 2.25

XXIII

With Nowhere to Go but Out[1]

Personally I felt a sort of half-shiver. Sleep out in this land he had been telling us about! Sleep out in the wildest, loneliest country in the world, surrounded by the very Redskins about whom he had earlier in the evening been reeling some pretty grewsome stories! He seemed to divine my thoughts. "The Indians are as peaceful as house cats now. The Navajos never gave us much trouble except when it came to horse-stealing."

The he looked at me in much the same way our friend the fire chief had in Rochelle, Illinois.

"You are not *afraid,* are you?"

"Oh, n-no! I think it's most enchanting!"

"Are you cold?" asked E. M.

"P-perhaps," I said weakly. "Besides if we are starting early I'd better go in and see about ordering provisions and things." Which last remark, I think, quite saved my face — at least it was meant to.

I did, of course, want to see Acoma, that exaltedly perched city of antiquity. I did want to get at least a glimpse of the Painted Desert, but my bravery of spirit was of a very halting quality. The only thought that bolstered me up was the possibility that I was really very brave, because I was not telling anyone but myself that I was scared to death at the thought of a night of homelessness in the middle of an Indian reservation. When we started the next morning I thought Celia looked less sturdy than usual. She said, "We are not going to spend the night anywhere, are we?"

And I said with my best effort at spontaneous gladness, "No, won't it be fun!"

---

1. This chapter did not appear in the *Collier's* article.

175

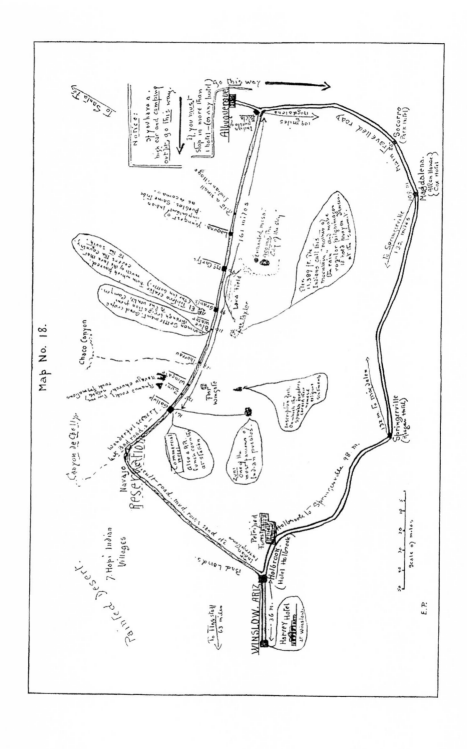

Map No. 18.

E.P.

Celia looked exactly as a beginner who is told to jump head foremost into the water in his first attempt to dive. E. M.'s attention was as usual entirely upon the car, and the probabilities of twistings and bumpings that the unknown roads might inflict upon his cherished engine. The question of nowhere to sleep was of little interest — still less importance. At all events we have seemingly enough provisions for ourselves and the machine to carry us to Alaska. Without doubt we can get motor supplies somewhere, but that is the one risk E. M. refuses to take and so we are starting off like a young Standard Oil agency, with forty-five gallons of gasoline, thirty-five in the tank and ten extra in cans. Also extra cans of oil. We have plenty of water for ourselves and some, too, for the car although we doubt whether alkali which ties the human stomach into a hard knot of agony at a taste would give the radiator a pain.

Our idea is to go, if we can, as far as Winslow. It seems rather funny that we, who nearly failed to stay intact over the well-worn Santa Fé trail, are branching into the unbeaten byway of the desert! We have taken our battered exhaust pipe off and shipped it to Los Angeles, and our sensation without it is one of such freedom that we feel we can surmount all obstacles.

Opposite: "Map no. 18. Albuquerque to Winslow": two alternative routes. They actually took the northern route, but added an alternative for travelers unwilling to camp out in the desert.

XXIV

Into the Desert

What has this land lived thorough? What sorrows have so terribly wasted, what cataclysms rent it, what courage exalted it! Stupendous in its desolation, sublime in its awfulness, it mystifies and dumbfounds at every turn. Smooth plains fall into an abyss, or rise in bleak rock spires. Firm, pebbled riverbeds suddenly shift to greedy quicksands; pools that look cool and limpid are boiling, or poisonous alkali. It suggests a theme of sculpture conceived by an Olympian Rodin, splendidly and gigantically hewn and with all the mystery of things not brought to a finite shaping.[1]

But like the Sleeping Beauty in the fairy-tale, the beauty sleeping in the Southwest is surrounded by a thorn hedge of hardships and discomfort that presents its most impenetrable thicket and sharpest spines to the motorist.[2] To see this wonderland intelligently or well, you ought really to be equipped with a camping outfit and go through on horseback. However, if you are willing to turn away from the main travel and strike west from Albuquerque, you can get a few compensating glimpses.

For miles and miles after leaving Isleta, a quite large settlement where there are many Indians and also many tourists, you go on and on and on over an easy gradually ascending road not unlike the long Platte Valley drive, but much more uninhabited. The once dangerous fording of the Puerco River is no longer a barrier to motorists, as there is a splendid new bridge that takes you smoothly over. From time to time you come to a few adobe huts or a lonely little packing-box railroad station, but your road stretches uneventfully on, until Laguna.[3]

---

1. Auguste Rodin (1840–1917) French sculptor, many of his best-known works such as *The Kiss* (1898) and *The Thinker* (1904) were originally conceived as part of his masterwork, *The Gate of Hell* which was commissioned in 1880 and never completed.

2. This complaint was not in the *Collier's* piece.

3. This paragraph did not appear in *Collier's*. Although the Puerco River is usually almost

"Across the real desert."

There is no need of going by motor to get a glimpse of Laguna, for you only have to sit on the observation platform — or even look out of a window of any train in the Santa Fé railroad. The pueblo of Laguna at a glance, is a collection of baked earth blocks piled steeply one behind the other against a sun-baked yellow hill at the side of the railroad track.

But to reach the Enchanted Mesa, and the sky-built city of Acoma, you must drive southward from Laguna across a stubbled prairie into a desert valley rimmed with distant cliffs like the walls of a vast garden. As you round a sand dune you come suddenly upon a gigantic round, flat-topped rock, like a titanic pink tree-stump — scarcely a reward for all those miles and miles of dreariness and intense heat, even though its flat-chopped top is a thousand feet clear above the surrounding plain. But when you visualize the story of that terrible storm that washed the great rock ladder away and left a village of women and children marooned upon that dizzy height until they starved or plunged off to a quicker death, it certainly grips you with its appalling awe.

It is a little wonder that the Indians think it haunted and accursed! For my part it seems miracle enough that anyone ever got up there at all even with a leaning rock supplemented with a notched tree ladder. Scaling such a cliff would be a feat of horror beside which circus thrillers,

dry, it is subject to flash floods. Both the original Puerco River Bridge and a later (1933) bridge are on the National Register of Historic Places.

looping gaps and dipping deaths would be a comparatively tame performance.[4]

A little way beyond the Enchanted Mesa crowned upon ramparts of
fantastic perpendicular crags arises Acoma, the skyland citadel of enchant-
ment. You know you can't be in such prosy place as Here, or within a
thousand years of Now. You are standing before the shadowy citadel of
some ancient Assyrian king, or more likely yet, you have journeyed into
the land of fairy-tales and have come to the castle of the King of the Iron
Mountain. Way, way above you, you see tiny figures of the sky inhabitants
inquisitively peering down. Several Indians come down from their soaring citadel and look you over. Finally one of the, very solemn and serious,
with his shirt-tail hanging out, motions, "Do you want to go up?"

You do, but how? There are only two paths, one hard and short, the
other long and easy! The easy one is as close to mountain climbing as the
ordinary person would want to undertake, though Indian mules and burros make it without difficulty. A burro, and a mule, and a mountain goat
must spring from the same species. You clamber, therefore, up the easy
road — a stiff, winding defile like the rock-hewn causeway to Valhalla in a
Metropolitan production of a Wagner opera, the trail narrowing as it
ascends until finally it is nothing but a narrow shelf at a precipice edge. If
you are rather light-headed and none too sure-footed you clutch tightly
to a stronger, steadier hand and turn your face cliff-ward as you shakily
venture the last of the ascent.

But your reward on top is a prehistoric Aztec citadel of communal
houses and occupied by people living exactly as their ancestors lived
hundred of years ago. An Indian communal house is really a honeycomb
of adobe boxes like a flight of gigantic steps; the row on top set back
from the one below so that the roof of the first floor makes the terrace
in front of the second, and the roof of the second a piazza in front of the
third. Against the wall of each story lean the typical ladders by which the
Hopi Indian always enters his home. The ground-floor rooms are usually entered through a hatchway in the ceiling from a room or a terrace
above.[5]

Acoma is really the sister of Santa Fé, who has never changed her
Indian ways. When the noble Spanish invader tried to make a conquest of
the whole family, Acoma met him at the top of her cliff-hewn staircase with
a battle-ax! I should think after that climb — the so-called "easy" way had

___

4. This paragraph was not in the *Collier's* piece.
5. This sentence, and almost all of the rest of the chapter (except where indicated), was
not part of the *Collier's* article.

not been built then — one of her brown babies could have pushed him off with a small forefinger!

To know anything at all about the lives or natures or customs of these people, you would have to see more than is possible to an average, ignorant tourist, who looks helplessly at their inscrutably serious faces. Even if by fortunate chance one of them invites you to mount a ladder and look into a dwelling or two, all you see is a small adobe room with bare walls, a bare floor and possibly a small, high window. There is a fireplace in one corner and maybe a string stretched across another with some clothes or blankets hung over it, or piled against a wall on the floor, a water jar or two, and some primitive cooking utensils. Except a few younger members of the community who have been to Carlisle, no one speaks a word of English.[6] Although in a few places such as the Grand Canyon or Albuquerque an Indian will let you take his picture for twenty-five cents, Mr. X. at Albuquerque had warned us not to photograph any Indians we might meet elsewhere. In such places as Acoma it might even be dangerous. Believing, as they do, that a photograph takes a portion of their life away from them, no wonder they object to a stranger's helping himself to a little piece of their existence.[7]

After leaving Acoma, you drive again long and tediously but without serious hindrance, all the way to Gallup.[8] At Gallup there is a hotel, a small frame, frontier kind of building. But by the time we reached it we agreed with Mr. X. that it would be more of an experience to spend the night under the stars. How much the beauty of the stars would have tempted us had the hotel been more inviting I am not very sure. Beyond Gallup you run into the Navajo Indian Reservation, your road having

---

6. The Carlisle Indian School in Pennsylvania, which was founded in 1879 and closed in 1918, was the first federally-funded school for Native Americans. Part of the policy of forced assimilation of Native Americans, a number of the students became ill and died, while others found pleasure and success in the sports program. The football team gained the school national prominence.

7. In a booklet published circa 1910 Frederick Monsen explains this idea: "An Indian will look at his photograph and recognize it an image of himself. He realized that he is still complete physically; hence this picture must be part of his soul, and if he should die his soul would be incomplete — hence his objection." *With a Kodak in the Land of the Navaho,* quoted in Dilworth, *Imagining Indians,* 119. By the 1920s the Acoma were more pragmatic about this, and in a 1927 *Couriers' Instructional Bulletin* one of the couriers wrote that she was not sure whether the $5 charged for taking photographs went directly to the chiefs, or to a communal fund. See Dilworth, *Imagining Indians,* 117–18.

8. Emily Post was fortunate, for when A.L. Westgard wrote his account of the routes to California in March 1915, he was not convinced that the new road from Albuquerque to Gallup would be open, despite the assurances of the State Engineer, so he proposed an alternative route going south via Socorro then west to Holbrook. The hotel she decided not to stay in was possibly the Rex, built c. 1900, which is now a museum.

ascended rather steeply through parklike woods of cedars, and the altitude again affects both lungs and carburetor, but even if it makes you gasp a little it is an essence of deliciousness as reviving as an elixir of life. You go past the road that leads to the wonderful Canyon de Chelly, but it is impossible for a motor — any kind of motor, even the littlest and lightest one — to go over it in the early spring, so you continue on until at last, coming out upon a mesa, you see spread below you the Painted Desert! It can be none other. You would be willing to take oath that a great city of palaces in all the colors of the rainbow lies spread before you. It is inconceivable that rock and sand and twilight alone create these turrets and ramparts and bastions of crimson, gold, blue, azure, indigo, purple, and the whole scene immersed in liquid mauve and gold, as though the atmosphere were made of billions and billions of particles of opalescent fluid. And as you stand in silent contemplation an Indian with scarlet head-band rides by on a piebald pony so that there shall be no color unused.[9]

At last when the vividness of colors begin to soften into vapory purples, deepening again to indigo, you gather a little brushwood and for the mere companionable cheerfulness make a campfire to eat your supper by. You probably heat a can of soup, roast potatoes, and finally, having nothing else to cool or heat for the present, hit upon the brilliant thought of boiling water, while the fire burns, for next morning's coffee. At least this is what we did, and poured it into a thermos to keep hot.[10] Also we climbed back into the car. Personally I have an abject terror of snakes, though there was very likely none within a hundred miles of us. For nothing on earth would I make myself a bed on the open ground. Also the seats of our car — there was at least one satisfactory thing about it — are only four or five inches from the floor, and sitting in it is like sitting in an upholstered steamer chair with the footrest up — a perfectly comfortable position to go to sleep in. So that bundled up in fur coats with the steamer blankets over us we were just as snug as the proverbial bugs in a rug. For my own part, though, the night was too beautiful out under that star-hung sky willingly to shut my eyes and blot it out. My former fears of prowling Indians, strange animals, spooks, spirits — or perhaps just vast empty blackness — had vanished completely, and instead there was merely the consciousness of an

---

9. The vivid description of the Painted Desert was part of the original article.

10. The first vacuum flask was made by Evangelista Torricelli in 1643 when he was trying to build the world's first barometer, but Cambridge scientist Sir James Dewar invented the Thermos flask as we know it in 1893, and patented it in 1903. It was an immediate success, and no early twentieth-century explorer was without his or her Thermos. Ernest Shackleton took his to the South Pole, Robert E. Peary to the North, and the Wright brothers carried one on their flights.

experience too beautiful to waste a moment of. I could not bear to go to sleep. The very air was too delicious in its sparkling purity to want to stop consciously breathing it. Overhead was the wide inverted bowl of purple blue made of an immensity of blues overlaid with blues that went through and through forever, studded with its myriad blinking lamps lit suddenly all together, and so close I felt that I could almost reach them with my hand.

I really don't know whether I slept or not, but the thing I became conscious of was the beginning of the dawn. Overhead the heaven was still that deep unfathomable blue. In the very deepest of its color the crescent moon and single star glowed with a light rayless as it was dazzling. Over near the horizon the blue lightened gradually to pale azure and deepened where it rested on the brown purple rim of the desert to a band of reddish orange, very soft, very melting. Gradually the moon and star grew dim like turned-down lamps against a heaven turning turquoise. Down in the valley hung a mist of orchid against which the black branches of a nearby cedar were etched in Japanese silhouette. Far, far on the north horizon the clouds of day were herded, waiting. Then a single cloud advanced, dipped itself in rose color and edged itself with gold; a streak of red, as from a giant's paint-brush, swept across the sky. A moment of waiting more and then the great blinding sun peered above the eastern mountains' rim and the clouds broke and scattered like cotton-wool sheep across their pasture skies. The moon turned into a little curved feather dropped from a bird's breast and the star a pinprick; yet in their hour, how glorious they were!

Celia and I tried to find a stream in which to wash our faces, but, failing in our search, we shared the water in our African bags with the radiator. The hot water in the thermos bottle poured over George Washington coffee did not delay us a moment in our breakfast-making, and it could not have been later than five o'clock when we were well off on our way.

It was an endlessly long day's run and difficult in places. I'm sure we lost our way several times, a perfectly dispiriting thing to do, as it was much like being lost in a rowboat out in the middle of the ocean. Except while still on the Reservation where we passed occasional Navajos we saw no living person or thing the rest of the day. Sometimes we went over rolling, stubbled prairie, fringed again with cedars and pines; next through a veritable desert of desolation with nothing but rocks and sand. Sometimes the road wound tranquilly through timbered glades; again came a straight, monotonous stretch of sandy trail. Then suddenly it twisted itself over a path of washed-out rock, or suddenly fell into an arroyo. Over and over these symptoms were repeated in every variety of combination. Finally we reached Holbrook, and we drove without any adventures over a traveled road to Winslow.[11]

For nothing would I have missed the experience. It was wonderful, all of it, yet no hotel seemed as enchanting as the Harvey, nor was any supper ever so good as the one they so promptly put before us.[12]

Of course, if we had had a breakdown we would have been marooned out in a wilderness! No living being knew our whereabouts and we might quite easily have been dust before anyone would have passed our way. If we had had different equipment we would certainly have gone further. Fortunately the most interesting (as well as the most difficult) part of the desert was all behind us, and as we also wanted to motor through California, we had no choice. The car was in a seriously crippled condition; any more arroyos and there really would be no more motoring for us this trip. So, all things considered, we hailed our freight car resignedly, put the motor on it and sent it ahead of us to Los Angeles, while we ourselves took the train to the Grand Canyon.[13]

EIGHTEENTH DAY'S RUN, ALBUQUERQUE TO WINSLOW SATURDAY MAY 22, 1915

Personal

Leave *Albuquerque*. Out in desert.
Winslow, Ariz. Harvey Hotel.

rooms, including meals	$10.50
Tips (most of luggage shipped with car)	$ 1.25
3 tickets *Winslow* to *Los Angeles*	$68.85
Extra tickets *Williams* to *Grand Canyon*	$22.50

---

11. Even Westgard regarded the first part of this road "pretty tough going."

12. Emily Post stayed at the original Harvey hotel in Winslow, which was a large, rambling two-story brick structure built in the late 1880s. It became the Harvey Girls' dormitory when La Posada was built, and was pulled down in the 1960s because the Santa Fe Railway did not want to pay the taxes and maintenance, and no one was willing to fix it up. La Posada, "the last Harvey Hotel in the West," and acknowledged as architect Mary Elizabeth Jane Colter's "masterpiece" was opened in 1930. Closed for many years, and under frequent threat of demolition, it was reopened in 1997. My thanks to Allan Affeldt, current owner of La Posada, for information on the earlier Harvey hotel in Winslow.

13. The Grand Canyon became a national forest in 1893, a game preserve in 1906, a national monument in 1908, and was to become a national park in 1919.

Motor

Albuquerque. Coleman Blank Garage

(A1 garage)

2 men, 4 hours each (night labor, double rate),

    mending leak in radiator, taking off exhaust,

    filling grease cups etc. $ 6.00

1 front spring shackle bolt $ .80

18 gals. gas in tank $ 5.40

10 gals. in cans $ 3.00

4 gals. oil $ 2.80

(First-class garage)

Winslow.

Car shipped via A.T. & S.F.R.R. Freight to Los Angeles.

    Perfect system for motor shipping, no crating and no delay.

Freight charge $151.20

By the way, a word about the Navajos whose dwellings in no way resemble the staired adobe pyramids in Acoma, Taos and Laguna. The Navajo huts—*hogans* they are called—are made of logs and twigs plastered with mud, not all over like an icing, but merely in between the logs as a mortar. They have no openings except a low door that you have to stoop to enter, and a smoke hole in the center of the domelike roof. Inside, if the ones at the Grand Canyon are typical, as they are supposed to be, they are merely one room with a fire burning in the center and blankets spread about the edge of the floor close under the slanting walls. Personally I feel rather embarrassed on being told to look in upon a group of swarthy figures who contemplate the intrusion of their privacy in solemn silence. In one of them a mother was rolling her plump brown baby on its swaddling board. When it was securely tied in place, although the father carried it outside in order to allow me to take its picture, I nearly got into trouble about it. The shutter of my camera had to be set first then released which made two clicks. When I paid the regulation quarter, he was furious and demanded double pay. I, on my side, thought I was being imposed upon, as he had himself volunteered to hold the baby for me for twenty-five cents. E. M., who divined the difficulty, quickly took the film pack out, and holding it open against the light, explained to the Indian, "Little click no picture." And the Navajo, being quite satisfied with the quarter, I then gave him a second one—a senseless, but commonplace proceeding.[14]

---

14. At this point there was a paragraph in the original article that was omitted in the book. Emily Post wrote: "Arrived at Winslow we hailed our freight car with joy, put   →

"Our chauffeur takes a day off at the Grand Canyon of the Colorado."

Meanwhile, comfortably lounging on the terrace overlooking the greatest of all great canyons, an old-timer is talking of "the good old days of Hance's camp before this high-falutin' hotel was built."[15] At his mere suggestion I become vividly aware that, after all, the way I like best to see anything is comfortably. Perhaps there might be an added awe if one stood alone at the brink of this yawning abyss, perhaps some of the gnarled roads and small clefts that seemed wonderful when we were crawling among them might have seemed dull little places from the terrace of a luxurious hotel, but being at heart — no matter how much I might pretend to be above the necessity of comfort — an effete Easterner, I very gratefully appreciate the genius if the man who built this hotel for such as I.[16]

---

the motor on it, dropped into our chairs at the Harvey Hotel, and mentally rhapsodized over the supper they put before us."

15. Captain John Hance, guide and storyteller, established a camp near the Grand Canyon in the 1880s. He, and it, became legendary. One tourist wrote: "All the way from Albuquerque you have heard of John Hance. You have read about him in all the guidebooks you have bought. People whom you meet tell you all about the flap-jacks he will cook for you at the canyon camp. You constantly hear references to "Hance's Trail," Hance's New Trail," "Hance's Old Trail," "Hance's Peak," and "Hance's Cabin," until you wonder if John Hance owns the Grand Canyon of the Colorado River. When you get to Flagstaff the air is still filled with confused murmurs of Hance. You come to have sort of a "See-Hance-and-die" feeling and are a little uncertain whether you have come thousands of miles to see the Grand Canyon or John Hance of Arizona." Edith Sessions Tupper. http://www.geocities.com/shioshya/hance/ppages/ppage5.html

16. Some visitors found spiritual renewal in places like the Grand Canyon; a later British visitor found "The Divine Intelligence very close" there; "it surrounds one like a consciously felt blessing." Not so Emily Post, who was far more interested in her creature comforts. See Mark Pepys, *Mine Host, America* (London: Collins, 1937), 194.

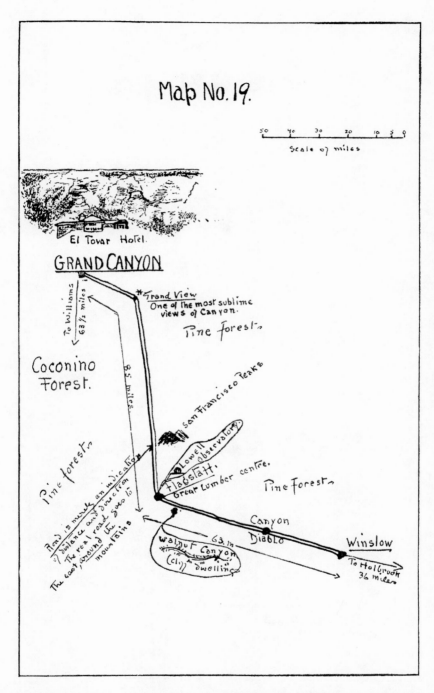

Map No. 19.

Scale of miles

El Tovar Hotel.

GRAND CANYON

To Williams 63½ miles

*Grand View
One of the most sublime
views of Canyon.

Pine Forest.

Coconino Forest.

85 miles

San Francisco Peaks

Pine forests

Lowell observatory

Flagstaff.
Great Lumber centre.

Pine Forest.

Road is merely an indication
of distance and direction
The real road goes to
the east around the
mountains

Canyon Diablo

Winslow

63 m.

Walnut Canyon
(cliff) dwelling

To Holbrook
36 miles

"Map 19, Winslow to Grand Canyon." Although she took the train, the conscientious Emily Post included a map of the sights a motorist might have seen.

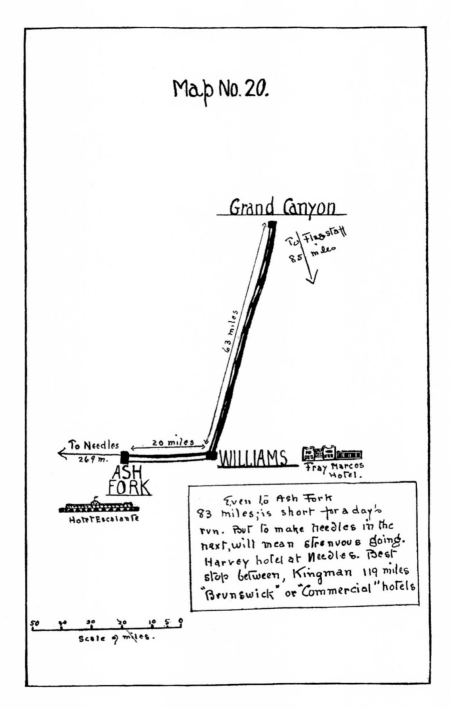

Map No. 20.

Grand Canyon

To Flagstaff 85 miles

63 miles

To Needles 269 m.

20 miles

WILLIAMS

Fray Marcos Hotel.

ASH FORK

Hotel Escalante

Even to Ash Fork 83 miles; is short for a day's run. But to make Needles in the next, will mean strenuous going. Harvey hotel at Needles. Best stop between, Kingman 119 miles "Brunswick" or "Commercial" hotels

50 40 30 20 10 5 0

Scale of miles.

"Map 20 Grand Canyon to Ash Fork"

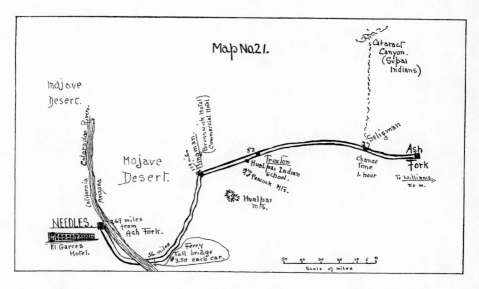

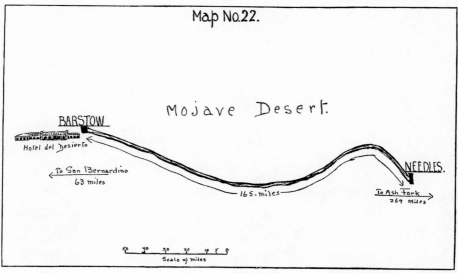

Top: "Map 21 Ash Fork to Needles"; *Bottom:* "Map 22 Needles to Barstow"

The amount of detail on maps 20, 21 and 22 suggests either very careful research, or that Edwin Post drove the car back to New York.

BY TRAIN, WINSLOW TO GRAND CANYON
MONDAY MAY 24 TO WEDNESDAY MAY 26, 1915.

Personal

Lunch, *Williams*	$ 3.30
Grand Canyon, Ariz. El Tovar Hotel.[17]	
2 rooms, bath between.	$10.00
1 room and bath including meals.	$ 5.00
Mule down *Angel Trail* (E. M.)	$ 4.00[18]
Moving pictures exhibited at studios of trip through Colorado River	$ 3.00[19]
Tips, per day, about	$ 1.25
Sundries, etc.	$ 1.80

Motor

Car on freight

---

17. Emily Post was staying in the El Tovar Hotel, which was opened in 1905 and cost $250,000 to build. It resembled a mixture of a Rhine castle and a Swiss chateau, and as a Flagstaff newspaper noted in 1902, "this is a combination never before attempted." The Fred Harvey Company was the concessionaire, and it was built by the Santa Fe railroad on twenty acres of land granted by the federal government. Its one hundred rooms had hot and cold running water, electric lights and steam heat, and its elegant restaurant served fresh salmon from the Pacific, fruit from California, and celery from Michigan, all shipped in on the railroad. Unlike the other Harvey hotels, the "Harvey Girls" at the El Tovar were allowed to fraternize with the guests, but though there were "a significant number of marriages" they were typically between the "girls" and other Harvey House workers, sightseeing car drivers or cowboys, rather than with the transitory, higher-class guests. See Rothman, *Devil's Bargains* 59, 78.

18. There is no comment from Ned Post on this experience; a contemporary traveler, on the other hand, described his mule ride in vivid detail. He wrote: "The trail clings to the sheer side of the dizziest, deepest chasm in the known world. One of your legs is scraping against the granite; the other is dangling over half a miles of fresh mountain air." Irving Cobb, *Roughing It Deluxe* (New York: Doran, 1914), 42.

19. In 1904, two years after they arrived at the Grand Canyon, Emory and Ellsworth Kolb purchased a photographic studio and relocated it to the rim. They started to photograph expeditions down the canyon, and in 1911 they filmed their rafting trip down the Colorado River. In 1915 they opened a showroom at the top of the Bright Angel Trail, which must be where Emily Post saw the movie. See Rothman, *Devil's Bargains*, 64–65.

XXV

Through the City Unpronounceable to an Exposition Beautiful

Says Los Angeles, "Whatever you do, don't call me Angy Lees"!

Laboriously E. M. wrote her name as she herself pronounced it, "Loas Ang-hell-less." With the piece of paper before me I can say it glibly enough, but in coming upon it unprepared, my only hope is to follow his flippant but very helpful suggestion and mentally dive through it. First, get *hell* as the objective plunge fixed in mind, then get *loas* (like a run-off), *Ang* (hit the springboard), *hell* (the dive), *less* (into the water).[1]

I am not very certain, though, that I want to call her at all. Perhaps we had the spleen, but the meaning and beauty of the city was quite as obscured to us as her name is to those having no knowledge of Spanish. Another thing that is even more obscured is why Los Angeles calls herself the City of Hotels? New York might as well call herself the City of Mosques, or Chicago the Citadel of Fortifications, or Colorado Springs the Seaside Resort! All the way across the continent in the various illustrated information books that are strewn for the edification of idle tourists around mezzanine writing-rooms, you read and read and read of Los Angeles hotels. Not a word does any one of these pamphlets say about the Southern capital's gigantically growing industries, fertile surroundings, automobile interests, millionaire mansions, peerless parks, or even the height

---

1. Apart from Emily Post's complaints about the cost of hotel rooms in Los Angeles, "Nowhere before, in the United States or Europe, have I met with such soaring room rates," she had little to say in *Collier's* about the city, or about Pasadena, until she got to the Mission Inn at Riverside, which she adored.

to which the June thermometer can soar. Each advertising line acclaims it solely as the City of Hotels.

"Which shall be *your hotel*?" reads one eulogy. "You only have to name your ideal, and choose whatever you like." "If you care most for food, there is the restaurant at the Van Nuys[2]; if you want a homey place to stop at, you have a score of smaller hotels to choose from. But of course if you want to find the most luxurious metropolitan hostelry on the entire continent, there is the Green and Gold lobby at the Alexandria." How the lobby in itself is supposed to so much contribute to your happiness and comfort, you have no idea. But each and every advertisement either begins or ends with a description and a full-page picture of this imposing hallway. To test the peerless perfection of this Blackstone rival is naturally irresistible and into its overwhelming gorgeousness you go! The gorgeousness is there quite as in the pictures, also it *is* in every way a perfectly up-to-date and luxurious hotel. You wonder, though, is the cost of food inordinately high? Are wages prohibitive? Is it merely monopoly or forces of circumstance beyond its control that allows the only strictly up-to-date hotel in the place to charge such prices? At Trouville, in the season, or Monte Carlo, your bill can be rather staggering, but at least you get the quintessence of exotic luxury and the most unlimited offerings in diversions that the purveyors to the spenders of the world can achieve. When, however, a commonplace city of extreme dullness asks you Monte Carlo prices, higher than the Ritz in New York or the Blackstone in Chicago, you find a certain much-advertised green and gold lobby illuminingly symbolical of the guests who would for any time stay there.[3]

2. Architects Octavius Morgan and J.A. Walls designed the Beaux-Arts style Van Nuys Hotel on West 3rd St. Opened in 1896, it was the first hotel in Los Angeles to have a telephone in every room and electricity throughout. It is now the Barclay Hotel.

3. The Alexandria Hotel still exists in downtown Los Angeles, but it has clearly seen better days. For many years it was a single-room occupancy hotel, though more recently there have been efforts to revive it. The hotel cost $1.1 million to build, and when it opened in February 1906, the *Los Angeles Times* reported, "...the grandeur of the interior is especially visible...The lobby and entrance to the dining room is a marvel of decorative art in marble, bronze, white and green." Three quarters of the 360 rooms had private baths, and the lowest rate in 1906 was two dollars a day, for a room, without any meals. Emily Post paid $7.00 for a double room with bath, which she described as "*inside* and *dark*," though her son's single room, which was "*very* small," was "perfectly good" at $4.50.

BY TRAIN, GRAND CANYON TO LOS ANGELES

Drawing room, Pullman	$14.00
Lower berth, E.M.	$ 4.00[4]
3 breakfasts	$ 2.60
Tip	$ .30
3 lunches	$ 3.15
Tip	$ .35
Los Angeles. Alexandria Hotel.	
1 hallboy (most luggage in car)	$ .25
Dinner (very simple; for three)	$ 7.80
Theater	$ 6.00
1 room and bath, *inside* and *dark*	$ 7.00
1 *very* small outside room and bath,	
but perfectly good room	$ 4.50
Breakfast and tips and luggage down	$ 2.70
Hiring a motor to move to *Pasadena*	
(while ours being repaired)	$10.00
Stopped with friends, but beautiful hotels in *Pasadena.*[5]	

Motor

Car on freight.
Los Angeles. Smith Bros.' Garage
  (highest class garage).
Result of desert:

1 front spring	$11.00
Tire and tube vulcanized	$ 2.50
Exhaust pipe brazed	$ 6.10
Exhaust pipe welded and repaired; install new gaskets and	
assemble; dismantle muffler and assemble; paint muffler	$21.50
2 gaskets	$ .90

---

4. Emily Post and her cousin Alice were traveling in greater comfort than poor Ned, who would have to sleep in a curtained cavern, dressing and undressing like a contortionist.

5. The Raymond Hotel at Pasadena was one of the great California resort hotels. Bostonian Walter Raymond, who owned Raymond and Whitcomb, nineteenth-century America's answer to Thomas Cook's touring company, first visited Pasadena in 1882; he immediately saw a market for wealthy New Englanders who wanted to get away from the winter cold. He opened his first hotel in 1886; after it was destroyed by fire in 1895 he replaced it with a much grander, three hundred-room building, which opened in 1901. It catered to people on Raymond and Whitcomb tours but closed during the Depression and was eventually demolished. The cottage, where Raymond and his wife lived until his death in 1934, was restored and reopened as a restaurant in the late 1970s.

Wash and polish	$2.50
21 gals. gas (8c!!)	$1.68[6]
1 gal. oil	$1.00
To charge battery	$ .50

To find anywhere else to stay is more than difficult. You run around to "This" one and to "That," and then to the whole advertised list, but your own "ideal" is not among them. So either you stay on where you are, and ignore the hole in your bank account or you go quickly on to the next place; or better yet move out to the beautiful suburb, for which one might say Los Angeles is famous and where half of the Los Angeles fashionables live. In other words, Pasadena. Pasadena, besides having many splendid hotels,[7] is a floral park of much beauty, a little too neat, perhaps, for real allure and possibly a little over-obviously rich. But its even squares of streets are splendidly bordered with palms or pepper trees. Here and there the center of the street is sentineled by a superb tree that you are glad the street builders had not the heart to cut down. Back of tropically verdant lawns are rows of homelike bungalows smothered in vines and there are many important and beautiful places that entirely compensate for the few crude garish ones that flaunt so much wealth and so little good taste.[8]

The Country Club is most charming, and in it a big room so appealing in color and furnishing that you feel irresistibly like settling yourself in the corner of one of the chintz-covered sofas and staying indefinitely.[9] Yet the same people whose own houses are so attractive will seriously take you to admire a horticultural achievement that, in its magentas and scarlets, purples and heliotrope, orange, Indian red and Paris green lacks no element of discord except an out-of-tune German band to play among its

---

6. Gas prices on the California coast were considerably lower than those elsewhere in the United States; in upstate New York they were paying 12 cents a gallon, and in the Midwest they paid as much as 22 cents a gallon.

7. See Map no. 23, page 308. (One of Emily Post's original footnotes.) This map is on page 196 in this edition.

8. The most noted architects in turn-of the-century Pasadena were Charles Sumner Greene and Henry Mather Greene; their masterpiece was the house they built in 1908 for David B. Gamble, of Proctor and Gamble, who retired to Pasadena in 1895. The Greenes were influenced by the aesthetic movement, John Ruskin, William Morris, Scandinavian wood and Japanese simplicity—little of which appealed to Emily Post, who had a strong preference for a mixture of French and colonial revival styles.

9. Charles Frederick Holder founded the Valley Hunt Club, one of Pasadena's most exclusive institutions, in the late 1880s. Club members, dressed in hunting pink, hunted rabbits and later foxes. On New Year's Day they held a great outdoor picnic followed by a hunt ball, and in 1890 they added a Tournament of Roses which by 1907 had developed into an elaborate downtown parade and a college football game.

"In a California garden." A black and white photograph cannot do justice to the riot of colors described by Emily Post.

glass globes. I don't really remember whether I saw any glass globes or not, but the disturbed visions that come back to me are of silver globes, iron stags, sea-shell fountains amid a floral debauch.

They say that when people paint their faces they lose their eye and soon put the whole paint box on. In the same way it may be that the brilliancy of the sunshine has affected people's sight and that they can't perceive color discords. All through Southern California you see combinations of color that fairly put your teeth on edge. Scarlet and majenta are put together everywhere; Prussian blue next to cobalt; vermilion next to old rose, olive-green next to emerald. Not only in flowers, but in homes and in clothes.

We dined the other night in a terra-cotta room hung with crimson curtains; one woman in a turquoise-colored dress wore slippers of French blue, another carried an emerald-colored fan with a sage-green frock![10]

The conversation — only some of it — was as queerly assembled as the colors. A Mr. Brown, to convince me of the high moral tone of Pasadena men, told me that, in Honolulu, a chief offered a friend of his two beautiful young wives. He laid special stress on their beauty of "form" and sweetness of disposition. Also he explained carefully that they were yellow

---

10. Emily Post was very interested in harmonious color — her book *The Personality of a House* which was published in 1930 and was, apparently her favorite, had a whole chapter on "The Principles of Color Harmony" and a color chart so the reader could be sure which colors "went" together.

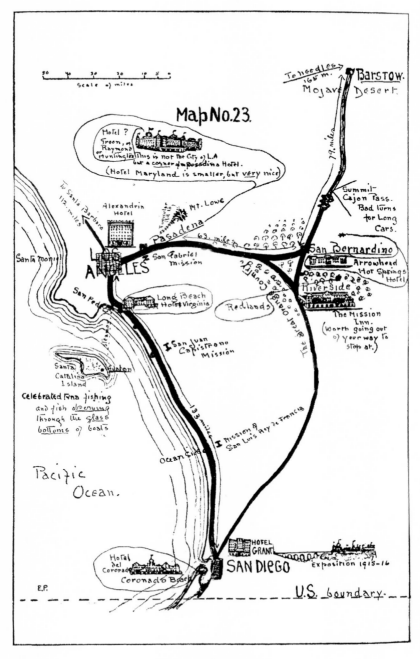

"Map 23 Barstow — San Diego — Los Angeles"

in color, not black. "But my friend explained to the chief that he was married. The chief said, 'What difference does that make? Do you want to insult my brotherly love for you?'" But the friend "insulted" and refused the little gold-colored wives. I waited for the rest of the story but there did not seem to be any rest. So I said, "And then —?"

"Well, that was just to show you," he answered proudly, "the high type of men we have out here on the coast."

I put this down as I heard it, although I myself don't see much point to it, even yet!

RESUMED MOTORING. SHORT RUN LATE IN AFTERNOON, PASADENA TO RIVERSIDE

Personal

Riverside. Mission Inn.
    (The *most* enchanting hotel!)

Dinner	$ 3.00
3 rooms, baths and food	$18.00
Tips and sundries	$ 3.60

I am trying not to say so much about hotels any more, but there is one I *must* mention — particularly after the failure we had with them in Los Angeles. Wanting to see the most famous orange grove in the country, we drove to Riverside and found quite by accident the most ideal hotel imaginable — the really most lovely place that ever was! So I must tell you that the Mission Inn at Riverside is worth traveling miles to stop at; a hotel of pure delight, in which the beauty of a Spanish palace and the picturesqueness of an old mission is combined with the most perfect modern comfort and at fair and reasonable rates. I don't believe anyone ever entered its hospitable doors without pleasure or left them without regret.[11]

From Riverside we made a loop back to Los Angeles and drove down to San Diego along the edge of the ocean all the way. The coast was one long succession of big ocean resort hotels on a boulevard that seemed too

---

11. The Mission Inn at Riverside started as a twelve-room adobe boarding house in 1876. In 1902, Frank Miller, son of the original owner, expanded it into a four-story U-shaped hotel surrounding a courtyard. He added the Cloister Wing, which included dramatic public spaces in 1910, and in 1913–14 added the Spanish Wing, designed by architect Myron Hunt. This incorporated a gallery to display Miller's collection of Spanish art, much of which is still on display throughout the hotel.

"This is not a gallery in a Spanish palace, but a gallery in the Mission Inn at Riverside, California."

smooth and perfect to be true. We had forgotten that such road smooth-
ness existed for our poor long-tortured engine to glide over.

The Fair at San Diego was a little Exposition Beautiful![12] The com-
posite impression was of a garden of dense, shiny green. Great masses and
profusions of orange-trees and vines against low one-storied buildings of
gray-white. Across a long viaduct under an archway and down a long
avenue, there was no other color except gray-white and green until you
came into the central plaza filled with pigeons as in St. Mark's in Venice,
and saw over one portico of the quadrangle of white buildings a single
blaze of orange and blue striped awnings—stripes nearly a foot wide of
blue the color of laundry blue, and orange the color of the most vivid fruit
of that name that you can find! Against the unrelieved green and gray this
one barbaric splash of color actually thrilled.

Down the next avenue hanging beside the balustrade of another building was the same vivid sweep of blue. Over a building around the corner
was a climbing amber rose, and just beyond it some pinkish-purple
bougainvillea, that beautiful but most difficult vine to put anywhere. There
were gardens and gardens of flowers but each so separated and grouped
that there was not a note of discord.

And how things did grow! Some of the buildings were already covered to their roofs with vines, and benches shaded by shrubs, that we treasure at home in little pots!

The San Diego Exposition was a pure delight. Its simplicity and faultless harmony of color brought out all its values startlingly.

A farmer—ought he be called a rancher?—said he thought it a
"homey" exposition. I doubt if the sentiment could be better expressed.
It was first and foremost designed to show by actual demonstration what
could be accomplished in our own land of the West. The citrus groves
were full sized; the fields of grain were big and real; instead of putting
reapers and harvesters in a large machinery hall, they demonstrated them
on a model ranch, so that anyone likely to be interested could see how they
were used.

---

12. The San Diego Exposition, which was organized to celebrate the opening of the
Panama Canal, caused a political ruckus that spread throughout California and may have
affected the 1912 Presidential election. The San Francisco planners tried to persuade the San
Diego group to abandon their scheme but they refused and it became a potent symbol of
local pride and boosterism. Unlike previous expositions such as that in Chicago in 1893,
the designers rejected classicism and opted for Spanish-style architecture. It opened on
December 31, 1914, after President Woodrow Wilson pressed a Western Union Telegraph
key at midnight Eastern time; the message traveled 3000 miles and turned on lights and set
off a firework display in San Diego. A crowd of more than 30,000 people surged through
the gates of what is now Balboa Park, singing, throwing confetti and waving banners.

The Indian exhibits were very complete — especially those of the Hopis.[13] There was a life-size model of the pueblo of Taos and miniature models of the other more famous pueblos, and examples of their arts and crafts.[14]

Otherwise the general impressions of the exhibits were much alike; bottles of fruit in alcohol, sheaves of grain, arches of oranges, and school children's efforts in art.

Of all the buildings, we liked Kansas best. We liked it from its three stiff clay sunflowers raised and painted over its plain little front door to its unending varieties of grains. And all because the old Kansan — not that he was so old, either — in charge of it loved his state and was so unaffectedly proud of it, that we caught the infection from him. We couldn't help it.

"Of course," he said, "I've only samples here but there's nothing that can grow in the soil that we can't grow in Kansas! These people out here talk about beautiful California, the 'ever-blooming garden of California,' and her 'sublime mountain scenery,' 'ocean-kissed shore' and what not. Now, for *my* taste, give me a land that is as flat as the pa'm of your hand — give me Kansas!"

An old woman came in while we were there. She poked all around, sniffed at the kaffir corn, at every variety of grain that could be stored in glass-fronted bins or arched into sheaves.[15]

"Land sakes!" she said. "Y'ain't got nothin' in here but chickin feed. Ain't yuh got nothin' t'eat?" And out she switched again.

"I suppose that old woman'd like me to keep a nice crock of doughnuts ready to give her, and a cup of tea, mebbe. Chickin feed, indeed! Well, when it comes to hens I like the feathered kind. You can put them in a pot and boil'em! Chickin feed! And its mighty fine chickin feed, I tell you, that a man can grown in the state of Kansas!"

Coronado Beach, the famous winter resort, is across the bay and reached in a few minutes by ferry from San Diego.[16]

---

13. Colonel David Charles Collier, the organizer of the San Diego Exposition, together with archaeologist Dr. Edgar L. Hewett of Santa Fe persuaded Edward P. Ripley, president of the Santa Fe railroad, to create an exhibition of Southwestern Indians. This was a more sympathetic image than at some earlier expositions, as the railroad wanted to promote tourism, and Hewett, unlike many of his eugenic and Social Darwinist contemporaries, saw the Indians as bearers of a simple yet graceful culture, which he wanted to both preserve and celebrate.

14. Significantly, Emily Post originally wrote that the Indian crafts "can really be better seen at San Diego than any traveler such as ourselves can see in going to the reservations." Somehow the theater was more authentic than the real thing.

15. Kaffir corn is an African sorghum, grown in the Southwest for grain and animal feed.

16. The very grand and turreted Hotel Del Coronado was opened in 1888. Created by

In San Diego itself a new apartment house, the Palomar, offers a novelty in automatic and economic living that is quite original. Single apartments, for example, rent for $65.00 a month and consist of a large living-room, a small dressing-room, a bathroom and a kitchenette. No bedroom! You dress in the dressing-room, and sleep in the living room in a disappearing bed, not a folding one, that in the daytime is rolled into an air chamber large enough to hold it intact. You can rent a room for your personal maid, or valet, but all of the service is furnished as in a hotel. Only instead of ordering your food in a restaurant, you do your own marketing and have it prepared in your own kitchen. Instead of paying your cook by the month, you hire one at twenty-five cents an hour whenever you want a meal cooked. No meals at home, no cook![17]

From the point of view of the stranger glancing about the streets, the chief diversion in San Diego seems to be moving pictures. The square which appears to be the central point around which the city is built, is lined with electric arched doorways displaying every lure of lithograph.[18] Besides the picture palaces are two drug-stores, and a funeral director's window, proffering the latest novelties in caskets. But the most lingering memory of San Diego, outside of her harbor, is of her school buildings. They are the last word in construction and equipment, Tudor in design, and very imposing.

When we left San Diego and all along the ocean the weather was deliciously cool, but as we went inland toward Pasadena it became hotter than anything you can imagine. It was a case of 116° in the shade and there wasn't any shade!

"How can the orange trees remain so beautifully green?" I heard Celia muttering. Twenty miles north of Los Angeles I looked at the unburnt hills and crisply standing live-oaks in wonder and amazement. I could actually see blisters forming on E. M.'s nose. Finally we panted up a big winding hill, a branch of the Coast Range of mountains, I suppose it was,

---

two Midwestern businessmen, Elisha Babcock and H. L. Story, who wanted it to be the "talk of the Western world," the grand opening was witnessed by thousands of people. Many years later it was to provide the setting for the Marilyn Monroe movie *Some Like It Hot.*

17. For a detailed account of experiments in living, see Dolores Hayden, *The Grand Domestic Revolution: A History of Feminist Designs for American Homes, Neighborhoods and Cities* (Cambridge, Mass., MIT Press, 1981). This paragraph did not appear in the *Collier's* article.

18. It seems rather extraordinary to have a display of funeral caskets in such a prominent place. In the *Collier's* article she located this square as the one "on which the General Grant Hotel faces." Although part of Horton Plaza is still a park, much of it is now taken up by an openair shopping mall.

"On a beautiful ocean road in California": even better than the French Riviera!

and as we dipped over on the other side, such a gust of cold sea wind greeted us that in five minutes, we, who had been gasping like dying fish, were wrapping our now shivering selves in coats!

Besides the life-giving coolness of the sea air, never, never was there a more beautiful drive than the one to Santa Barbara. Not the Cornici of France — not even the Sorrento to Amalfi of Italy.[19] Mountains on one side, the ocean on the other, curving in and out of bays each more lovely than the last, and on a road like linoleum. I thought I should like to live where I could drive up and down that road forever!

Editor's Note: Post and her party drove to San Diego on Monday May 31, and left on Thursday June 3, 1915.

---

19. These European comparisons were added in the book version.

Personal

San Diego. U.S. Grant Hotel[20]

Dinner	$ 3.00
Tip	$ .35
(Average day)	
Hallboys, luggage up and down	$ 1.75
Chambermaid	$ .75
3 rooms and baths	$14.00
3 entrances exposition (night)	$ 1.50
Electric chair	$ 2.00
Breakfast (3)	$ 2.95
Exposition, 3 entrances (morning)	$ 1.50
Electric chair (*whole day and held all 3 of us*)	$ 4.00[21]
Lunch at Exposition restaurant (3)	$ 1.50
Tip	$ .30
Indian Village	$ .75
Panama Canal (3)	$ .75
Various sideshows etc.	$ 6.30

Motor

White Star Motor Co.

Storage, 3 days	$ 1.50
20 gals. gas	$ 3.20
1 gal. oil	$ .80
Wash car	$ 1.50

---

20. U.S. Grant, Jr. (1852–1929), son of the 18th president, was a Harvard-educated lawyer and real estate developer who did much to build up the city of San Diego. His hotel, which cost $1.9 million, opened in 1910 after numerous delays, and boasted 437 rooms, most of which had private baths; there was also a roof garden, a palm court, and a beautiful ballroom on the ninth floor. It is still operating as a hotel and is now on the National Register of Historic Places. See Evelyn I. Banning, "U. S. Grant Jr., a Builder of San Diego," *The Journal of San Diego History* Vol. 27, no. 1 (Winter 1981).

21. One of the great delights of the San Diego Exposition was the "electriquettes," motorized wicker chairs, which could whirl visitors around the exhibits at three and a half miles per hour.

XXVI

The Land of Gladness

Light-hearted, happy, basking in the sunshine, her eyes not dreamily gazing into the past, nor avariciously peering into the future, but dancing with the joy of today — such is California! It is not only the sun of heaven shining upon California that makes her the garden-land of the world, but the sun radiating from the hearts of her people. Golden she certainly is — land of golden fruit, land of golden plenty, daughter of the golden sun.

If you have millions and want to learn a million ways to spend them; if you are a social climber and want to scale the Western Hemisphere's most polished pinnacle; if you want to become worldly, cynical, effete, go to New York. New York is the princess of impersonality, the queen of indifference. Your riches do not impress her; without any, you do not exist. You can come or go, sink or swim, be brilliant, beautiful or charming, she cares not a whit. "What new extravagance do you bring to amuse me?" she asks, bored even before she finishes asking.

"What are you ambitious to do?" asks Chicago. "What are you trying to be? Can I help you?"

"Welcome to the land of sunshine!" says smiling California. "If your heart is young, then stay with me and play!"

There are plenty of reasons why they liken Santa Barbara to Nice, Cannes or Monte Carlo. When we arrived in our rooms at the Hotel Potter we could hardly believe we were not on the Riviera, not merely because of the white enamel and shadow chintz furnishings of our rooms looking out upon the palm-bordered esplanade to the ocean just beyond, but because only in Continental watering places do friends send — or could they possibly find for you — bouquets of welcome like that. Against the gray wall above the writing-table a great sheaf bouquet of the big, pale-pink roses you associate with France, combined with silver violet thistles, gladiolii in a chromatic scale of creams and corals, and in such profusion that

204

"Under Santa Barbara skies": presumably outside a friend's house.

they were standing in a tall vase on the floor. The third bouquet was of apricot-colored roses, heliotrope and white lilies.[1]

As a matter of fact, the Riviera bears the same resemblance to Santa Barbara that artificial flowers bear to the real. The spirit of one is essentially artificial, insidiously demoralizing. The spirit of the other is the essence of naturalness, inevitably rejuvenating.[2]

Instead of spending your every waking moment in electric-lighted restaurants and gambling rooms, you live in the sunshine, and in the open. Every house, nearly, has its patio or open court, and no matter what your occupation may be, you seldom go indoors. Carrying the love of outdoors even to concerts and theatrical performances, the owner of a very beautiful garden has built a theater, of which the stage is a terrace of grass, and the scenery evenly planted trees. In spite of some of the pretentious villas, the keynote of the Pacific coast is still naturalness. Affectations have really no place.[3]

---

1. The six hundred-room Potter Hotel was opened in January 1902 and destroyed in a fire in April 1921. The site is now Ambassador Park. The hotel was constructed on Burton Mound, a prehistoric Chumash Indian site. After archaeologists investigated the site some artifacts were taken to the Smithsonian Institution in Washington DC while others remain in the Santa Barbara Museum of Natural History.

2. For an interesting study of tourism in Nice, see Robert Kanigel, *High Season: How One French Riviera Town Has Seduced Travelers for Two Thousand Years* (New York: Viking, 2002).

3. This paragraph and the following six, including the anecdote about the olives, were not in the *Collier's* version.

One afternoon at a fruit ranch, we found ourselves next to a woman who for twenty minutes extolled the perfection of her long years of living in Italy. With her hands affectedly clasped and gazing at the feathery olive-trees, she exclaimed:

"Ah! That takes me so back to my beloved Sicily, and the mornings when I used to walk along the olive groves and eat ripe olives before break-fast."

To offer strangers olives picked from the trees is a pet joke of Californians no less than the Italians. The uncured fruit is as bitterly uneatable as quinine.

"Oh, do you like fresh olives?" This gleefully from the host. "Let me pick you some!" In a few moments he returned with a fruit-laden branch. With bated breath, everyone watched as she plucked one and — gamely, ate it!

To look at the orange, lemon, walnut and olive groves out here you would think failure in crops an impossibility. Put any kind of a little shoot in the ground and you can almost stand beside it and wait for it to be grown. But perhaps the land's perfection is a proof of skilled industry after all. At least one of the greatest of the orange-growers in the State told us: "Come out and run a ranch for fifteen seasons and you will find fifteen reasons why you can fail."

Ordinarily, though, in the conversation of people here, the personal equation is left out. Californians seldom if ever accentuate their own share in the success of anything.

Everywhere else the enthusiastic inhabitants speak of their state and of their city as a man speaks of his success in business, or a woman speaks of her new home — not only with pride in the thing accomplished but with a satisfaction that comes from their personal effort toward its accomplishment.

The Chicagoans, I remember, for instance, in their pride in the Wheaton Country Club, seemed to feel that their planting and building and making a beauty spot out of a sand heap was the most admirable thing about it.

The only parallel to the attitude of the Californians that I can think of is that of the Italians. Living in their land is merely a great privilege that God has given them, and the beauty of it is a thing that has always been — a thing with which mere man has had little to do.[4]

The picture that the visitor remembers first, last and best in Santa Bar-

---

4. The rest of this chapter was not in the original *Collier's* piece.

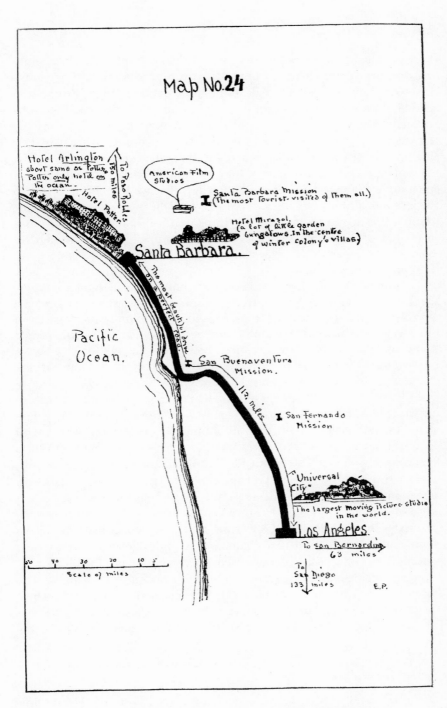

"Map no. 24 Los Angeles to Santa Barbara" Thursday June 3, 1915.

bara is of a succession of low mountain ledges capped with white, pink, gray or terra-cotta villas, surrounded by tropical gardens and overlooking a sapphire-colored ocean gleaming in perpetual sunlight. Nothing in all of Italy, not on the road from Sorrento to Amalfi, not even at Taormina in Sicily, is there any scene of land and water more beautiful. Of the villas, most are impressive, a few are admirable, and one, in particular, is like a fifteenth-century Italian gem of the first water transplanted by magic, gardens and all, from the heart of Italy. No other place has quite the atmosphere of this one — that sense of nobleness that we have been taught to believe is made only by centuries of mellowing on an already perfect foundation. It is not an imitation. Everything in it is real and everything in it is old except the garden, which looks the oldest of all. Perhaps, though, in a land where green things crowd an average year's growth into every week, it is small wonder that an effect of centuries can be acquired in a decade.

I don't know whether we missed them, but among all the glorious gardens of lawns and hedges and trees, we saw scarcely any flower gardens; and the few we saw screamed in hideous discords of magenta, scarlet and purple. As in Pasadena, the riot of sun and color seems to make people blind to color discord. An exception, however — the only one we saw — was in the gardens of the Mirasol, which reminds me, by the way, that the Mirasol is a sort of post-impressionist *ne plus ultra*, in hotel-keeping.[5]

To begin with, its groups of little white bungalows neatly set within its white picket-fenced enclosure, is more like a toy village than any possible suggestion of a hotel. Each little bungalow is low and white, with boxes of flowers under every window and a general smothered-in-vines appearance. So much for the outside. Inside each holds several bedrooms, one or two bathrooms, and perhaps a private sitting-room, all of them super-modern in their furnishings, and each room looking out upon a vista of garden that matches its own color scheme. A rose-chintz sitting-room, for instance, looks out on a rose garden; a lavender bedroom opens on a garden in which there are none but lavender flowers, and a yellow one looks out on a vista of yellow. All of the decoration is rather over-stenciled and striped, but the bedroom bungalows are really enchanting. The public rooms, dining room, public sitting room and tearoom, are in a bigger house, the orange and blue interior of which suggests nothing so much as the setting of a Bakst ballet.[6] The walls, curtains, table cloths, decora-

---

5. El Mirasol, on the site of the former Huerter residence, eventually burned down and the land became a park.

6. Leon Bakst (1866–1924) was a Russian painter and co-founder, with Sergei Diaghilev, of the Ballet Russe. Famous for his rich, exuberant colors, one of his most celebrated designs was for *Sheherazade* (1910).

tions, chairs, napkins and the waitresses' aprons are all apricot orange, and the stenciling and stripes and floor and waitresses' dresses are blue. There is a tearoom in which gorgeous cockatoos—live ones!—live in blaze of orange surroundings. The details are all carefully done, most of them are effective, and certainly unusual. For our own parts we thought the bedrooms lovely; the highly polished indigo floor paint an inspiration, and the orange-colored table linens amusing; but when it came to filigreed silver breast-pins glued into the drawing-room mantel, it was the one touch too much!

Editor's Note: Post and her party drove to Santa Barbara on Thursday June 3, and left on Sunday June 6, 1915.

Personal

Lunched in car on road.
Santa Barbara. Hotel Potter.

3 rooms and baths, a day, including meals (none of which we took; lunched and dined out every day)	$21.00
Bringing the coffee to room and tip	$ .45
Lunch to take with us the day we left	$ 1.50
Ice-cream at druggist's in thermos jar	$ .30
Sundries and telegrams	$ 3.10

Motor

Santa Barbara. El Camino Real Motor Co.

25 gals. gas	$ 2.50
Storage, 3 days	$ 1.50
Oil (1 gal.)	$ .80

XXVII

The Mettle of a Hero

An explosion shook the town, then came the fire engines. Everybody ran and of course we ran too. We saw a big, Colonial house in a blaze, then a second explosion! And a thick mass of smoke blew off the roof. People ran hither and thither in wild excitement; a fireman dashed into the flames and carried out a dying girl; her face was bleeding and her clothes were in burnt shreds. More dying people were miraculously saved, then suddenly like a huge screen the whole house fell flat. It had no behind and no inside and the whole scene was only the "movies." The injured face of the heroine was only red paint and the house a property one built for the purpose.[1]

"This is nothing," said a member of the company to me, "if you want to see something exciting, go to the chalk cliffs just on the road to Santa Maria tomorrow morning. We're going to work on the 'Diamond From the Sky.' That's our star over there! You don't want to miss any pictures when he is in it."[2]

I saw a young man leaning against a telegraph pole chewing a straw. He looked almost too lazy to be alive.

---

1. Emily Post was a little ahead of the crowd here, as by the 1930s, according to one historian of tourism, "every tourist hoped to see movies being made," and "tours of various studio departments and the inspection of various movie sets were mandatory." Jakle, *The Tourist*, 32–33.

2. *Diamond From the Sky*, directed by Jacques Jacquard and William Desmond Taylor, was shown in 32 episodes in 1915. The star was William Russell (1886–1929) who was born in New York, was a child actor, and then studied law at Fordham University, where he was on the football team and a champion swimmer. He became a lawyer but his legal career was short and unsuccessful and after stints as a boxing coach and a lifeguard, he returned to acting. At 6 feet 2 inches and 203 pounds, and as an all-round athlete with dark good looks, he worked on numerous films until his death from pneumonia in 1929. Lottie Pickford (1895–1936), sister of the more famous Mary Pickford, played the "gypsy heroine" in *Diamond From the Sky* which also starred Charlotte Burton, who later married (and divorced) Russell.

210

"He's always like that!" said the member of the company. "You wouldn't think there was an ounce of go in him! He's always whittling a stick, or chewing a straw, and if he was to be killed, he'd never move a muscle!"

"He looks kind of comatose, doesn't he?" said the manager, who overheard. "Well, you go out to the chalk cliffs at about eleven tomorrow if you think he's comatose, and see him come to."

Naturally we went. We found the place easily by the number of people gathered at the spot. A shelf road was cut on the face of the high chalk cliffs, above a seventy-foot sheer drop into the water. We saw the comatose one, looking just as indifferent as ever, get into a car and start for the narrow road up on the edge of the cliff. Then another followed him. At a word from the director, they raced across the high narrow shelf, the comatose one swerved to the very edge, toppled and plunged over the abyss! No stopping the picture at the brink and putting a dummy in his place. A feeling of such nausea caught me I could not look to see him land. How he escaped with his life he alone knew. The car struck the rocks and smashed to pieces, but they say he threw himself like an eel clear of the wheel and safely into the water. They then fished him out, he got into another car just as he was, and started home as though nothing had happened. When we reached a railroad track where they were going to take another picture, the same actor was to drive so near the track that the locomotive might in the picture seem to hit the car. The camera man was ready to turn the crank of his camera, the locomotive was almost at the crossing, when dash! went the devil-driver toward the track. Stop? Nothing of the sort. He met it as a ram meets an enemy, head on. The locomotive carried his mangled self and wrecked machine up the track. The engineer, shaking as with the palsy, almost fell out of his cab. The company and we, too, rushed up to where the wrecked machine and injured man lay. Blood was streaming from his head, his arm distortedly twisted under him, and he was writhing in pain, but when the camera man reached him all he said was:

"This'll be great stuff! Make a close-up quick!" They made the pictures and then he lost consciousness.

Although decorated with many bandages, he is up and about, looking as comatose as ever.

We went to a film rehearsal at the Flying A. In front of us sat the heroine, the hero, the villain, and all members of the company.[3] The director read the words that would be printed between sections of the finished reel

<hr>

3. For an account of the American Film Manufacturing Company, more familiarly known as the Flying A Studio, see Stephen Lawton, *Santa Barbara's Flying A Studio* (Santa Barbara, California: Fithian Press, 1997).

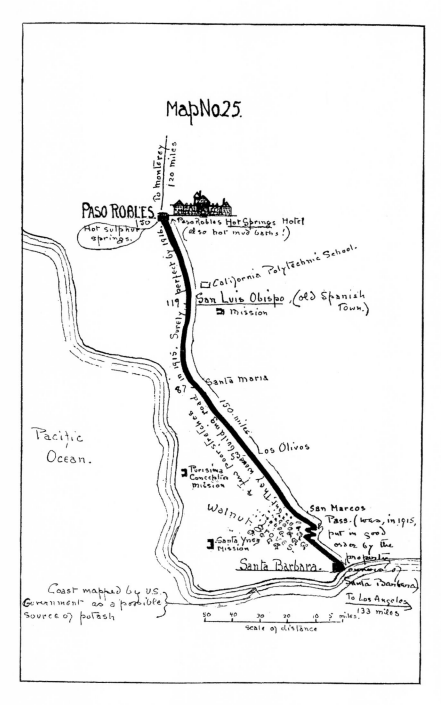

MapNo.25.

To Monterey 120 miles

PASO ROBLES. 50

Hot sulphur springs.

↑ Paso Robles Hot Springs Hotel (also hot mud baths!)

119   Surely perfect by 1916.

☐ (California Polytechnic School.

<u>San Luis Obispo</u> (old Spanish Town.)
🏠 Mission

87   87 in 1915.   150 miles

Santa Maria

The poor stretches of Camino Road.   53 miles

Los Olivos

■ Purisima Concehlín mission

Walnut

San Marcos Pass. (was, in 1915, put in good order by the property owners.)

■ Santa Ynez Mission

Santa Barbara. ■

(Santa Barbara.)

Pacific Ocean.

Coast mapped by U.S. Government as a possible source of potash

To Los Angeles 133 miles

50   40   30   20   10   5 miles.
Scale of distance

"Map 25 Santa Barbara to Paso Robles" Sunday June 6, 1915.

and the pictures were shown in negative only. Every now and then the actors made a few remarks such as, "That's a fine action, Steve"; "Gee, Steve, that's great!" "I like Flora down by the brook"; "Nice scene Flora!" Finally the heroine died.

"Nobody can die with so much sob stuff as Flora," said our friend in a whisper.

Flora heard and answered: "Some time I'd like a part that I don't have to die in. That's the seventeenth time I've died this season."

Of the many moving picture plants we saw, the Flying A was the smallest but most interesting. The difference between the Universal City and Flying A studio is that between Barnum's Circus at the Madison Square Garden and the Little Theater — or better, the Grand Guignol in Paris. The Universal City is a gigantic organization that can produce anything from tiger-hunting in the jungle to plays like "Quo Vadis."[4]

But why — Oh, why don't the moving picture people have someone to show them how the houses of the socially prominent really look? Where do they devise the manners, customs, and nightmare interiors that could not be found outside of the society atmosphere of Dingy Dunk or Splashville except in the "movies"?

Leaving Santa Barbara about two o'clock we arrived at Paso Robles long before dark. The next morning, however, we left early in order to spend part of the day with some friends who have a cattle and alfalfa ranch about midway to Monterey. I should think the cattle would all topple over dead and the alfalfa shrivel to cinders. Cool California? The thermometer was easily 120, and that cloudless sky a blinding blaze of torture. Our friends were quite tranquil about it. "It *is* pretty hot here just now. You see we are pocketed between the hill ranges, but it is beautifully mild all winter."

To us the mild winter did not seem to compensate, since we could not understand anyone's surviving so long as until then.

---

4. Universal City was very new when Emily Post was in California. In March 1915 Carl Laemmle opened a movie studio on a former chicken ranch and invited visitors to watch movies being made. Paying a quarter for a box lunch and a seat on the bleachers, visitors could shout and cheer at the silent movies under production. *Quo Vadis*, based on a historical novel published in 1896 by Polish author Henryk Sienkiewicz, was adapted into a play in 1901, an opera in 1909, and filmed in 1912, 1924, 1951 and 1986. The 1912 Italian version, directed by Enrico Guazzoni, was one of the first full-length films ever made, but it was not made at Universal City.

Twenty-Fifth Day's Run, Paso Robles to Monterey Monday June 7, 1915

Personal

Paso Robles, Cal. Paso Robles Springs Hotel[5]
    Rooms with baths and two meals; no luncheon charged for $12.75
    Lunched at the R's on our way. Much further *out* of
      our way than we thought, and had supper at *Salinas*;
      had cocoa, toast and omelette, plenty of it and
      very good for 75c. for three.

Motor

Paso Robles. Pioneer Garage
    15 gals. gas $ 3.30
    Storage $ .50

That afternoon's drive was the hottest I hope ever to have to live through. To put your hand on unshaded metal was to burn it, as though on a hot flat-iron. The main road, El Camino Real, was good all the way to Salinas, but the branch road from there to Monterey was bumpy and bad until within a mile or so of our destination.

Of Monterey and its peerlessly beautiful seventeen-mile ocean and cedar drive, there is no need to write. Like Niagara and the Grand Canyon, it has been written about and photographed in every newspaper and periodical in the world. Also, as was the case further south, hot as it might be inland, the coast was deliciously cool. The weather changed fortunately by the time we again drove inland and up the perfect boulevard to San Francisco. They tell me, however, that so far as the neighborhood of San Francisco is concerned no one need ever dread heat, a scorching temperature being unknown. Wind you may have, and sometimes fog, but extremes of either heat or cold, never! Besides other blessings in this par-

---

5. The Paso Robles Springs Hotel was opened in 1889, and a hot springs bathhouse added in 1906. Many famous people came to the hotel — the hot springs (which provide two million gallons of 124 degree water a day) eased the arthritis of concert pianist Ignace Paderewsky, and when Major League baseball teams used Paso Robles for spring training, members of the Chicago White Sox and the Pittsburgh Pirates soaked their aching limbs in the springs. The hotel, which was supposedly fireproof, burned down in 1940, but was rebuilt and renamed the Paso Robles Inn in 1942. The grand ballroom, the only room to survive the fire, was restored in 2000.

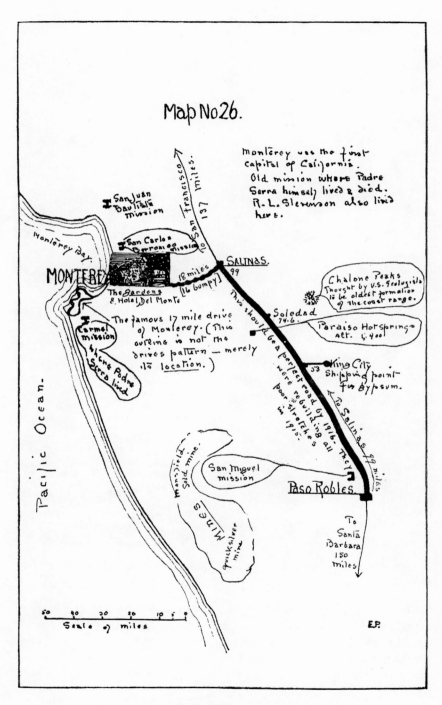

Map No 26.

Monterey was the first capital of California.
Old mission where Padre Serra himself lived & died.
R. L. Stevenson also lived here.

San Francisco 137 miles.

San Juan Bautista Mission

Monterey Bay.

San Carlos Borromeo Mission

MONTEREY

SALINAS. 99

18 miles [16 bumpy]

The Gardens & Hotel Del Monte

Chalone Peaks Thought by U.S. Geologists to be oldest formation of the coast range.

Soledad 74.6

Paraiso Hotsprings alt. 1,400.

Carmel mission where Padre Serra lived

The famous 17 mile drive of Monterey. (This outline is not the drive's pattern — merely its location.)

This should be a perfect road of 1916. They were rebuilding all poor stretches in 1915.

53 King City Shipping point for gypsum.

To Salinas 49 miles.

Pacific Ocean.

Mansfield Gold mine.

San Miguel mission

Mines

Quicksilver mine.

Paso Robles.

To Santa Barbara 150 miles

50 40 30 20 10 5 0
Scale of miles

E.P.

"Paso Robles to Monterey" Monday June 7, 1915.

Top: "Ostrich Rock, Monterey, California"; *Bottom:* "On the seventeen-mile drive at Monterey."

ticular spot of this wonderful land you can also choose your own temperature. If you like warm weather, walk in the sun. If you like cold
weather, walk in the shade. On the former side of the street, you will find
a muslin dress just right; on the latter you will be comfortable in a sealskin coat. This is not a joke, as I had always thought it to be, but quite
true.

Twenty-Sixth Day's Run, Monterey to San Francisco Tuesday June 8, 1915.

Personal

Monterey. Hotel Del Monte.[6]

Rooms (perfectly *vast*) and baths, American plan	$18.00
Tips and breakfast tray	$ 2.50
Lunch to take with us	$ 1.60
Sundries	$ 2.00

Motor

Monterey. Hotel Del Monte Garage.

14 gals. gas	$ 3.08
Storage	$ .50
Oil	$ .90

---

6. One of the earliest California resort hotels, the Del Monte at Monterey was built in 1880, rebuilt in 1888 after a fire the previous year, and after another fire in 1924 destroyed the middle section, partially rebuilt, leaving the 1888 wings intact. Since World War II it has belonged to the US Navy, and now forms part of the Naval Postgraduate School.

XXVIII

San Francisco

Just as it is often for their little tricks or failings that we love people best, so it is with San Francisco. You may find her beautiful as she rises tier on tier on her many hills above the dazzling waters of the bay, you must admire the resolution and courage with which, out of her annihilation, she has risen more beautiful than before; but you love her for a lot of human, foolish, adorable personalities of her own, such as the guileless way she stuccoes the front of her houses, leaving their wooden backs perfectly visible from behind or at the side — a pretense deliciously naïve, as though she said: "I am putting a lovely front of concrete where you will see it first, because I think it will please you!"[1]

Her insistence upon loading your pockets with pounds of silver cartwheels, instead of a few dollar bills, is not quite so enchanting — but maybe when your muscles and pocket linings become used to the strain, you learn to like her silver habits too.[2]

And in her methods of building she has no "fashionable section," but mixes smart and squalid with a method of strange confusion peculiar to herself. The value and desirability of the land is entirely proportionate to the altitude or view, and not to convenience of location or neighborhood. On the top of each and every hill, on the "view side," perches Mr. Millionaire. If the hill slopes down gently, the wealth of his neighbors decreases gently also, but as the descent is likely to be almost a cliff, Mr. Poorman's shanty, as often as not, clings to Mr. Richman's cellar door.

And then there are her queer-looking cable-cars — with "outside" seats

---

1. The next six paragraphs were not in the original *Collier's* piece.
2. The Morgan silver dollars (named after their designer George T. Morgan) were authorized by the Bland-Allison Act of 1878, continued in production until 1904, and were reissued in 1921. They were, apparently, called cartwheels because of their size and their shiny surface and were mostly used in the West.

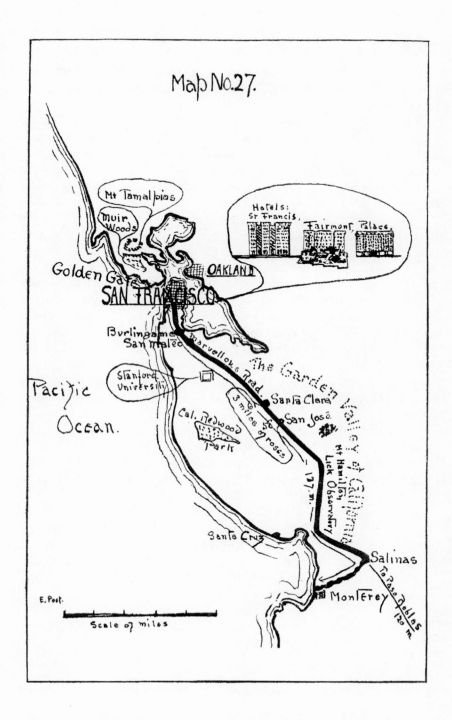

Map No. 27.

Mt Tamalpias

Muir Woods

Hotels:
St Francis, Fairmont, Palace.

Golden Gate

OAKLAND

SAN FRANCISCO

Burlingame
San Mateo

marvellous Road.

Stanford University

Pacific

Ocean.

3 miles of roses

Cal. Redwood Park

The Garden Valley of California

Santa Clara

San José

Mt Hamilton
Lick Observatory

127 m.

Santa Cruz

Salinas

To Paso Robles
130 m.

Monterey

E. Post.

Scale of miles

"Map 27, the last day's run, from Monterey to San Francisco, Monday June 8, 1915."

facing the sidewalk, as in an Irish jaunting car — pulled up and let down the terrific hills on their wire ropes. The cable-car was, in fact, originated on the hills of San Francisco.[3]

Many streets are so steep that they have a stairway cut in the sidewalk, and in the center, the crevices between the cobblestones are green with grass. The streets are divided into those you can drive up and those you can't. In motoring to an address ten blocks away, instead of driving there directly as in any other city of the world, you have to take a route not unlike the pattern of a wall of Troy.

Also, as there are scarcely any names posted up on any corners, and the traffic policemen order you about for no seeming reason but their own sweet will, it is just as well for a stranger to allow twice as much time to get anywhere as would ordinarily be necessary. We were trying to go to the Hotel St. Francis for lunch.[4] "You turn down Post Street," said one policeman. We certainly made no mistake in the name of that street. When we got to it and tried to go down, another shouted at us, "What's the matter with you? Don't you *know* you can't go down Post Street!" I don't yet know the solution unless there is one section of Post Street you can go down, and another section that you can't. But I do know, however, that at the end of a little while you get so confused turning around three times for every block that you go forward, that your sense of direction seems very like that of a waltzing mouse in a glass bowl.

One thing, though, delays are not as annoying as they would seem. Californians take life too tranquilly to begrudge you a little while spent in trying to solve the hill and traffic mysteries. In fact, nothing could harass or annoy anyone long in a land where the spirit of gladness is the first and only thing that counts.

Where gigantism, self-inflation, or personal ambitions play a prominent part in the characteristics of other states, the Californians are merely happy — happy about everything, happy all the time. Their optimism is as unfailingly golden as their metal, their fruits, their grain, their poppies.

In a corner of the orange country, lava poured over the soil. Were they down-hearted? Not a bit.

---

3. The first successful cable car was tested in San Francisco on August 1, 1873. It was the brainchild of a London-born Scot, Andrew Smith Hallidie (1836–1900), who arrived in California in 1852. After an unsuccessful stint as a gold prospector, he turned to engineering, building suspension bridges and manufacturing wire cable. Hallidie became a US citizen, and a regent of the University of California, as well as playing an active part in the scientific life of San Francisco.

4. The St. Francis Hotel was opened in 1904 and withstood the 1906 earthquake, but not the succeeding fire. It was rebuilt and is still one of the grandest hotels in San Francisco.

"For all we know," said they, "we may find we can grow something new in it that we've never tried before."

In Pasadena the heat was stifling. It required all the breath I could muster to ask weakly of a land owner:

"Do you think there is any likelihood of *more* of this weather?"

"Yes. Oh, yes indeed," he beamed. "It is generally cool until the first of May, and then it gets pleasant just like this."

In San Francisco it rained all through May without ceasing. "Too wonderful!" they said. "The Eastern tourists will see the country so beautifully washed."

But we have heard that their gladness had one vulnerability, they could not bear to speak of earthquakes. Therefore, curious as I was to hear something about them, I did not dare to ask. Drinking my coffee one morning in San Mateo where we were stopping with the B.'s my bed suddenly shook so that my coffee spilled. In a moment Mrs. B. rushed into my room in joyful excitement:

"Did you feel the earthquake? Wasn't it a wonderful one! I was afraid you would go back to New York and never know what they are like!"

All that day everyone we saw spoke of the earthquake in much the same way, as though some delightful happening had occurred for our special benefit. Instead of shying away from the subject they reveled in it; advised us if we ever felt a severe one to run and stand in the doorframe. Even if the whole house comes down the doorways, it seems, are perfectly safe. Then they drove us to a beautiful estate that was directly over a fault and to prove what a *real* earthquake could do, they showed us a stone wall that had been shifted four feet, and an orchard of trees that had been picked up bodily and planted elsewhere. They added casually that the house, of course, was new, the other having been quaked to the ground.

But "How *terrible*," exclaimed nearly everyone to us, "to live as you do in a country where they have *thunderstorms!*"[5]

There is, however, one small matter that upsets them curiously. To us, it was a phenomenon not unlike the elephant's terror of a mouse. Never call Californians Westerners. They get really excited and indignant if you do. They live on the Pacific Coast — not in the West. For my own part they are children of the golden sun; call them what you please!

I think it is a rather universal habit to dismiss any unusual features in the lives of others by saying: "Oh, but they are a different sort of people from us!"

---

5. Emily Post added the rest of this chapter for the book version. The only similarity concerns the two women who were now bold and fearless, whereas back in New York they were frightened of their own shadows.

When we first crossed the Rio Grande and heard of two women who had gone out camping in the Rocky Mountains alone, and when later we saw a group of unmistakably well-bred people — each riding astride of a little burro and each leading a second burro laden with camping things, we thought, "What an extraordinary people Westerners are! We are brothers and yet it is impossible to believe that we spring from the same stock." Later on, however, we learned the difference was geographical and not ethnological. And the realization came this way:

A Mrs. R. used to be the most nervous and timid woman I ever knew. Six years ago, living on Long Island with twelve servants in her house, she used to lock herself in her bedroom immediately after dinner if her husband was out, because she was too nervous to sit in the front part of the ground floor alone. I remember distinctly that she once left a dinner party at about half-past nine because, with her own coachman driving, she was afraid to go late at night through the woods. About four years ago her husband and she moved to California. Last year she bought a ranch ten miles from the nearest station and seven miles from the nearest neighbor. And this same woman who used to be scared to death in a house full of people, with neighbors all around, now sleeps tranquilly in a ground floor bungalow with every door unlocked, every window open, and her servants' quarters half a mile away. She drives her own motor everywhere, and thinks nothing of dining with a neighbor fifteen or twenty miles distant, and coming home at midnight though Mexican settlements alone!

Another New York girl, Pauline M., who certainly was as spoiled as pampering could make her, went once long ago to a Maine hotel and never stopped talking about how awful the rooms were and how starved she was because of the horrible food. Twenty years ago she married a Californian and her house in San Francisco is a luxurious as a house can well be, but when we arrived she had gone to the mountains to camp, and telegraphed us to join her. We did not do that, but we motored out to lunch. Having always associated her with Callot dresses[6] and marble balustrades, I expected the make-believe "roughing it" of the big camps in the Adirondacks.[7] As we arrived at a small collection of portable houses dumped in a clearing we saw our fastidious friend in heavy solid boots, a drill skirt, flannel shirt, kneeling beside a fire cooking flapjacks. She used to be beautiful but rather anemic; her sauntering, languid walk seemed always to be

---

6. The three Callot sisters ran one of the most celebrated Paris couture houses of the early twentieth century.

7. From the 1890s wealthy New Yorkers, tired of Newport, "camped" in large, comfortable lodges, taking with them their servants and many changes of clothes.

dragging a five-yard train and her face was set with a bored expression. The metamorphosis was startling. She looked younger than she had at twenty and she put more life and energy in her waving of her frying-pan in greeting than she would have put in a whole New York season of how-do-you-do's.

Even the Orientals seem affected by the spirit of this land's gladness. The Chinaman of San Francisco is a big, smiling and apparently gay-hearted individual — none the less complex and mysterious for all that.

Frankly, the people out here who fascinate me most of all are the Chinese. From the two or three that we have seen in friends' houses, a Chinese servant must be about as easy to manage as the wind of heaven; you might as well try to dig a hole in the surface of the sea as to make any impression on him. He is going to do exactly as he pleases and in the way he pleases. Of course, his way may be your way, in which case you are lucky. Also it must not be forgotten that his faithfulness and devotion, when he is devoted, is quite as unalterable as his way. Of the two or three individual ones that we have seen in friends' houses, one at least will never be forgotten by any of us. His serene round face was the personification of docility, and he moved about in his costume of dull brocade like some lovely animate figure of purely decorative value. Why have we nothing in our houses that are such a delight to the eye?

I have forgotten what we had for luncheon — caviar canapé, I think, and with it finger bowls.

"No, Chang, not finger bowls yet," I heard Mr. K. say. So Chang removed them, only to bring them back again with the next course.

"There is no use," laughed Mr. K. to me, "he will keep bringing them back no matter how often I tell him to take them away. He always does, and we just have to have them from the beginning through."

Mr. K. carved on the table — Chang probably insisted on that too — and asking me whether I preferred dark or white, put the breast of a broiled chicken on a plate. The Celestial one in green brocade instead of passing it to me, deftly picked up a fork, placed the chicken breast back on the platter, took a second joint instead, and saying severely:

"*Him* likee leg pliece!" carried the plate to Mr. K.'s mother. Company or no company, Chang served her always first.

Also the K.'s told me that Mrs. K., senior, was the only member of the household whose personal wishes he invariably respected. He is also the slave of the K. baby, but to the rest of the family he behaves exactly as a chow, or a Persian cat, or any other purely decorative independent household belonging.

China is the place for old women to live in! They receive all the attention and consideration that is shown in our own country only to the most young and beautiful.

Mrs. S., whose husband was for many years chargé d'affaires in the American legation in Pekin, is the most enthusiastic champion of everything Chinese. "If a Chinaman is staying under your roof, you need have no uneasiness on the subject of his good intentions," she said this morning. "No Chinaman will stay in your employ if he does not like you." As an example, she told us that while she was in Pekin the head boy of another legation was taken to task about something in front of some of the under servants—a situation of great indignity. The occurrence happened in the midst of the serving of a meal. The Chinaman quietly laid down the dish he was holding and left the room and the house. In less than ten minutes he presented himself before Mrs. S. and announced he had come to live with them. For nothing would he go back to the other legation, and having chosen Mrs. S. as his *tai tai* (lady) in her particular service he stayed. One New Year's he presented her with a miniature pig, stunted in the way that the Japanese stunt trees or else just a little freak. It was only a foot long, but full grown, and as black as though it had been dipped in shoe polish.[8]

One day in San Francisco, I went out shopping in the Chinese quarter with Mrs. S. The sensation may be imagined of an American lady suddenly speaking fluent Manchu Chinese. Such a grinning and gesticulating and smiling as went on! And the whole neighborhood gathered suddenly into the discourse.

Understanding not a single syllable, I could only watch the others, but even more than ever, they fascinated me.[9]

In San Francisco we rushed early each morning to the Exposition and spent no time anywhere else. Every now and then someone said to Pauline, with whom we were stopping, the mysterious sentence: "Have you taken them to Gump's?" And her answer: "Why no, I haven't!" was always uttered

8. This was probably an Asian Potbelly Miniature Pig, also known as Chinese or Vietnamese Potbelly Pig. Although they were not widely kept as pets in the United States until the 1980s, it seems as though Mrs. S. was given one in China. They were descended from the wild boars that once roamed throughout China. Around the 10th Century AD, these boars were domesticated and used as both pets and food throughout Southeast Asia. They can be seen on tapestries from these early periods and archeological excavations have also produced bones from these pigs.

9. Emily Post was one of many tourists who went to San Francisco's Chinatown for exotic excitement. The Raymond and Whitcomb tours often included visits to Chinese churches, theaters, teahouses and shops as well as opium dens and gambling joints. Amy Bridges, who toured in 1882, noted that "one of the party gave a Chinaman two bits (25cts) to smoke [opium] for us and we watched with interest." Quoted in Shaffer, *See America First*, 280.

in that abashed apologetic tone that acknowledges a culpable forgetfulness. Finally one day instead of driving towards the Exposition grounds we turned towards the heart of the city.

"Where are we going?" I asked.

"To Gump's!" triumphantly.

"To Gump's? Of all the queer-sounding things, what is to Gump's?"

"Our most celebrated shop. You really must not leave San Francisco without seeing their Japanese and Chinese things."

Shades of dullness, thought I, as if there were not enough shops in New York! As for Oriental treasures, I was sure there were more on Fifth Avenue at home than there are left in Asia. But Pauline being determined, there was nothing for us to do but, as E. M. said, "to Gump it!"

Feeling very much bored at being kept away from the Exposition, I entered a store reminiscent of a dozen in New York, walked down an aisle lined on either side with commonplace chinaware. My first sensation of boredom was changing to irritability. Then we entered an elevator and in the next instant I took back everything I had been thinking. It was as though we had been transported, not only across the Pacific, but across centuries of time. Through the apartments of an ancient Chinese palace, we walked into a Japanese temple. And again into a room in a modern Japanese house. You do not need more than a first glance to appreciate why they lead visitors to a shop with the unpromising name of Gump. I am not sure that the name does not heighten the effect. If it were called the Chinese Palace, or the Temple of Japan, or something like that, it would be like telling the answer before asking the conundrum. As in calling at a palace, too, strangers, distinguished ones only, are asked to write their names in the visitor's book.[10]

In this museum-shop each room has been assembled as a setting for the things that are shown in it. Old Chinese porcelains, blue and white, sang de bœuf, white, apple-green, cucumber-green and peacock-blue, are shown in a room of the Ming Period in ebony and gold lacquer.[11]

10. See Carol Green Wilson, *Gump's Treasure Trade: A Story of San Francisco* (New York: Thomas Y. Crowell, 1945). Wilson writes of Emily Post's visit: "When she returned to the East and recorded her experiences in her book *By Motor to the Golden Gate*, she introduced the beauty she had found in Gump's to a widespread circle of readers." (119). Gump's store was at 250 Post Street when Emily Post visited; in 1995, under new ownership, it moved a block away from Union Square to 150 Post Street.

11. The Ming Dynasty was founded in 1368 by the Buddhist monk Zhu Yuanzhang, and replaced the Mongol Empire's control of China. Administration was centralized, the power of the bureaucrats (the Mandarins) rose, and it was a period of refined lifestyles governed by complex systems of etiquette. The most famous artifact of the period was the exquisite Ming porcelain. On the other hand, the items Emily Post describes here seem to come →

The windows of all the rooms, whether in the walls or ceiling, are of translucent porcelain in the Chinese, or paper in the Japanese; which provides an indescribable illusion of having left the streets of San Francisco thousands of miles, instead of merely a few feet, behind you.

The room devoted to jades and primitives has night-blue walls overlaid with gold lacquer lattices and brass carvings and in it the most wonderful treasures of all. They are kept hidden away in silk-lined boxes, and are brought out and shown to you, Chinese fashion, one at a time, so that none shall detract from the other. We wanted to steal a small white marble statuette of a boy on a horse. A thing of beauty and spirit very Greek, yet pure Chinese that dated back to the oldest Tang dynasty![12] There was also a silver, that was originally green, luster bronze of the Ham Period, two thousand years old, and a sacrificial bronze pot belonging to the Chow Dynasty, B.C. 1125.[13] The patina, or green rust of age, on these two pieces was especially beautiful. I also much admired a carved rhinoceros horn, but found it was merely Chien Lung, one hundred and fifty years old, which in *that* room was much too modern to be important.[14]

In one of the Japanese rooms there were decorated paper walls held up by light bamboo frames, amber paper *shoji* instead of windows, and the floors covered with *tatami*, the Japanese floor mats, two inches thick. You sit on the floor as in Japan and drink tea, while silks of every variety are brought to you.[15]

We saw three rugs of the Ming Dynasty that are probably the oldest rugs extant. The most lovely one was of yellow ground, with Ho birds in blue. And there was an *ice-cooler* of cloisonnée, Ming Period. They brought the ice from the mountains and cooled the imperial palace — years ago. Yet to hear Europeans talk, you'd almost be led to believe that ice is an American invention.[16]

---

from several different periods of Chinese history: while the blue and white was probably Ming (unless it was the blue and white created for the export trade in the seventeenth and eighteenth centuries), the *sang de boeuf* glaze, which needed a higher firing temperature, was invented during the Qing dynasty in the eighteenth century.

12. The Tang dynasty lasted from 616–906 A.D.

13. She probably meant salver, not silver. The Han dynasty lasted from 206 B.C. to 220 A.D. while the Zhou dynasty was much earlier, namely 1100–771 B.C.

14. Qianlong reigned from 1736–1796.

15. Shoji screens are made of rice paper stretched over wooden frames, while tatami mats, which are made of woven straw, are still widely used in Japanese homes.

16. Cloisonné is an enameling technique developed in the sixteenth century. Ice, transported from mountains or frozen lakes and packed into icehouses had been used for hundreds of years, and the Chinese had probably been the first to discover that a container placed in brine would stay cool because evaporating salt water absorbed heat. Artificial

We were shown old Chinese velvet wedding-skirts and a tapestry of blues, with silver storks and clouds of an embroidery so fine that its stitches could only be seen through a magnifying glass, and poison plates belonging to the Emperor Ming that were supposed to change color if any food injurious to His Majesty were served on them.[17]

One of the most beautiful things was a Caramandel screen of the Kang Hai Period, in a corridor that is shared only with an enormous lacquer image of the Buddha.[18]

We were told that a rather famous collector went out to see the Fair. On his first day in San Francisco— he was stopping at the St. Francis which is only a stone's throw across the square — he went idly into this most alluring of shops and became so interested he stayed all day. The next day he did the same, and the third morning found him there again. Finally he said with a sigh: "Having come to see the Exposition, I *must* go out there this afternoon and look at it, as I have to go back to New York tomorrow."[19]

I don't know if this is an average point of view, but it is a fact that was vouched for, and also that his check to the detaining shop ran into very high figures.

In the suburbs of San Francisco, Burlingame, I suppose, compares most nearly to Newport, of our Eastern coast, Sewickley of Pittsburgh or Broadmoore of Colorado Springs.[20] It is a community of big handsome

---

refrigeration, using the rapid expansions of gases was, in fact, developed by Americans. Although the first person to demonstrate such a method was William Cullen at the University of Glasgow in 1748, he did nothing with his discovery, and an American inventor, Oliver Evans, designed the first refrigeration machine in 1805; another American, Jacob Perkins, made the first practical refrigerator in 1834, though German engineer Carol von Linden patented the process of liquefying gas in 1876. African American inventor Thomas Elkins took the process a stage further in 1879 when he patented an improved refrigeration system, which was designed to keep human corpses cool.

17. These small plates were inserted several times into each dish, as it was believed that poison would cause them to change color. Even if the color remained unchanged, eunuchs were then expected to taste the dishes, just to be on the safe side.

18. Gang Hai (1475–1541) was one of the best-known poets of the Ming period; famously devoted to wine, women and song, his poetry is said to have contributed to changes in attitudes toward passion and sensuality. A Coromandel screen was large, with up to 12 folding leaves. The frame was made of ebony and the panels were incised black lacquer, which was often painted gold, and decorated with jade and other semi-precious stones, shell or porcelain. The panels usually portrayed Chinese landscapes, but for the export market European hunting or nautical scenes were sometimes depicted.

19. It is not clear who this visitor was, but one prominent buyer during the Exposition was T.B. Walker (1856–1928) of Minneapolis. The lumber magnate purchased many pieces of porcelain, which he donated to the galleries bearing his name. See Wilson, *Gumps's Treasure Trade*, 119.

20. Sewickley Heights is a few miles northwest of Pittsburgh. After air pollution →

places occupied by the rich and fashionable. It strikes you, though, how much simpler people are in habits, in taste, in attitude, than in the East. Suggest anything on a house-party in Burlingame or San Mateo, or Ross, and instead of being answered "What for?" or "Oh, not just now!" the response is a prompt and enthusiastic, "Fine! Come on!"[21]

Young women and men in San Francisco, though many have more money to spend than they know what to do with, demand less in the way of provided entertainment than New York children in their earliest teens. A dozen of San Francisco's most gilded youths stood around a piano and sang nearly all one evening. After a while someone played, and the rest danced. At Newport they would have danced, more likely than anything else, but the music, even if thought of at the last moment, would probably have been by an orchestra. One afternoon they pulled candy, and every day they swim in someone's pool. Today at the J.'s, tomorrow at the H.'s. The girls play polo as well as the men and all of them, of course, drive their own cars.[22]

In the J.'s garden they have ladders against the cherry trees and everyone wanders out there and eats and eats cherries—and such cherries! In the first place we haven't any such cherries, and in the second, can you imagine a group of Newport women climbing up ladders and clinging to branches rather than let the gardeners gather them?

But it isn't the standing on cherry-tree ladders, or the doing of any actual thing, that makes the essential difference between the people of the Atlantic and the Pacific Coast. It is the land itself, perhaps—the sunshine, the climate, that pours a rejuvenating radiance upon the spirit of resident and visitor alike.

Even at the end of a little while you find yourself beginning to understand something of the oppressive grayness that settles upon the spirit of every Californian when away from home. Which reminds me of a young

---

forced local moguls out of their palatial homes in Allegheny City (now the Pittsburgh's North Side), many of them followed the Allegheny Country Club when it moved into the country in 1902. Here they built summer "cottages" to rival those at Newport, Rhode Island or Southampton on Long Island.

21. Burlingame and San Mateo are on the Bay, southeast of San Francisco; Ross is a small town in Marin County.

22. According to *Polo in India*, by Captain G.F. Younghusband, published in 1873, English women played polo. He described a match in which four married women played against four single women, each team having one male player, who could only hit the ball to help move the game along and support the women's play. After many delays in action and a break for tea and a meal, the women were recorded as "astonishingly good, considering the inexperience of the players". The ladies rode sidesaddle on the offside to get a clean hit. Quoted at http://www.katerri.com/html/wiph-tw.html

"The portico of a California house" with a fine view of the hills in the background.

Italian girl whom I found one day crying her heart out on a bench in the Public Gardens in Boston. To me Beacon Street is one of the most beautiful streets I have ever seen, especially where the old and most lovely houses face the green of the Public Gardens, and the figure of this sobbing girl was doubly woeful. To every question I could think of she shook her head and sobbed, "No." She had not lost anyone, no one had deserted her, and she was not hungry, or cold, or houseless, or penniless. "But, my dear, what *is* the matter?" I implored. Finally, almost strangling with tears, she stammered: "B-boston is so *u-ugly!*"

Mrs. M., a Californian married to a New Yorker, had seemed to us rather negative, a listless silent figure who trailed through New York drawing rooms more like a wraith than a live woman. We happened to be at her mother's when this pale, frail young person returned home for a visit and came very much to life! She hung cherries on her ears, covered her hat, and filled her belt with poppies, and came running up the terraces of their very wonderful gardens, her arms outstretched and shouting at the top of her voice:

"California, *my* California! I'm home, home, *home!*"

Does anyone ever feel like that about New York? I wonder! Does anyone really love its millionaires' palaces, its flashing Broadway, its canyon streets, its teeming thoroughfares, its subway holes-in-the-ground into which men dive like moles, emerging at the other end in an office burrow — sometimes without coming up into the outdoors at all? Or are the sentiments composed more truly of pride that has as much egotism in the consciousness of more square feet of masonry crowded into fewer square feet of ground; more well-dressed women, more automobiles; bigger crowds — sprucer-looking crowds; more electric signs; more things going on; more business; more amusements; more making and spending; more losing and breaking, than, one might almost say, all the other cities of the world together?

All of which makes typical New Yorkers contemptuous of and dissatisfied with every other city. But as to whether they *love* it, as the people of Chicago or San Francisco do — do they? Do we?

For anyone to look out upon New York's immensity and spread out his arms and say: "My city! My home!" would be almost like looking overhead and saying, "My sky, my stars!" *Almost*, wouldn't it?

I wanted to lead up to a story of a California bride's impression of New York. Instead of which I seem to have arrived in New York, but left the bride at home!

The story was told to me by Mr. B., himself a New Yorker, but whose wife and stepson were Californians. Last winter the stepson brought his wife to New York on their wedding-trip. This is what Mr. B. told me:

"She had everything we could give her, but spent the afternoon at matinées and galleries and shopping; her evenings at the play or the opera and a cabaret afterward, and her mornings in bed. Finally I said: "Why don't you want us to have some dinners for you, so that you can meet some people? You can't know much about a city if you meet no one."

"'Oh,' she said, 'the people look so queer.'

"'How, queer?'

"'Why, so — so well-dressed and so horrid — their faces aren't kind, and they don't seem to smile at all.'

"But I insisted on taking her up Fifth Avenue to see the fine houses. No enthusiasm. Finally I said:

"'But surely, the V. house is wonderful!'[23]

"'I suppose so,' she said, 'but like all the rest it is just stone and mortar

23. Six Vanderbilt houses were built on Fifth Avenue between 51st and 58th Streets between 1878 and 1882, and in 1897 Alice and William Vanderbilt built the largest of them all, on the corner of 57th Street. In 1915 all were still standing, though not for long; the introduction of income tax in 1913 meant that such examples of conspicuous consumption were less affordable, even for the very rich.

stuck up in a crowded, noisy street, and the newspapers blow up around the door.'

"Then she stopped, and seeing how disappointed I was, patted me on the arm: 'You know,' she said, 'I was born and grew up in an orange grove, and you people stifle me. I want to go home.'"

XXIX

The Fair

The Fair will be over when this account is published, but it was so dominant a part of San Francisco at the time we — and all the thousands of others — were there I haven't the heart to cut the pages out.[1]

With merely a phrase you can make a picture of the little fair at San Diego; cloister-like gray buildings with clumps of dense green, and a vivid stroke of blue and orange. But to visualize the Pan-American Exposition in a few sentences is impossible. You could begin its description from a hundred different points and miss the best one, you can say one thing about it and the next moment find you were quite wrong. In the shade or fog, it was a city of baked earth color, oxidized with any quantity of terra cotta; in the sun it was deep cream glowing with light. If you thought of half the domes as brown, and others as faded green you found, the next time you saw them, that they looked like a bit of the sky itself, and the brown ones glimmered a dull, yet living, rose.[2]

Seeing it first from a distance, coming down upon it from the hill streets of San Francisco, you see a biscuit-colored city with terra-cotta roofs, green domes and blue. Beyond it the wide waters of a glorious bay,

---

1. The Panama-Pacific International Exposition ran from February 20, 1915 to December 4, 1915. It seems that paying visitors continued to attend for eleven more months, the last one being recorded on November 16, 1916, at 3:30 in the afternoon. A total of 18,876,438 people visited the fair, which even made a profit, as revenues exceeded expenses by more than $1.3 million.

2. Unlike most previous expositions, the Panama-Pacific made no attempt to create new architectural forms; instead organizers tried to create a unified, modernized form of Oriental and western buildings to showcase the various exhibits. The Exposition site covered 635 acres of drained swampland to the east of the Presidio. Architect Edward Bennett devised a plan which included high walls to shield the site from the fog and the wind, and color designer Jules Guerin looked to ancient Rome in his decision to use an ivory-pink imitation travertine marble, such as Paul E. Denneville had already used at New York City's Penn Station. Landscape designers, sculptors and artists all had to work within his prescribed palette of nine colors, so nothing would clash.

rimmed with far gray-green mountains. But you were luckiest if you saw it first when the sun was painting it for you, which was invariably unless there was a fog, or perhaps you looked down upon it at night when the scintillating central point, the Tower of Jewels, looked like a diamond and turquoise wedding-cake and behind it an aura of prismatic-colored search-lights—the most thrilling illumination possible to imagine.[3]

Or entering one of its many gates you wandered like an ant through bewildering chaos. Not that it lacked plan; its architectural balance was one of the most noteworthy things about it. But there were so many courts, so much detail.[4] Gradually, you noticed that there were eight great exhibition palaces, and a ninth, the Palace of the Fine Arts, like a half-circle at the end.[5] You perceived that the buildings of the separate States and foreign nations trailed off like a suburb at one end, and that the Zone was a straight street also by itself.[6] Among the thousands of embellishments, you noticed perhaps the lovely statues of Borglum's "Pioneer," Fraser's "End of the Trail," Daniel Chester French's "Genius of Creation," the adventurous bowman on the top of the Column of Progress, nor could you miss the nations of the West and East, and figures of the rising and the setting sun.[7]

The murals of Brangwyn no chair boy would let you pass.[8] Each one

---

3. The Tower of Jewels stood 435 feet high, and glittered with glass beads resembling rubies, emeralds, sapphires and aquamarines. Two large eagles perched on the top, to symbolize power, and on either side of the tower were colonnades, fountains, and historical plaques.

4. The original version of this paragraph included this critical sentence: "much too trimmed is your first impression; if they would only take everything away and bring it back one at a time so you would see and appreciate it." *Collier's* September 18, 1915.

5. The semi-circular Palace of the Fine Arts is the only building still standing. It now houses the Exploratorium.

6. The Zone was the amusement area of the Exposition, at the eastern end of the grounds. It included a roller coaster, other rides and amusement arcades.

7. Emily Post admired "Pioneer" by Solon Borglum (1868–1922). The son of Danish immigrants who settled on the Great Plains, Borglum depicted a crusty old frontiersman, rifle held high. "The End of the Trail" by James Earle Fraser (1876–1953) showed a dispirited Native American on an exhausted pony; the piece was first shown in 1894, and reflected an entirely different viewpoint from Borglum's celebration of the individual pioneer. Daniel Chester French (1850–1931), sculptor of the massive statue of Abraham Lincoln at the Lincoln Memorial, was apparently not pleased that his allegorical "Genius of Creation" was placed in front of the palace of machinery. He thought it merited a more central place. The Column of Progress, which was based on Trajan's column in Rome, was topped by Hermon A. McNeil's statue of "The Adventurous Bowman." The bowman was shooting his arrow out over the Pacific, as a none-too-subtle representation of the spirit of imperialist America.

8. She wrote: "it is the easiest exposition to get about in. Besides all the varieties of Push chairs, bicycle, electric and boy-walking chairs, the latter are the only ones allowed inside the buildings." *Collier's* September 18, 1915.

pushed you in front and backing off to give you the proper distance, declared that they cost five thousand dollars, *"each one."*[9]

We were admiring their vital animation, for they pulsated fairly with energy and life, as well as color, when suddenly from the sublime to the ridiculous, E. M. remarked: "That's curious! The men have just taken their shirts off." Then Celia and I wondered too, why every male figure was brown as a berry as high as a shirt sleeve would roll up, and as white as a person always sheltered from the air over the rest of his body?

We also wondered about the four women who clung to the corners of gigantic boxes on top of the beautiful Fine Arts colonnade. Each of the boxes suggested the coffin of a very fat Mormon and his four wives weeping for him. There was *something* hidden up there that the clinging women were afraid to take their gaze away from, but what it was we had no idea.[10] All of which levity reminds me that in Paris I watched two tourists as they hurried eagerly down the long gallery toward the Venus de Milo. Arrived at its base one of them leaned over the guard rail, stared at the marble, and exclaimed:

"Why, Gussie, she's all pock-marked!"

My criticism of a work as notable as the Pan-American Exposition is probably much like the above. Beautiful as much of it is, I wish they had left a few unfilled niches, a few plain surfaces, but they are filling them fuller every day. When we first came, the little kneeling figure on her peninsula in front of the Fine Arts Temple and her reflection in the lagoon gave an impression of a dream. While we were there, they filled every archway with imposing sculptures until it looks merely like a museum.[11]

I found myself driving around and mentally taking things away. The

---

9. Frank Brangwyn (1857–1956), a Belgian-born artist who worked in London, was the only non-American muralist, and the only one of the one of the nine muralists commissioned to work for the Exposition not to paint onsite. His eight panels, which represented the ancient elements of fire, earth, air and water, were installed in the Hall of Abundance, where they were much admired, and not only by Emily Post and the chair boys. Since 1932 the panels have been in the Herbst Theater of the San Francisco War Memorial and Performing Arts Center. There were several methods of transportation within the Exposition. Visitors could walk, take the intramural railway, or ride in an electric or a hand-propelled chair.

10. Emily Post was looking at the "Weeping Women" sculpted by Ulric Ellerhusen. According to the website for the Exploratorium, now housed in the Palace of Fine Arts, "Some say they were intended to express Contemplation; others the melancholy of life without art." Apparently architect Bernard Maybeck intended them to be only partially seen, but his plan for covering them with vines was abandoned as a cost-cutting exercise. *http://www.exploratorium.edu/history/palace/palace_2.html.*

11. Emily Post is referring to Robert Stackpole's figure of Venus, which was in the lagoon in front of the rotunda. There was such an abundance of art and statuary that an annex to the Palace of Fine Arts had to be built.

lovely old eucalyptus trees, the only planting that was on the grounds before the Fair, seemed almost to have heard me, for they were not to be kept from taking everything off that they could, and untidily strewing the ground with their discarded clothing.

One thing, however, was hard to understand or forgive; of all the courts, especially at night, the one which had the most imaginative appeal was the Court of Abundance. At the four corners of a square pool were standards of erect green cobras holding brasiers filled with leaping flames of tongues of silk blown upward by concealed fans and red and yellow lights; in the center of the pool was the Fountain of the Earth, a work of highly imaginative beauty in which, above four panels of symbolic figures in high relief, the globe of the earth was set in a rose-colored glow surrounded by a mystic vapor, made by a gentle escapement of steam, and *then* at one side they had planted two Maltese cross standards of blatant electric lights![12]

On the subject of the exhibits, everyone has read about the Ford cars that are assembled on a conveyor. Beginning at one end as pieces of metal and running off the other under their own power.[13] That was undoubtedly the most interesting exhibit to the public in general, but to many others the Sperry Flour display was quite as ingenious and if anything more interesting. They had a whole row of little booth kitchens to show how all the nations of the world use flour.[14]

A camper tossed flapjacks over a campfire; a Mexican made anchillades and tomales; a Swede, a Russian, a Chinaman, a Hindoo and four or five others made their national wafers and cakes and gave samples away! In the center at a bigger oven was baked home-made American bread and cake and pies, of such deliciousness that everyone who passed by looked as longingly as the proverbial ragamuffin in front of a baker's window.[15]

---

12. This highly critical description was not in the *Collier's* version. The central fountain in the Court of Abundance was by Robert Aitken; a contemporary account suggests reservations, saying it did not really fit the spirit of the place. While its figures were "magnificently virile" it was only at night "when, through clouds of rising steam, the globe of the Earth glows red like a world in the making, and from the forked tongues of the flaming serpents flames pour out on the altars set around the pool, — only then does the fountain become mystic. Even then it suggests cosmogony, mechanics, physics, which are not romantic, except insofar as there may be romance of the intellect." Ben Macomber, *The Jewel City* (San Francisco: John J. Newbegin, 1915) available online at http://www.books-about-california.com/Pages/The_Jewel_City/The_Jewel_City_Chap_07.html

13. Eighteen Model T's were built every day on the world's smallest assembly line.

14. The Sperry Flour Company, which began in Stockton, California in 1852, was one of the Pacific Coast's largest millers. In 1929 it became part of General Mills.

15. In *Collier's* the list of "ethnic" cooks included "a colored mammy [who] bakes Johnny cake and corn pone." September 18, 1915.

There was always a crowd, too, watching the manufacture of white
lead paint by the Fuller Company, and going through the staterooms of a
section, full-sized, of an Atlantic steamer.[16] Perhaps the greatest interest
of all was shown in a model United States post-office, with bridges crossing above, so people could look down and see all the details of sorting and
distributing.[17]

One thing you noticed — nearly all San Franciscans were personally,
or through some members of their family, interested in the Fair. Everyone
gave dinners on the Zone, either on the balcony of the Chinese restaurant — that had nothing Chinese about it except its Chinese ornamenta-
tion on the front of the building — or at the Old Faithful Inn of the
Yellowstone.[18] The illuminations at night were very soft and subdued, all
the lanterns were turned dark side to the Concourse and light side to the
buildings.[19]

In the Zone there were few new attractions, and fewer worth seeing.
The best were the Panama Canal, the Painted Desert, and Captain, the
mind-reading horse.[20] A woman mind-reader, who took turns with the
horse, was equally remarkable.[21]

---

16. Lead carbonate or white lead was used as a white pigment for many years. Recently,
because of the risk of lead poisoning, it is seldom used indoors, though red lead, or minium,
a scarlet, crystalline powder, is used in the protective paint for structural iron and steel.

17. Mail sorting was still done by hand until the 1950s, although some early experiments
occurred in the 1920s.

18. In *Collier's* Emily Post added here: "we also lunched at the Inside Inn, a hotel in the
grounds. The Fairmount, the Palace and the St. Francis are naturally more luxurious in
every way, but for those who have come out here to see the exposition, nothing could be
better than to stop on the spot and in a very nice hotel."

19. A journalist writing in the *San Francisco Examiner* asked "Wouldn't it be ridiculous
to "do" the Zone in evening clothes?" to which a local socialite, Mrs. Marshall Hale, replied
that she planned to wear an informal "tailored gown" stating that "fashion should give way
to pleasure and convenience." Quoted without date or further attribution on a PBS website dealing with a documentary film on photographer Ansel Adams. http://www.pbs.org/
wgbh/amex/ansel/peopleevents/e_exhibition.html

20. The most famous mind reading horse was "Clever Hans" the subject of a ground
breaking scientific paper in 1907, whereby Oskar Pfungst (1874–1932) a German psycholo-
gist, demonstrated that the horse was responding to imperceptible signals by his owner or
by other individuals who knew the answer. When the questioner did not know the answer
the horse failed miserably. The paper was published in translation in the United States in
1911 as *Clever Hans (the Horse of Mr. Van Osten)* (New York: Henry Holt, 1911).

21. In *Collier's* Emily Post had a lot more to say about the woman mind reader, who she
clearly found intriguing. "We went to hear her half a dozen times, but could make nothing of her system. Either it is genuine mind reading or she and her Asiatic partner have a
code that is unlimitedly complicated in its apparent simplicity. She is blindfolded and her
confederate repeats unvaryingly the same questions. "What is this lady thinking?" "What
is the name?" "Come now, what is the number?" yet she answers numbers of six figures,
long sentences on every subject under the sun. We tried her on every question that we could

The queen of the Samoan village, clad literally in a short skirt, a Gaby Deslys head-dress, a string of beads and a dazzling smile, had not only great audacity but a fascinating personality that was literally bubbling over with the old Nick.[22] We were crazy about her, a fact she saw perfectly well, for in the garden afterward, when she had discarded her gorgeous head-dress and donned a modest piece of sash tied around her chest, she came straight to us and shook hands as a child might, who, amid a crowd of strangers had singled out a friend. That is all there is to tell, as we couldn't speak Samoan, nor she English.[23]

A few months ago, in the midst of a daring flight, the wings of the famous Beachey's aeroplane crumpled and plunged into the sea. The aviator was strapped into his machine in such a way that, if he still lived, he could not free himself.[24]

Le roi est mort! Vive le roi!

And the new king was Art Smith. At eleven o'clock at night, the siren blew and thousands crowded about the open field to see him start. Up and up and up he went until, at several hundred feet up, a torch suddenly burned at the back of the machine which swept the sky, leaving a trail of

---

think of beforehand — she answered every one. Once the man merely pointed to a book in my hand, my earrings, my hair, a feather on a hat, and each time he said only "This?" She told him what he was pointing at as fast as he could point."

22. Gaby Deslys (1881–1920) was a French dancer who was also very popular in the United States. She is said to have introduced the first "striptease" dance in a Broadway musical. She was to spy for the French in World War I, and to die of pneumonia in 1920.

23. Laura Ingalls Wilder visited the Exposition in September 1915 and commented on the Samoan dancers. She wrote: "Samoa, you know, are South Sea Islands belonging to the U.S. There were several girls and men, dressed, or rather undressed, in their native costume... They wore necklaces and strings of beads and rings... Their skin was a beautiful golden color where it was not tattooed and their voices were soft and musical. The girls are very pretty and some of the men are fine-looking. They danced their native dances and sang their island songs. In all this dancing and singing they never touched each other and they danced in every muscle of their bodies, even their fingers and toes... I did enjoy every bit of it." These letters to her husband were published in *West From Home* in 1974 and are quoted at *http://www.sanfranciscomemories.com/ppie/visitors/liw/laura.html*

Another contemporary commentator was a little more skeptical: he wrote: "All these people are genuine and live in primitive style on the Zone, though, to tell the truth, they are quite likely to use college slang and know which fork to use first." Macomber, *The Jewel City,* chapter XX.

24. Lincoln Beachey (1887–1915), born in San Francisco, was one of America's first aviators. He gained international fame after he flew across the Niagara Falls in 1911, and in November 1913 he became the first American aviator to loop a plane — a feat he repeated more than one thousand times over the next twelve months. He was heavily involved in the Panama-Pacific Exposition, flying his bi-plane as part of the pre-opening publicity and again during the opening ceremony. He died a month later during an aerial exhibition at the Exposition.

fire like a comet's tail, looped and double looped and curved and twisted and wrote "ZONE" across the sky.[25]

But really to see the feats of this aeronaut who far exceeded Beachey's daring, you had to go to the Aviation Field on a day when he flew at five. You saw, if you were early enough to stand near the ropes of the enormous enclosure, a young boy apparently, very small, but stockily built, walk casually out of the crowd standing back of the machine, wave good-bye to a young girl, his wife, and get on a sort of bicycle on the front of his bi-plane without any apparent strapping in, except the handle of the steer-ing-wheel that he pulled close in front of him. Across the wide grass field he gradually arose, soared higher and higher, until at half a thousand feet or more, he dipped and swooped, then somersaulted round and round and round in a whirling ball, then flying upside down dropped nearly over your head, then rose again, flying backwards, sideways, fell, arose, dipped — like a bird gone mad. At last he came swooping down and alit at the end of the great green field.

Very young and small, Art Smith walked the whole length of the field between fifty thousand shouting, waving human beings. No hero of the Roman Stadium, no king coming to his own, has lived a greater moment than the young birdman lived every day. Boyishly his mouth broke into a wide smile, he doffed his cap, bowing to the right and to the left, and the applause followed him in a series of roars. At the hangar his young wife ran out and kissed him. He had been spared to her once again.[26]

---

25. Indiana-born Art Smith (1890–1926) had been obsessed by flying since his late teens. After several false starts, and after his father had mortgaged his home to supply the money to build Art's first plane, (and after the bank foreclosed and they lost the home), Art started to make some money by flying exhibitions, and in October 1912 eloped with his sixteen-year-old girl friend Aimee Cour — possibly the first aerial elopement. His plane had to make an emergency landing, and the couple were injured; nevertheless, someone found a minis-ter and they were married from their hotel bed. Over the next two years Aimee traveled with him as he made a comfortable living, and in 1915 he got his big break when he took over as stunt flier at the Panama-Pacific Exposition after Beachey's death. Unfortunately the marriage did not last, and Smith was killed in a plane crash at the age of thirty-six. See Rachel Roberts, "The Smash-Up Kid: Fort Wayne Aviator Art Smith," *Indiana Historical Society* (2000), online at http://www.indianahistory.org/pub/traces/artsmith.html

26. This last paragraph was not in the *Collier's* piece.

XXX

"Unending Sameness" Was What They Said

Of course you can't see the Fair in a day, or two days, or three. And if you stay long in San Francisco, you won't want to leave at all. Up and down and around the hills, you constantly see houses that you wish you could immediately go and live in. For in what other city can you sit on a hillside — only millionaires sit on hilltops — with a view of sea and mountains below and beyond you? Where else, outside of a Maxfield Parrish picture, is there a city rising gayly on steep sugar-loaf hills, and filled with people whose attitude of mind exactly matches their hilltops?[1]

In many other cities people live in long narrow canyons called streets, under a blanket of soot, signifying industry, and they scurry around like ants carrying great mental loads, ten times as big as they are, up steep hills of difficulty, only to tumble down with them again. The people of countless other cities are valley people, their perception bounded by the high walls of the skyscrapers they have themselves erected in the name of progress. The San Franciscans, too, are building in the valley towering office buildings in which they work as earnestly for their living as any others elsewhere, but in spirit they are still hill-people, and their horizon is rimmed not by acquisitive ambition, but by sea and sky.[2]

When we started, I had an idea that, keen though we were to undertake the journey, we would find it probably difficult, possibly tiring, and surely monotonous — to travel on and on over the same American road, through towns that must be more or less replicas, and hearing always the

---

1. The artist and illustrator Maxfield Parrish (1870–1966), sometimes called "the common man's Rembrandt," was the most popular and successful American artist of the first third of the twentieth century.

2. The next six paragraphs were not included in the *Collier's* piece.

same language and seeing the same types of people doing much the same things. Everyone who had never taken the trip assured us that our impression in the end would be of an unending sameness. Sameness! Was there ever such variety?

Beginning with New York, as that is the point we started from, New York was built, is building, will ever be building in huge blocks of steel and stone, and the ambitious of every city and country in the world will keep pouring into it and crowding its floor space and shoving it up higher and higher into towering cubes. New York dominates the whole of the Western hemisphere and weights securely the Eastern coast of the map, and because of this weight and importance, New Yorkers fancy they are the Americans of America, but New York is not half as typical of America as Chicago; and that is where you come to your first real contrast.

Omnipotent New York, in contrast to *ambitious* Chicago. Chicago is American to her backbone — active, alive and inordinately desiring, ceaselessly aspiring. Between New York and Chicago is strung a chain of cities that have many qualities, like mixed samples of these two terminal points. But beyond Chicago, no trace of New York remains. Every city is spunky and busy, ambitious and sometimes a little self-laudatory. (New York is not self-laudatory; she is too supremely self-satisfied to think any remarks on the subject necessary.) Leaving the country of fields and woods and streams, you traverse that great prairie land of vast spaces, and finally ascend the heights of the mighty Rocky Mountains.

"On the famous 'staked plains' of the southwest."

The next contrast is Colorado Springs, which is as unlike the rest of America as though St. Moritz itself had been grafted in the midst of our continent. All through New Mexico and Arizona you are in a strange land, far more like Asia than anything in the United States or Europe. A baked land of blazing sun, dynamic geological miracles, a land of terrible beauty and awful desolation, and then the sudden ascent to the height of steep snow and conifer-covered mountains, looking even higher than the Rockies because of their abrupt needle-pointed heights. And finally, the greatest contrast climax of all, the sudden dropping down into the tropically blooming seacoast gardens of the California shore.

It goes without saying that only those who love motoring should ever undertake such a journey, nor is the crossing of our continent as smoothly easy as crossing Europe. But given good weather, *and the right kind of a machine*, there are no difficulties, in any sense, anywhere.

There couldn't be a worse tenderfoot than I am, there really couldn't. I'm very dependent on comfort, having little strength, less endurance, and hate "roughing it" in every sense of the word. Yet not for a moment was I exhausted or in any way distressed, except about the unfitness of our car and its consequent injuries, a situation which others, differently equipped, would not experience.

I suppose the metamorphosis has come little by little all across our wide spirit-awakening country, but I feel as though I had acquired from the great open West a more direct outlook, a simpler, less encumbered view of life. You can't come in contact with people anywhere, without unconsciously absorbing a few of their habits, a tinge of their point of view, and in even a short while you feel you have sloughed off the skin of Eastern hidebound dependence upon ease and luxury, and that hitherto indispensable details dwindle — at least temporarily — to unimportance.[3]

---

3. The material printed in the *Collier's* articles ended here with this paragraph.

XXXI

To Those Who Think of Following in Our Tire Tracks

For the benefit of those who are planning such a trip and in answer to the many questions that have been asked us since our return, we have compiled the following pages:

The subject of car equipment, driving suggestions, garage and road notes, I have left to E. M., who has written part of this chapter.

At the end of the book is a small outline map of the United States and the route we took marked on it with divisions, each indicating a day's run. On separate pages are enlarged, detailed diagrams of these divisions, drawn to uniform scale, giving general road surfaces, points of historical or topographical interest, and thumbnail outlines that suggest the types and relative sizes of the hotels they represent. Each little symbol means a modernly, even a luxuriously equipped house; good food, good rooms and private baths. The mileage between all these best hotels is clearly indicated, so that a tourist can plan the distance he likes to run at a glance.

East of the Mississippi there are plenty of high-class hotels, and although fine ones are building in every state of our country, in many sections of the West those dependent upon luxuries will still have to go occasionally long distances a day to get them.

From New York to San Francisco, by way of the Rocky Mountains and Los Angeles, is about 4,250 miles; which divides itself into about four weeks' straight running, including the side trips to the Grand Canyon, to San Diego and Monterey, but not including extra days to stop over. To make it in less would be pretty strenuous, but perfectly feasible.[1] Allowing

---

1. This works out at an average of a little over 150 miles a day. They were actually on the road for 27 days out of a 54-day journey.

no time out for sight-seeing, accidents or weather delays, we arrived in San Francisco in four weeks' running time, including the run to San Diego (two days), but we skipped a stretch of Arizona and Southeastern California, a distance that would have taken about three days, which would have made our own entire distance time twenty-nine days.

Some days we drove thirteen or fourteen hours, others we drove only three or four. We never ran on schedule, but went on further or stayed where we were as we happened to feel like it, excepting, of course, our one breakdown and the two times we were held over by rain. When roads were good and the country deserted, we went fast, but the highest the speedometer ever went for any length of time in the most uninhabited stretches was fifty miles an hour. At others it fell to six! For long, long distances, on account of the speed laws or road surfaces, we traveled at eighteen to twenty. Between thirty-five and forty is the car's easiest pace where surface and traffic conditions allow. East of Omaha we were never many hours a day on the road. Between Omaha and Cheyenne, and again between Albuquerque and Winslow, finding no stopping places that tempted, we drove on very long and far.

To the Man Who Drives
by E. M. Post, Jr.

If I were starting again for the West, I should want an American car. A *new* car of almost any standard American make would be better for such a trip than the best foreign one.

In the first place, our own cars have sufficient clearance — ten inches. In the second place, spare parts are easy to get. Especially is this true of the moderate priced cars, which are sold in such large numbers that even the small country garages must carry supplies for them. But the important advantage is sufficient height. There are many places, particularly in New Mexico and Arizona, where with a low car you will have to fill in ruts so that your center can clear the middle of the road; and you will have to pile earth and stones on the slopes of some of the railroad crossings, so as not to "hang up" on the tracks.

Beyond the state of Colorado, which has magnificent mountain roads, if your car is a foreign one, you should have extra-sized wheels put on it to lift the frame high enough. Of course, you *can* get through, by destroying your comfort and temper, in road building, and jacking the machine over places impossible to pass otherwise, and arriving in a very battered condition in the end. Another qualification besides height in favor of an

American car, is endurance. American manufacturers have solved the problem of building machinery that needs little care and can be jolted without injury, where the more complicated European machinery under like treatment goes to pieces.

With a foreign car you are furthermore at a disadvantage in using metric tire sizes. You can always get the standard American sizes, which in the tubes will fit your metric casings all right, and for that matter you could probably at a pinch and temporarily use a standard casing. Metric sizes can be found in such places as New York, Chicago, Los Angeles and San Francisco, but shoes have a way of exhausting themselves without regard to your position on the map.

At Los Angeles or San Francisco you can get your metric equipment for the return trip so that if you start with new tires all around and two spares, you should have no need of buying tires on the road. Mine are, according to average American equipment, way under size for the weight of my car, and my six shoes carried me through easily. In fact there was New York air in two of them when we arrived in San Francisco.

In the matter of what to carry: New tires of course. For any but a very heavy car two spare shoes are plenty. Tubes you can buy anywhere. I only had five punctures all the way — and no blow-out. More than two extra shoes would be a hindrance because of their weight. A small shovel is sometimes convenient but not necessary east of New Mexico, and with a high car not necessary at all. African water bags are essential west of Albuquerque, but not before.[2] Fifty or a hundred feet of thin rope may be very useful if you happen to strike mud or sand stretches, especially if two cars are making the trip together. In the way of spare parts, I should suggest a couple of spark plugs, extra valve and valve spring, fan belt, extra master links for a chain-drive car. Tire chains with extra heavy cross-pieces for all wheels are indispensable through the Middle West in case of rain. And see that the tools that have been "borrowed" from your tool kit have been replaced. Repairs on the road are aggravating enough, not to be made more so through lack of tools. Now that people carry spare rims and almost never seem to put in a new tube and pump it up on the road, they neglect to carry a pump and a spare tube, but if you should have three flat tires in one day, you will appreciate a spare tube and an old-fashioned tire pump that works!

I carried thirty-five gallons of gasoline in my tank, which gave me a radius of three hundred and fifty miles on a tank full, with which I was

2. These were canvas water bags.

never in any danger of running short.[3] I should say that a two hundred-mile radius would be plenty, except across the desert. You *can* buy it even there, but at three or four times the regular rate. You may go many miles before you come to a hotel, but gasoline you can buy anywhere. Good shock absorbers all around will probably save you a broken spring or two. It will probably pay to look over your springs after each day's run and if a leaf is broken, have a new one put in before attempting to go on.

In the Middle West, automobile associations or highway commissioners do magnificent work. Roads are splendidly sign posted, and in the dragged roads districts, the rain no sooner stops than the big four- and six-horse drags are out. Follow a rainstorm in a few hours, and you will find every road ahead of you as smooth as a new-swept floor. Hence for the patient motorist, who can spare the time, there is always an eventual moment when there are good roads.

A few of the bad roads of the Southwest are so rocky that you literally have to clamber over them, but about seventy per cent of the road across New Mexico and Arizona, in which I include the road across the Mohave Desert that I covered later, is a fair, and occasionally fast, natural road.[4] The streams are generally easy to get through, and at those that are sandy or too deep, the automobile association keeps teams standing on purpose to see you through.[5]

A Few Suggestions on Driving

Don't try to drive from New York to San Francisco on high gear. You will often have used "first" by the time you strike the Rocky Mountains. Don't, then, subject your bearings to an unnecessary strain by forcing your motor to labor as it must, if too steep a hill is taken on too high a gear. See that your hand brake can lock your wheels. On a five-mile grade one brake may burn out, and on most cars in this country the hand brake is next to worthless from lack of use and care. Letting the engine act as a brake is a good practice on long descents.

On going through sand or mud that looks as if it might stop you, change into a lower gear and don't lose your forward momentum. It is eas-

---

3. Thus he expected the car to do ten miles to the gallon of gas, though the average was a little less.

4. While Emily Post and her cousin Alice took the train back to New York, Ned Post drove the car, at least part of the way.

5. Or the local Native Americans...

ier to keep a car going than to start it again. Fording through streams instead of crossing on bridges is common in the Southwest and many of the streams have bottoms of quicksand character. Before fording a stream make sure the water is not going to come above the height of your carburetor. Then start and stay in first until you are out the other side. The idea is to go through at a constant speed with no jerk on the wheels.

In high altitude your carburetor will need more air, as there is less oxygen in a given volume of atmosphere than at sea-level. This means also that a gasoline motor has considerably less power in Colorado than at sea-level. Don't be discouraged and think your car is failing you when you find you have to crawl up a long hill in "second," upon which you think you ought to "pick up" on "high." Not only is your motor less powerful than at home, but the *hill is steeper than it looks.* When you get back to sea-level it will run as well as ever.

The hardest thing for a stranger to guess seven or eight thousand feet up in the air is height, grade or distance. You see a little hill, a nice little gentle incline about half a mile long at most; then gradually from the elevation of your own radiator out in front of you, you get some idea of the steepness of grade and you find from your speedometer when you get to the top, that it was a short little stretch of three miles.

One other point: on high altitudes you will have to fill your radiator often. Water boils more quickly, and this added to the long stiff grades will cause a lot of your cooling water to waste in steam — even in a car that at normal altitude never overheats.

Repair Work on the Road

You will find a few garages anxious to please, beautifully equipped and capable of the finest work. The garages of Europe are not to be compared with our best ones. Garage equipment of the newest is to be found frequently, and all the way across the continent. The greater majority of the garages are neither good nor bad; and again a few — a very few only — are incompetent, careless and lazy, the men having the attitude that they are doing you a favor in robbing you.

If you know enough about your car to do your own repairing, or know what should be done well enough to superintend others, you will have no trouble. Furthermore, if you actually oversee everything that is done — you *know* that your car is all right and you don't have to hope that nothing has been forgotten by a man who knows that he is not going to be the one to suffer if his work is not what it should be. Also you know your car's weaknesses and in driving can save them. I find garage men who take pride in their garages glad and willing to serve an owner who takes that much interest in his machine.

On rare occasions, a first-class man resents your persistent superintendence, as though it were a slur on his ability or good intentions. There was a case in the Marksheffel garage in Colorado Springs—it was one of the best, by the way, that I have ever encountered. The car had been driven over 30,000 miles without ever being taken down, and without other care than my own.[6] And before going into such an uninhabited country as the desert, there were several parts that I thought it safer to put in new.

Taking the crank case off and fitting new gaskets, two men worked on it until late in the night. I did not do any of the work myself this time, but stood watching the men, so interested in the efficient way they were doing the job, that I was unconsciously silent. At the end of about two hours, one of them burst out with:

"I guess you've had some pretty tough experiences with dishonest garages—is that it?"

"No," I told him, "that was not it, but that I always wanted to know the exact condition of my engine. Otherwise I might get into serious trouble on the road somewhere." The situation being thus explained, his former resentment melted entirely, and a few hours later we parted warm friends.

In the case of this particular garage, as well as those that are listed in the garage expense accounts, you can certainly leave the repairs to them, unless your engine is to you what a favorite horse is to a lover of animals— something whose welfare you do not want for a moment to be in doubt about.

On the whole, to a man who has had any driving experience at all, and who chooses a proper car, most particularly if it is a new one, the trip will not present any difficulties. And the experiences he may have will prove an incomparable school for his driving and for his ability to tackle new problems with the means at hand.

---

6. This seems an extraordinarily high mileage for a two-year-old car, given the state of the roads in 1914–15. According to his biography of his mother, Ned Post drove the (new) car from London to southern France just before war broke out, then talked his way out of it being commandeered for the army. It was then shipped back to the United States in August or September 1914, and the Posts set out on their journey in late April 1915.

XXXII

On the Subject of Clothes

We had far too many! They were a perfect nuisance! Yet each traveler needs a heavy coat, a thin coat or sweater, a duster and a rug or two, and there is a huge bundle already. Then possibly a dressing case for each, and surely a big valise of some sort, either suit-case or motor trunk. Added to this are innumerable necessities— Blue Books, a camera, food paraphernalia, an extra hat — most women want an extra hat, and men too, for that matter — and though goggles and veils are worn most of the time, they have to be put somewhere. All of these last items go too wonderfully in a silk bag such as I described as having been given us. It was of taffeta, made exactly like an ordinary pillow-case with a running string at one end; it was about twenty inches wide and thirty inches long. E.M.'s straw hat, Celia's extra hat, and mine all went in it, beside veils and gloves and other odds and ends. It weighed nothing; it went on top of everything else and, tied through the handle of a dressing-case by its own strings, was in no danger of blowing out. Why hats traveled in it without crushing like broken eggshells, I don't know, but they *did*.

Offering advice for clothes for a motor trip is much like offering advice on what to wear while walking up the street. But on the chance that in a perfectly commonplace list there may be an item of use to someone, I have inventoried below a list of things that I personally should duplicate, if I were taking the trip over again:

First: A coat and *pleated skirt* of a material that does not show creases. Maltreat a piece first, to see. With this one suit, half a dozen easily washed blouses and a sleeveless overwaist of the material of the skirt, which worn over a chiffon underblouse, makes a whole dress, instead of an odd shirt-waist and skirt. These underblouses are merely separate chiffon linings with sleeves and collars, and half a dozen can be put in the space of a pound candy-box — yet give the same service as six waists to your dress.[1]

---

1. A "waist" in this context is a blouse or a bodice.

On an ordinary motoring trip such as over the various well-worn tours of Northeastern States or the Pacific Coast or Europe, where you arrive in the early afternoon with plenty of time to rest for a while and dress for dinner, several restaurant or informal evening dresses may be useful, but crossing the continent, unless you stop over several days in cities where you have friends, in which case you can send a trunk ahead, it is often late when you arrive, and any dressing further than getting clean and tidy does not strongly appeal to you. Besides one suit and blouses, a very serviceable dress to take would be a simple house dress of some sort of uncreasable silk. There is a Chinese crêpe that *nothing* wrinkles—not to be confused with many varieties of crêpes de chine that crease like delicate plants at a mere touch.

If I expected to go through towns where I might be dining out, I would add an evening dress of black jet or cream lace — two materials that stand uncreasingly any amount of packing. Otherwise my third and last would be a silk skirt and jacket — the skirt of black and white up and down stripes with white chiffon blouses, and the jacket black. The taffeta should be of the heavy soft variety that does not crack or muss. The skirt should be unlined and cut with straight seams gathered on a belt; a dress that folds in a second of time and in a few inches of space. With the coat on, it is a street dress; coat off (with a high girdle to match the skirt), it is whatever the top of the blouse you wear makes it.[2]

A duster is, of course, indispensable. A taffeta one is nice, especially when you want something better-looking, but on a long journey taffeta cracks, dirt constantly sifts through it and it can't be washed as linen can.[3] In the high altitudes of the Southwest, a day of tropical heat is followed by a penetratingly cold night. The thermometer may not be actually low and the air seem soft and delicious, but it sifts through fabrics in the way a biting wind can, and you are soon thankful if you have brought a heavy wrap. When you need it, nothing is as comfortable as fur. I took an old sealskin coat and I don't know what I should have done without it. On my personal list, a mackintosh has no place. If it rains, the top is up, and to keep wind out, I'd rather have fur.

Nor are shoes under ordinary fortunate circumstances important. But on my list are "velvet slippers." Scarcely your idea of appropriate motoring footwear, but if your seat is the front one over the engine, you will find velvet the coolest material there is—cooler than buckskin, or suède, or kid

---

2. By "a high girdle" Emily Post means a broad belt.
3. Silk taffeta is a smooth, tightly woven fabric with a dull sheen and a distinctive rustle. It was first woven in 3rd century Persia when it was called "Tafftah."

or canvas— much! And if you want to walk, your luggage, after all, is with you.

Every woman knows the kind of hat she likes to wear. But does every woman realize, which Celia and I did not, that a hat to be worn nine or eleven hours across a wind-swept prairie must offer no more resistance than the helmet of a race driver? A helmet, by the way, made to fit your head and face is ideally comfortable. A hat that the wind catches very little won't bother you in a few hours, but at the end of ten, your head will feel stone-bruised. An untrimmed toque, very small and close, and tied on with a veil is just about as comfortable as a helmet.[4] It has the disadvantage of having no brim, but yellow goggles mitigate the glare, and it is the brim, even though it be of the inverted flower-pot turn-down, that is a pocket for wind that at the end of a few hours pulls uncomfortably.

A real suggestion to the woman who minds getting sunburnt, is an orange-colored chiffon veil. It must be a vivid orange that has a good deal of red in it. Even with the blazing sun of New Mexico and California shining straight in your face, a single thickness of orange chiffon will keep you from burning at all. If you can't see through chiffon but mind freckling or burning, to say nothing of blistering, sew an orange-colored veil across the lower rims of your goggles and wear orange-colored glasses. Cut a square out of the top so as to leave no sun space on your temples, and put a few gathers over the nose to allow it to fit your face. Fasten sides over hat like any veil. The Southwestern sun will burn your arms through sleeves of heavy crepe de chine, but the thinnest material of orange — red is next best — protects your skin in the same way that the ruby glass of a lantern in a photographer's developing room protects a sensitive plate.

Wear the thinnest and least amount of underwear that you can feel decently clad in, so as to get as many fresh changes as possible in the least space, because of the difficulty in stopping often to have things laundered. What they put in the clothes in Southern California I don't know, but in any mixture of linen and silk, the silk has been apparently dipped in blue dye. A cream-colored silk-and-linen shirt of E. M.'s that happened to have the buttonholes worked in silk, is now a stippled green with buttonholes of navy blue. It is rather putting your belongings to the test of virtue — as those that are pure silk wash perfectly well. If I were going again I should take everything I could of thin crêpe de chine. It seems to be very easy to launder, and is everywhere returned in a clean and comfortably soft condition, whereas linen often comes back uncertain as to color and feeling like paper.

---

4. A toque is a woman's brimless hat, made of a soft fabric, and designed to fit closely to the head. The word is an adaptation of the Old Spanish *toca*, which meant headdress.

Emily Post devised a veiling system which incorporated a pair of goggles. Such equipment was necessary on early, dusty roads.

Although of more service on boats or trains, or in Europe where private baths are not often to be had, a black or dark silk kimono and a black lace bed-cap, if you ever wear bed-caps, are invaluable assets to anyone who dislikes walking through public corridors in obvious undress. My own especial treasures, acquired after many unsuccessful attempts, are a wrapper cut the pattern of an evening wrap, of a very soft, black silk brocade. It rolls up as easily as any kimono, and takes scarcely any space. The cap is a very plain "Dutch" one, of thread lace with a velvet ribbon around it. A wrapper that isn't obviously a wrapper, is sometimes very convenient. You could make believe it was an evening wrap, if you were very hard pressed.[5]

And above everything, in traveling you want clothes that are uncomplicated. The ones that you get into most easily are the ones you put on most often. Underblouses, such as I have described above, are a perfect traveler's delight, because there is no basting in, or trying to clean collars, cuffs, etc. A fresh underblouse with lace trimming, rolled like a little bolster, measures one and half inches by seven.

And remember: Plain skirts crease in half-moons across the back, pleated or very full ones don't. An orange veil prevents sunburn. Western climate is very trying to the skin, so that you need cold cream even if you don't use it at home. A lace veil of a rather striking pattern is at times of ugliness a great beautifier.

Clothes for men are a little out of my province. E. M. had some khaki flannel shirts, breeches and puttees that seemed to be very serviceable.[6] At

---

5. A delightful vision, Emily Post going out for the evening in her dressing gown.
6. Puttees (from the Hindu word patti, a strip of cloth) were either a strip of cloth wrapped round the leg from ankle to knee, or leather leggings.

least he was able to spend any amount of time rolling on the road under the machine, and still brush off fairly well. He had a sweater and an ulster and two regular suits of clothes to change alternately at the end of the day. His evening clothes, tennis flannels, etc., were sent through by express.

To send one hundred and fifty pounds from New York to San Francisco costs fifteen dollars.

Food Equipment

Don't take a big, heavy, elaborate lunch basket. If you want to know what perfect comfort is, get a tin breadbox with a padlock, and let it stay on the floor of the tonneau. In the bottom of it you can keep tins of potted meats, jars of jam, and a box of crackers, some milk chocolate, or if you like better, nuts and raisins. And on top you can put everything you lay your hands on! Books, sweaters, medicine case, and a pack of oiled paper to wrap luncheons in. We had a solidified alcohol lamp, a ten-cent kettle, and thermos bottles, a big thermos food jar, which we filled with ice cream if the day was hot, and one of the bottles with cocoa if it was cool. Coffee (if you put cream in it) has always a corked, musty taste, but cocoa is not affected, neither is soup. Food tastes better if you don't mix your bottles. Keep the jar for ice cream, if you like ice cream, a bottle for cocoa or soup, and two for ice or hot water. On long runs in the Far West, a canvas water bag is convenient. You can buy one at almost any garage, and it keeps water quite wonderfully fresh and cool.

On top of our permanent supplies we put the daily luncheons we took from the hotels: sandwiches, boiled eggs and fruit and the above-mentioned cocoa or ice cream. Cocoa we bought at the hotels, but our favorite place to buy ice cream was at a soda-water fountain.

The tins in our bread box we hoarded as a miser hoards gold — as a surplus that we might need to keep us alive; and, as is the common end of most misers, when we got to San Francisco and our journey was over, the greater part was still left — to give away.

EXPENSES

The following[7] pages of actual expenses copied out of our diaries may be useful as a table of comparison by which other travelers can form an idea of what their own are likely to be.

For some, the trip will cost more, but on the other hand, it can be done for much less. In every case we had the kind of rooms that are assigned to those who, without questioning the price, asks for "good outside rooms with baths." Undoubtedly, there were in many cases more expensive ones to be had, but in all cases there were cheaper ones.

Our restaurant bills, however, were comparatively light. We seldom ordered more than three dishes each, and the restaurant charges to people of very substantial appetite, will run more rather than less.[8] On extras, of course, anyone could add or subtract indefinitely, but the details noted may serve as a scale of current charges.

The garage bills speak for themselves. Each man knows how far his car can go on a gallon, and how often he wants it washed. No one can count his repairs in advance, but our garage bills, however, were certainly very much heavier than average. E. M.'s car is at best an expensive one to run, and on this trip it was at its worst, having been driven without overhauling for two years.

---

7. In Post's book, all the expense sheets were placed at the end, as were the sketch maps. I have placed them in the text.

8. Emily Post was writing in the days of eight-course meals.

XXXIII

How Far Can You Go in Comfort?

This was the original query that we started out to answer, and second "How long did it take you?" is the question that has been asked us more often than any other.

Interpreting "comfort" as really meaning "luxury," you can go, so far as roads are concerned, only to Pueblo. So far as *high-class* hotels are concerned, there are two inhospitable distances. The first from Omaha, Nebraska, to Cheyenne, Wyoming; the second between Albuquerque, New Mexico and Winslow, Arizona, over three hundred miles.[1] Between Ash Fork, Arizona, and Needles, California, the distance is one hundred and ninety-one miles, which over those roads is a long distance, but perfectly possible to make in a day. Also it is by no means necessary to motor across any of these sections, unless you choose to. Putting a machine on a freight train is a very different matter from putting it on a boat and shipping it to Europe. In the latter case, you have to have a crate made as big and clumsy as a small house; then there are always delays and complications about catching boats, and altogether it is something of an ordeal. But to send a motor across our own country, for as short or as long a distance as you please, is very simple. You have only to drive it to the railroad station, roll it on an automobile freight car with a door at the end, as in a small garage, take the next passenger train yourself and skip as many or as few miles as you choose. In America, automobile freight is wonderfully efficient and is about as fast as ordinary express. (At least the Santa Fé service is.)

We spent only two days at the Grand Canyon and the car arrived in Los Angeles at the same time we did. There is only one deterrent to fre-

---

1. See Map no. 18, pp 302–303. (Emily Post original footnote).

quent freight shipments: the cost. Automobiles weigh a good deal and the freight charges are by the pound. From Winslow, Arizona, to Los Angeles— distance of 613 miles—costs $151.20 for a car weighing 4,000 pounds. A 2,000–pound car would cost, of course, exactly half that amount. If you don't want to go into the desert where hotels are great distances apart and roads are not the smoothest in the world, a 3,000–pound car costs $133.20 from Albuquerque, New Mexico, to Barstow, California, after which there are plenty of good hotels and beautiful California roads. The above freight rates will be of interest to very few, as except in case of accident or some unseen conditions no one who can help it, will want to see their car, housed like a lonesome and abandoned dog, on a freight. If it is a very crippled car, that is different; it is more like leaving it in a nice cot in a hospital, where it can't get hurt any more.

But on the subject of cross-continental freight, by which many people may want to ship their cars home, the Transcontinental Freight Company's offices in Chicago, New York, San Francisco, etc., have a special rate for through shipment of automobiles that is a very good thing to know about. They ship three automobiles in one freight car, and for cars weighing 4,500 pounds and *over*, they charge a maximum rate of $225.00, or $5.5 — a hundred pounds, from New York to San Francisco or vice versa. A car weighing 3,000 pounds would cost $165.00.

The sole objection to this consolidated car load shipment is that they only send out the cars when they have three auto consignments, and you may have to wait a few days for the other two car spaces to be filled. Also their service is only between the most important terminal points. If you live somewhere in the middle distance between these terminal cities, it might be cheaper, as well as more convenient, to ship by regular railroad freight.

SOME DAY

Some day we are going back. Celia, E. M., and I have planned it. We must have plenty of time, and take our whole families with us, so that she will not have to hurry home to a husband, and I will not have to rush on without pause, in order to get home to a younger son. When we go again we are going in two cars— one to help the other in case of need, and, if possible, a third car to carry a camping outfit — and camp! Celia and I both hate camping, so this proves the change that can come over you as you go out into the West. I say "out into," because I don't in the least mean being tunneled through on a limited train! The steel-walled Pullman carefully preserves for you the attitude you started with. Plunging into an uninhabited land is not unlike plunging into the surf. A first shock! To which you quickly become accustomed, and find invigoratingly delicious. Why difficulties seem to disappear; and why that magic land leaves you afterwards with a persistent longing to go back, I can't explain; I only know that it is true.

The taste we had of the desert has something so appealing in the reminiscence of its harsh intensity by day, its velvet mystery at night — if only we could have gone further into it! We couldn't then and now it is lost to us, three thousand miles away!

Appendix

Emily Post's Journey,
April 25–June 8, 1915

		miles	hotel
Sunday April 25	New York to Albany	160	Ten Eyck, Albany NY
Monday April 26	Albany to Fort Plain	95	Utica, Utica NY
Tuesday April 27			Utica, Utica
Wednesday April 28	Utica to Buffalo	214	Statler, Buffalo NY
Thursday April 29	Buffalo to Erie (via Niagara)	93	Lawrence, Erie NY
Friday April 30	Erie to Cleveland	102	Statler, Cleveland OH
Saturday May 1	Cleveland to Toledo	120	Secor, Toledo OH
Sunday May 2	Toledo to South Bend	162	Oliver, South Bend IN
Monday May 3	South Bend to Chicago	102	Blackstone, Chicago IL
Tuesday May 4			Blackstone, Chicago
Wednesday May 5			Blackstone, Chicago
Thursday May 6	Chicago to Rochelle	77	Collier Inn, Rochelle IL
Friday May 7			Collier Inn, Rochelle
Saturday May 8[1]	Rochelle to Davenport	103	Black Hawk, Davenport IO
Sunday May 9	Davenport to Cedar Rapids	100	[unnamed hotel]
Monday May 10	Cedar Rapids to Des Moines	150	Chamberlain, Des Moines IO
Tuesday May 11	Des Moines to Omaha	158	Fontanelle, Omaha NE
Wednesday May 12			Fontanelle, Omaha
Thursday May 13	Omaha to Grand Island	155	Palmer House, Grand Island? NE
Friday May 14	Grand Island to North Platte	163	Union Pacific, North Platte NE
Saturday May 15	North Platte to Cheyenne	230	Plains, Cheyenne WY
Sunday May 16	Cheyenne to Colorado Springs	185	Antlers, Colorado Springs Co
Monday May 17			Antlers, Colorado Springs
Tuesday May 18			Antlers, Colorado Springs
Wednesday May 19	Colorado Springs to Trinidad	137	Cardenas, Trinidad CO

---

1. This is the only date specified in the text; the other dates were calculated by using her maps and descriptions. Although she said they planned to set off on a Saturday, it seems likely that their departure was delayed, given the problems with maps, routes and luggage, and a Sunday departure fits the information given in the book.

		miles	*hotel*
Thursday May 20	Trinidad to Las Vegas	136	Castenada, Las Vegas NV
Friday May 21	Las Vegas to Albuquerque	137	Alvarado, Albuquerque NM
Saturday May 22	Albuquerque to Winslow	161	night in desert
Sunday May 23	to Winslow continued	(?)	Harvey, Winslow AZ
Monday May 24	to Grand Canyon by train		El Tovar, Grand Canyon AZ
Tuesday May 25			El Tovar, Grand Canyon
Wednesday May 26	train to Los Angeles		on Pullman
Thursday May 27			Alexandria, Los Angeles CA
Friday May 28	Los Angeles to Pasadena	10	with friends in Pasadena CA
Saturday May 29			with friends in Pasadena
Sunday May 30	Pasadena to Riverside	63	Mission Inn, Riverside CA
Monday May 31	Riverside to San Diego	200	U.S. Grant, San Diego CA
Tuesday June 1			U.S. Grant, San Diego
Wednesday June 2			U.S. Grant, San Diego
Thursday June 3	San Diego to Santa Barbara	245	Potter, Santa Barbara CA
Friday June 4			Potter, San Diego
Saturday June 5			Potter, San Diego
Sunday June 6	Santa Barbara to Paso Robles	150	Paso Robles Springs Hotel CA
Monday June 7	Paso Robles to Monterey	117	Del Monte, Monterey CA
Tuesday June 8	Monterey to San Francisco[2]	1552	with friends in San Francisco

---

2. Emily Post documents driving a total of 3,900 miles (although she mentioned 4,250 miles in the text). As she also documents the purchase of 453 gallons of gas, this works out at a little less than nine miles per gallon.

Index

by Jane Lancaster

Acoma, pueblo of 171, 171n15, 175; difficulty of access to 180; photography and 181; *see also* pueblos
"The Adventurous Bowman" (Hermon A. McNeil) 233n7
Africa 160; Biskra, 162, 162n3; Cairo, 159, 161; Sahara compared with Arizona 162–163
African water bags 5, 24, 183, 244
Albany, New York 21, 25, 28–29, 30, 33, 104n1
Albuquerque, New Mexico 7, 8, 167–174; road to 137, 164
Alexandria Hotel, Los Angeles 191–193
Alice in Wonderland 27–28
Alvarado Hotel, Albuquerque 165–170; Indian Exhibition Room at 168, 170, 170n14; *see also* Harvey Company; Harvey Girls; Native Americans; Post, Emily
Amana Colonies (Pennsylvania Dutch) 91n4
America the Beautiful 131n9
American Automobile Association 16, 16n11, 16n13, 20n33, 164n1; in Colorado Springs 137, 137n19
Ansco Photographic Company 104, 104n3
Antlers Hotel, Colorado Springs 131, 131n9, 132, 139
Arizona 4, 8, 17, 241, 254, 255; cave dwellings in 163; health resorts in 127n3, 131n10, 132n12, 135n16; Native Americans in 170n13; Emily Post's preconceptions of 161; roads in 243, 245; suffrage in 160n7; University of 170n14, 186n15
Atchison, Topeka and Santa Fe Railroad: and Grand Canyon 190n19; and Harvey Company 146n6, 165–166, 168n12; and health tourism 127n3, 131n10, 200n14; "invents" Southwest 161n2, 179; Posts' car on freight 185; and Royal Gorge 141n1; and San Diego Exposition 200n13
Austen, Jane 39
automobile clubs *see* American Automobile Association; Westgard, A.L.
automobiles *see* cross-continental motoring; Ford; Lincoln Highway; Posts' car; women as motorists

Babcock, Elisha 200n16
Bajada Hill 147, 147n10, 156, 164, 164n1
Bakst, Leon 208, 208n6
Banting, William 106n9
Bates, Katherine Lee 131n9
Beachey, Lincoln 237, 237n24
Beadleston, Alice 1, 4, 20, 24n30, 40; and Bajada Hill 164; and camping 175, 177; as "Celia" 58; and jitney driver 98; and North Platte 113; and picnic hamper 71
Belasco, David 166, 166n7
Bennett, Edward 232

"black and white craze" 54, 99, 106, 106n11
Black Hawk Hotel, Davenport Iowa 86, 86n4, 87–88, 89, 94
Blackstone Hotel, Chicago 61–64, 69, 75; picnic in 73–74; "smoke-filled room" in 61n1
Blue Book 15, 16n11, 28, 248; unreliability of 58–59
Bonaparte, Jerome, at Niagara Falls 42n17
Boosters 7, 66, 66n1, 199n12
Borden, Gail 74n5
Borglun, Solon, *Pioneer* 233n7
Boston: compared with California 228–229; compared with Chicago 68–69; compared with Italy 229; cowboy from 151–152, 152n15, 153–154
Brainard, Eleanor Hoyt 95, 95n5
Brangwyn, Frank 233–234, 234n9
Brentano's 17
brittle bread (Swedish bread) *see* food
Broadmoor, Colorado 128–129, 133, 227
Brown, Thomas 94n2
Bryan, Ohio 53n32, 54
Bryan, William Jennings, and Welch's Grape Juice 37n4
Buffalo, New York 22, 37–45, 49, 63, 257
Buffalo Bill (William Frederick Cody) 113, 113n3, 121
buffalo meat 14n3, 113n3
Burlingame, California 227–228
Burns, Ken 13n1
Burr, Theodosia, at Niagara Falls 42n17

cable cars 218, 220, 220n3
Cadillac 31, 31n4, 28n8
California 191–239 (passim), 245–255; characteristics of 204, 206; expositions in 3, 6; gardens in 195, 241; gas prices in 194n6; heat in 213, 250; routes to 16, 17–18, 164n1; transformations wrought by 7, 222–223, 228–229
Californians, characteristics of 220–22, 228–231
Callot Sisters 222, 222n6

camping: elite 135–135, 135n16, 222–223; "gypsying" 105n5; Emily Post and 8, 105, 173, 175, 178, 182–183, 255; women and 162–163, 222–223
Captain, the Mind Reading Horse 236; *see also* Clever Hans
Carlisle Indian School 181, 181n6
carpet sweepers 95; *see also* Hoover, William H.
Carson, Christopher "Kit" 136, 136n17
cash register, Emily Post's delight in 33, 33n6
Castle, Irene Foote, 167n9; *see also* clothes
Cedar Rapids 9, 92, 93, 94–96; bakers' convention at, 96
Celia *see* Beadleston, Alice
chauffeur, gendered meanings of 25n2
Cheyenne, Wyoming 121–126; Cadet Corps 123, 123n12, 124–125; Frontier Days 125, 125n14; Emily Post's disappointment in modernity of 121, 123; *see also* Kendrick, John B.; Plains Hotel
Chicago 61–70, 75; characteristics of 204, 206, 240; compared with Boston 68–69; Golf Club 68n4; newspapers 83; Emily Post's liking of 69–70; and routes to the West 18n20, 21n24, 22–23; and silver picnic set 5, 71; Society in 67, 69, 135; typicality of 240; White Sox 214n5; Worlds' Fair 37n4, 188n12; *see also* Palmer, Mrs. Bertha (Potter); Saddle and Cycle Club
Chicagoans, enthusiasm admired by Emily Post 8, 61, 66, 68, 69–70
Chinatown, San Francisco 224, 224n9
Chinese: artifacts 225–227; Emily Post's attitudes to 223–224; servants 7, 223–224
Cleveland, Ohio 4, 22, 23, 43–51, 53; *see also* Johnson, Tom; Kang Hai Dynasty; Ming Dynasty; Statler Hotels; Tang Dynasty
Clever Hans 236n20
cliff dwellings 162, 162n6, 163
clothes 55–57, 248–252; for camping 222; "Castle cut headdress" 167; dusters 57n7, 248, 249; hats 82–83, 250; men's 56; Emily Post's criticisms of 48–49, 82–83, 106; Emily Post's

praise of 107; veils 5, 23, 40, 56–57; at the Zone in San Francisco 236
Cody, William Frederick *see* Buffalo Bill
Colfax Springs 97, 97n2
Collier, Colonel David Charles 200n13
Collier, Robert 11n1
Collier Inn, Rochelle, Illinois 79, 79n6, 81, 81n1, 84n5
Collier's Weekly 2, 3–4, 8, 11n1, 95; and automobile advertising 3; and Julian Street 37n5; and Mark Sullivan 20n22
Colorado Springs 126, 127–140, 191; architecture in 129n6; attitudes of wives in 134–135; compared with St. Moritz 241; as fashionable resort 128–130, 227; garage in 247; Emily Post's expectations of 127; roads 126; and tourism 139n23; and tuberculosis 127n1, 130n7; *see also* Antlers Hotel
Colter, Mary Elizabeth Jane 167n10, 184n12
"comatose one" *see* Russell, William
Comstock Lode 17n18
Coronado Beach, San Diego 200, 200n16
Cortéz, Hernán 157n2
Council Bluffs, Nebraska, compared with Brooklyn 105
cowboys 7; from Massachusetts 151–154; Emily Post and 135, 143, 145, 145n4; in Santa Fé 159
crêpes Suzette 34, 34n9
cross-continental motoring 3, 15–22
Crowninshield, Frank 22n5

dancing: after tea 61; club, in Chicago 67; complaints about 36; Native American 167; tango 34, 34n10, 87
Daniels, Josephus, and Welch's Grape Juice 37n4
Davenport, Iowa 6, 79, 86–89
Davis, Louise Hitchcock 4, 13n6; *see also* women motorists
decalcomania 42, 42n16
De Kalb, Illinois 77, 77n3
Denver, Colorado, 119, 126, 136, 139
Des Moines, Iowa 6, 88, 90, 97–103, 117; Capitol 97, 98, 98n4, 100; Cham-

berlain Hotel 98, 98n5, 99, 100; civic pride in 99–100; population of 99; Speedway 98n5; stuffed buffalo in 97–98; topsy-turveyness of 98–99
desert: damage to car in 6, 193; gas supplies in 245; lack of accommodation in 255; Painted 173n18; 175, 182, 236, Emily Post and 4, 6, 178–184, 256; and traveling in 17, 23; *see also* Africa; camping
Deslys, Gaby 237, 237n22
Dewar, Sir James 182n10
Dixon, Winifred 163n7
Dorgan, Thomas Aloysius, "TAD" 2, 21n24
Dreiser, Theodore 45n24
"drummers" 62, 62n2, 63, 103; on North Platte 112
duster *see* clothes

earthquakes, in California, attitudes to 221
Eden Musée 162, 162n5
Edwards (Post's butler) 23
"electriquette" 6, 203
Elting, Victor M. *see* Saddle and Cycle Club
El Tovar Hotel 190, 190n17; *see also* Native Americans
Enchanted Mesa 173, 173n17, 179–180
Erie, Pennsylvania 34, 45, 49, 51
Erie Canal 21n24
Escoffier, Auguste 106n7
etiquette, Chinese 225n11; Emily Post book on 1, 2–3
Europe, Emily Post and 2, 15; *see also* France; Italy; Monte Carlo
expenses 6, 15n7; at Blackstone Hotel 62; Emily Post's lists of 29, 34–35, 43, 49–51, 53–54, 75–76, 84, 87–88, 103, 110–11, 115, 117, 125–126, 139–140, 145–146, 174, 184–185, 190, 193–194, 197, 202–203, 209, 214, 217; for ensuite rooms 99; for lobster salad 73; in Utica 33n7, 34n10; expositions, Chicago 37n4, 199n12; San Diego 199–200; San Francisco 232–238

Fell, Doctor 94, 94n2
Fisher, Carl 16n2, 77n2; *see also* Lincoln Highway

Fishkill, New York 28

food: picnic 71–75; Emily Post's criticisms of 62, 89, 95, 223; Emily Post's praise for 33–34, 47; protopuffs 72, 72n2; service of 223; travel diet 105; at Woman's Rest Room 89–90; *see also* hard tack; pemmican; picnics; thermos

Ford: automobile 23, 25n33, 31, 31n3, 31n4, 37, 79n6, 146, 147, 147n9, 235; plant 4, 37n5; at San Diego Exposition 235, 235n13

Ford, Henry 16n17

fords (across rivers) 137, 144–145, 155–156, 178, 246; the Hon Geoffrey G — and 144–144n3, 144–145

Fort Plain, New York 31–35

France: houses compared with 135; poor coffee reminiscent of 62; Statler restaurant compared with 46, 46n25, 47; U.S. hotels compared with 204; U.S. roads compared with 36, 51, 77, 202

Fraser, James Earle, *The End of the Trail* 233, 233n7

freight trains, cars on 4, 16, 254–255; from Rochelle 83–86; from Winslow 184, 185, 190, 193

French, Daniel Chester, *The Genius of Creation* 233, 233n7

Fuller Company 236, 236n16

G —, The Honorable Geoffrey 138, 143–144; car blows up 144; and wading valet 144

Gang Hai *see* Kang Hai

garages 29, 43, 51, 54, 76, 88, 103, 111, 117, 126, 146, 197, 203, 209, 214, 217; Coleman Blank, Albuquerque 185; Fort Plain Motor Company 31–33, 35; Hoffman and Adams, Fort Plain 31; Mark Sheffell Motor Company, Colorado Springs (also Marksheffell) 139–140, 247; Santa Fé Transcontinental 174; Smith Brothers, Los Angeles 193–194

Garfield, James A. 45n23, 46

gasoline: consumption 6, 245n3, 244, 246, 258n2; prices 6, 29, 194n6; stations 3, 16n11, 245; supplies in desert 244

Geneva, New York 37–39, 43

George Washington coffee 183

Germans, hostility from 91, 91n3, 91n4, 92

"gilded youth" 228

Gladding, Effie Price, 16n14; *see also* women, as motorists

Google 9

Gramercy Park, 1 21

Grand Canyon 6, 161, 181, 184n13, 186–190, 242; Native American buildings at 167, 167n10, 185; *see also* El Tovar Hotel, Kolb Bothers

Grant, U.S., Jr. 202n20, 203

Gulf Refining Company 16n11

Gump's 224–227, 225n10

Hance, John: camp 186; legend of 185n15

hard tack, 14n4 71, 72

Harte, Francis Brett 104, 104n1

Harvard, 1 5, 148, 153

Harvey, Fred 146n6

Harvey Company: collection of Native American material culture 168n12; Mary Elizabeth Jane Colter and 167n10, 184n12; hotels 3, 146, 146n6, 146n7, 161, 165–167, 170, 170n14, 174; and myth of the West 161n2, 165n3, 166n5; Santa Fe Railroad and 146n6, 165–166, 168n12; Herman Schweitzer and 168n12; *see also* Alvarado, El Tovar

Harvey Girls 7, 146n6, 165–166; fraternizing with guests 190n17

Hearst, William Randolph 3, 21n29, 168n13

Henzie, George "String" *see* Rochelle Fire Chief

Hewett, Edgar L. 160n6, 200n13

Hodge, William T. 101, 101n9

Hoffman, Roland 31n3

Holbook, Arizona 173, 184

Hoover, William H. 95n4

Hopi (Moqui): at Acoma Pubelo 180–181; at Grand Canyon 167n10; Snake Dance 169–170, 170n13

hotels: complaints about by Emily Post 34n10, 47, 63–64, 95, 117; interior design of 28n6, 33, 54, 204–205; mentioned by Emily Post: Alexandria, Los Angeles 192, 192n3, 153;

Alvarado, Albuquerque 165–174, 170n14; Antlers, Colorado Springs 131, 131n9, 139; Black Hawk, Davenport 86–88, 86n4; Blackstone, Chicago, 61, 61n1, 115, 192; Brown's Palace, Denver 139, 139n22; Cardenas, Trinidad 146; Castenada, Las Vegas 146; Chamberlain, Des Moines 98–99, 98n5, 100, 103; Christman, Bryan 54n32, 54; Collier, Rochelle 79, 79n6, 81, 81n7, 84; Coronado, San Diego 200, 200n16; De Monte, Monterey 217, 217n6; El Tovar, Grand Canyon 190, 190n17; Fontanelle, Omaha 104, 104n2, 106, 107, 115; Jefferson, Iowa City 89, 89n1; La Posada, Winslow 184, 184n12; Lawrence, Erie 36; Mirasol, Santa Barbara 208, 208n5, 209; Mission, Riverside 197, 197n11, 198; Oliver, South Bend 53n33, 54; Onondaga, Syracuse 33; Paso Robles Springs, Paso Robles 214, 214n5; Plains, Cheyenne 121, 121n10, 125–126, Potter, Santa Barbara 204, 205n1, 209; Raymond, Pasadena 193n5; Rex, Gallup 181; Secor, Toledo 51, 51n30; Seneca, Geneva 39, 39n8, 43; Statler, Buffalo 40, 40n12, 41, 41n14, 41n15; St. Francis, San Francisco 220, 220n4; Sherry's, New York 106, 106n7; Statler, Cleveland 46, 46n25, 47, 49, 61; Utica 33–35; Vail, Pueblo 153, 154, 145n5, 192, 192n3; Van Nuys, Los Angeles 192, 192n2; plumbing and 33n8, 63, 95; praised by Emily Post 34, 40–41, 47, 62, 75; Ritz, comparisons with 21, 62, 81, 106, 106n7, 192; *see also* Harvey Company; Statler Hotels
Hudson River Valley 21, 25–28
Huerfano River 144

Illinois 4, 8, 86; landscape of 101, 103; mud in 91–92; spirit of 135
Iowa 101, 118
Iowa City 89–90
Isleta, Pueblo of 1 71, 173n16, 178, 180–181
Italy: comparisons with 62, 161, 199, 202, 206, 208; Emily Post in 15n9

Jackson, Horatio Nelson 13n1
Japanese: artifacts 225–226; servants 128–129
jitney 6, 97n3; ride in Des Moines 97–98, 103
Johnson, Tom 48n29

K., Governor *see* Kendrick, John B.
kaffir corn 200, 200n15
Kang Hai (Gang Hai) 227; 227n18
Kansas 17; building at San Diego Exposition 200
Kendrick, John B. 123, 123n11
King Leo Peppermint Candy 137, 137n20
Kipling, Rudyard 130n, 132, 132n13, 163
Kodak 145n4, 181n7
Kolb Bothers (Emory and Ellsworth) 190, 190n19

ladies' dining room 104, 110; entrance to hotel 58–59
"the lady who was traveling with is" *see* Beadleston, Alice
Laguna, pueblo at 173, 178, 178n3, 179
Las Vegas, New Mexico 146, 146n7, 151, 154, 156
Lincoln Highway 3, 14n5, 16, 16n12, 16n14, 17, 18, 18n20, 77n2, 77n3, 83, 86, 115, 118n7; Emily Post disappointed by 77–78
Lincoln Memorial 77n2
Los Angeles 4, 147, 185, 191–192
luggage: Alice Beadleston and 5, 24, 28, 71; porters and 29, 35, 43, 73, 75, 87, 184, 193, 203; problems with 55, 56, 250, 257; sending ahead 13

macadam 19, 19n21
manifest destiny 7
Mann, Colonel William D. 2
Maybeck, Bernard 234n10
Mayflower 158
McCall's 2
Mentor, Ohio 43, 43n22, 43n23
Mexicans 148, 159; adobe villages and 155; at ford 155–156
Midwest 5, 7; compared with New York 95–96; gas prices in 194n6;

impressions of 103; weather in 12n3; *see also* Rochelle

Miller (head waiter at the Blackstone) 74

Ming Dynasty 225, 225n1, 226

Mirasol Hotel, Santa Barbara, harmonious color schemes of 208, 208n5, 209

Mission Inn, Riverside 197, 197n11, 198

Mississippi River, crossing of 87, 87n5

Missouri River 18, 105, 117

Mix, Tom 104n1

Moctezuma 157n2

Monroe, Marilyn 200n16

Monte Carlo: and Alexandria Hotel 192; and Colorado Springs 130; and Santa Barbara 204

Monterey 214, 216, 217, 217n6, 242,

Morgan silver dollars 218, 218n2

Motor Magazine 3, 164n1

movies: *Diamond in the Sky* 210, 210n1, 210n2; at Flying A Studios 211, 211n3, 213–213; interior design in 213; and Emily Post attends 29, 35, 53, 82–83, 84, 110, 146; Emily Post feels part of 141; Emily Post's assumptions 104, 143; TAD and 21; and Universal City 213, 213n4; and Westerns 104, 104n1

mud *see* roads

Nast, Condé 4

Native Americans: adobe villages and 154, 155; Apache 136; crafts 167, 168, 168n11, 168n12, 169; Hopi 167n10, 169–170, 170n13, 180–181; Navaho 167–169, 168n11, 171, 181; in New Mexico 151; photography 181, 181n7, 185; and Pueblo Revolt 158, 158n3, 159; at San Diego Exposition 200; *see also* Harvey Company; pueblos; Schweitzer, Herman

Navaho (Navajo) *see* Native Americans

Nebraska 118–119

New Mexico 17, 136n17; cliff dwellings in 162–163; compared with Asia 241; reconquest of 158, 158n3; roads in 137–138, 149–150

New York: attitude of wives in 134–135; characteristics of 204, 240; compared with Chicago 66–67, 69–70; compared with Midwest 95–96; fash-

ion in 167; hotels in 34n10, 41, 63, 74, 101, 192; Emily Post's love for 229–230; Society in 11n1, 17, 17n18, 223; women 107, 222

New Yorkers, characteristics of 99, 228, 230

Newport, Rhode Island 128, 130, 227, 228

Niagara Falls 6, 45; bridal couples at 42–43; museum at 41–42; romance at 42n17; tourism at 42n18

North Platte, Nebraska 18, 112–115; and Buffalo Bill 113, 113n3; as "City of Ishmael" 112

O, Mrs. (Tessie Fair Oehlrichs) 17, 17n18, 112

Omaha, Nebraska 8, 104–111, 119; attitudes in 109–110, 134; automobiles in 105; Country Club 109, 109n14; cyclone 107, 107n12, 108–109; Farnum Avenue 107n2, 109; Fontanelle Hotel 104, 104n2; 106–110; Society in 107–109

Oñate, Don Juan d' 157, 157n2, 171n15

Painted Desert *see* desert

Palmer, Bertha Honoré (Mrs. Potter) "Mrs. X." 67, 67n2

Palmer, General William Jackson 127n1

Palomar Apartments, San Diego 201

Panama-Pacific International Exposition 3, 7, 232–238, 239; colors of 232, 232n2, 233; Court of Abundance at 235, 235n12; dates of 232n1; manufacturing exhibits at 235, 235n13, 235n14, 236, 236n16, 236n17; Palace of Fine Arts at 233, 233n5, 234, 234n10, 234n11; Emily Post's favorite attractions of 235, 236, 237; Samoan Village at 237, 237n22; stunt flying at 237, 237n24, 238, 238n25; style of 232n2; Tower of Jewels at 233, 233n3; Laura Ingalls Wilder and 237n23; Zone at 233–234

"Parlor Snake" 134, 134n5

Parrish, Maxfield 239, 239n1

Pasadena 45n23, 191n1, 193; clashing colors in 194–195, 208; Country Club in 194, 194n9; odd moral tone of 195, 197; splendid hotels in 193, 194n5

Paso Robles 213, 214, 214n5
Pasteur, Louis 74n5, 106n9
pemmican 14
The Personality of a House (Emily Post) 195n10
Petrified Forest 173, 173n18
Pickford, Lottie 210n2
picnic set: silver, 1, 5, 23, 24; christened 27–28; freighted back to New York 71; replaced with tin bread box 71
picnics: in Blackstone Hotel 73–74; with cowboy 151–154; in desert 182, 183; first 27
pig (Asian Potbelly Miniature) 224, 224n8
Pikes Peak, Colorado 127n1, 131n9, 132
Plains Hotel, Cheyenne 121, 121n10, 125–126
Plainsville, Ohio 58, 58n2
Platte River 18, 119–120, 120n9, 137
Pomander Walk 39; apartments 39n8
Post, Edwin M. 2, 15n9
Post, Edwin M., Jr., "Ned" 1, 5; at Angel Trail, Grand Canyon 190; attitude to his car 90; and clothes 56, 251–252; driving style 45, 45n24, 46; and garage mechanics 82; as "grimy mechanic" 57; at Harvard 5, 153–154; hatlessness of 83; and mud 78; use of chains 78–79, 90
Post, Emily Price: and architecture 27n4, 39, 47, 51, 194n8; assumptions about the "Wild" West 12, 104, 119–120, 121, 123, 127, 138, 143, 161; attitudes to Chinese 223–234; attitudes to desert 178–184; attitudes to Midwest 85–86, 135; as author 2, 3, 4, 11n2; and chocolate 34, 71; and comfort 4, 186, 241; and design 2, 194–195, 213, 233, 233n4, 234–235; early life 2–3; friends' advice to 5, 13–14, 23, 24, 74; metamorphosis of 8, 241, 255; as tourist 2, 7, 15, 15n9; *see also* camping; Chicago; Chinese; clothes; cowboys; desert; Europe; food; hotels; Native Americans; Panama-Pacific Exposition; Rochelle
Post, Emily, Institute 2–3
Post, George W. 40n12
Post, Ned *see* Post, Edward M., Jr.

Posts' car: breakdown of 30–35; comfortable to sleep in 182; driving tips for 245–246; exhaust pipe, problems with 22n27, 24, 25, 149, 156, 174, 185, 193; gas consumption of 177, 244–245; make of 5, 22n27; repairs to 6, 31, 33, 35, 43, 76, 103, 139, 185; shipped to Los Angeles 177; unsuitability of 5, 149, 241, 243, 244–245
prairie schooners 138, 143
Price, Bruce 2, 15n9
Price, Josephine Lee 2
Pueblo, Colorado 8, 137, 141–142, 143n2, 145; compared with Pittsburgh 142; Emily Post's assumptions about 161
Pueblo Revolt 158, 158n3
pueblo style 167n10; *see also* Colter, Mary Elizabeth Jane
pueblos *see* Acoma; Enchanted Mesa; Isleta; Laguna; Taos
Puerco River 178, 178n3
Pullman car 6, 8, 14, 14n5, 90, 193
Puppen Fée 125, 125n14

railroads 120n9; freight car on 83–85; Kansas Pacific 113n3; New York Central 21n24; Union Pacific 18, 112n2, 115, 115n4, 125n14; and Western tourism 14n5, 125n14, 200n13; *see also* Atchison, Topeka and Santa Fe Railroad
Ramsey, Alice 4, 18n20
"a rather famous collector" *see* Walker, T.B.
Raton 137–138, 138n21; Pass 147, 148n11
Raymond and Whitcomb 15n7, 131n9, 193n5, 224n9
refrigeration 226, 226n16
restaurants: in Blackstone Hotel 61–62, 73; chicken dinner disaster in 58–60; Chinese 236; costs 29, 34, 43, 49, 53, 54, 75, 84, 87, 103, 110, 115, 125, 139, 145, 174, 184, 190, 193, 197, 202, 209, 214, 217, 253; dress in 48–48, 249; good, according to Emily Post 39n10, 51, 101, 192; in Harvey hotels 146n6, 165–166, 190–191; infrastructure of 3, 4, 115n4, 205; in Paris 46, 46n25; at the Ritz 106n7; service in 47
Reynolds, Sir Joshua 118

Rio Grande 117, 164n1, 222
River to River Road 86, 118
Riverside, California 191n1, 197, 197n11
roads: bad 14n5, 119, 148, 245, 254; in
    California 199, 202, 210, 211, 214,
    255; to California 17–18, 164n1, 242;
    in Colorado 139n23, 141, 243; con-
    versations about 4, 8, 16, 18–19, 21,
    117–118, 136–138, 147, 152, 154; in
    desert 178, 179–183, 245; dragged 118,
    118n7, 119, 245; good 12n4, 30, 36, 39,
    51, 53, 89, 126, 141, 243, 245, 254; in
    Iowa 89–90; maps 16n11; in moun-
    tains 141, 148, 186; muddy 73, 77–79,
    88, 90–91; in Nebraska 118–119; in
    New Mexico 148–151, 148n11, 156,
    164, 171, 180, 243; in Ohio 43, 45;
    optimism about 22–23; Route 66
    164n2; safety 16n15; signs, lack of 22,
    22n26, 245; see also American Auto-
    mobile Association; fords; France;
    Lincoln Highway; macadam; River to
    River Road; Westgard, A.L.
Rochelle, Illinois 77–87, 79n6; Fire
    Chief (George "String" Henzie) 7, 79,
    79n1, 83, 91; Posts lose face 83; Posts
    regain face 85–86; spirit of 135
Rocky Mountains 119, 120, 240–241
Rodin, Auguste 178, 178n1
Roosevelt, Theodore 20n22, 61n1,
    105n5; and Rough Riders 146n7; and
    Snake Dance 170n13
Royal Automobile Club 92, 92n5
Royal Gorge Loop 141, 141n1
Russell, William 210n2; as "comatose
    one" 210–211

Saddle and Cycle Club 67–68, 68n3
Salem, Massachusetts 134
San Diego, California 3, 201, 201n18,
    202–203, 242, 243; Exposition 6, 199,
    199n12, 200, 232
San Francisco 3, 6, 16, 17, 218–231, 239,
    244, 245; cable cars in 218, 220,
    220n3; driving in 220; Exposition
    site 232–233; "gilded youth" in 228;
    local involvement in Exposition 236;
    St. Francis Hotel in 220; weather in
    214, 216; see also Gump's; Panama-
    Pacific International Exposition
San Mateo, California 228

Santa Barbara, California 204–209;
    better than Italy 208; outdoors life in
    205; Potter Hotel in 204–205, 205n2
Santa Fé 6, 7, 138, 147, 157–164; fiesta
    158n3, 160n6; hotel 161; "invention"
    of 160n6; legend of 167n1; Plaza 159;
    Emily Post's assumptions about 161;
    roads 156; trail 17, 177
Santa Fé Railroad see Atchison,
    Topeka and Santa Fé Railroad
Schweitzer, Herman 168–173, 168n12
Scott, Blanche 4
"See America First" 3, 7, 15n7, 162n4,
    224n9
Sewickley, Pennsylvania 227, 227n20
silver picnic set see picnic set
Simla, India 130, 130n8
Simpson, Bill 136, 136n17
slimming 72, 72n3, 106, 106n9; see also
    Banting, William
Smith, Art 237–238, 238n25
speed limits 16; in Nebraska 112n1,
    118–120; in Ohio 45, 45n21, 51–53
Sperry Flour Company 235, 235n14
Sphinx 160
Standard Oil Agency, 177
Statler, Ellsworth M. 40n12
Statler Hotels 5, 40–41, 43; in Buffalo
    40, 40n12, 41, 43, 63n5; in Cleveland
    46, 46n25, 62; clothes in 48–49,
    delivery of newspapers in 41, 41n15;
    restaurants in 46–47, 49; service
    codes of 41, 41n14
Street, Julian 4, 37, 37n5, 47n26,
    48n29; on Colorado Springs 129n6;
    on hotel rooms 65n5; on Royal
    Gorge Loop 141n1
Sullivan, Mark 4, 20n22
Syracuse, New York 21, 25, 37; Pottery
    Company 42m 42n16; salt 37n7

TAD see Dorgan, Thomas Aloysius
Tang Dynasty 226, 226n12
Taos pueblo 155; at San Diego Exposi-
    tion 200
t.b. see tuberculosis
Tennyson, Alfred, Lord 86, 86n2
thermos 71, 182, 182n10, 183
Tiffany, Louis C. 3, 9
tips 29, 35, 43, 49–51, 53–54, 75, 84,
    88, 103, 110–111, 115, 117, 125–126,

139–140, 145–146, 174, 184–185, 190, 193–194, 197, 202–203, 209, 214, 217

Toledo 51–54; art museum in 51, 51n31, 53–54

tourism: in America 36; automobile 4, 12n4, 92, 146–147; and camping 105n5; changes in 14n5; embarrassment and 181, 185; impact of bad experiences in 60; at Niagara Falls 42n18; promoted by railroads 127n3, 131n10; as theater 7, 165–167, 200; *see also* Native Americans; Post, Emily; Raymond and Whitcomb

tourists: and health 127n3, 131, 131n10; ignorant 234, literature for 191; Emily Post as 5, 6, 69; and "See America First" 3, 7

Town Topics 2

transcontinental motorists *see* Davis, Louise Hitchcock; Jackson, Horatio Nelson; Ramsey, Alice

traveling time 242, 242n1, 243

Trinidad, New Mexico 146–147, 151

Truly Emily Post (Edwin Post) 15n9, 130n8

tuberculosis 7, 127n1, 128, 128n4, 129; and Colorado Springs 127n1, 130n7; history of 129n5; recklessness and 132–135

Tuxedo Park 2, 24n33, 67n2

Universal City 213, 213n4

U.S. Post Office 236, 236n17

Utica, New York 21, 30, 33–35, 37, 42; hotel 33, 33n8, 34, 34n8, 35

valet: Hon. Geoffrey G —'s 144; Japanese 129; service in hotels 35, 51, 75, 139, 201

Vanderbilt houses 230, 230n23

Vargas, Diego de 158, 158n3, 159

vaudeville, Native Americans and 166–167

Versailles, Palace of, compared with Colorado Springs 135–136

Vogue 39

vulcanization 88, 88n9, 103, 193

Walker, T.B. 227n19

Walter's Concert Band 87n7

Warner Speedometer 28m 28n8

weather: blizzard in New Mexico 151, 154–155; complaints about heat 213–214; contrasts in California 201–292, 214, 216; cyclone in Omaha 107, 107n12, 109; mud in Illinois 77–86; mud in Iowa 89–94; rain 12n4, 14n6, 73, 77, 90, 94, 221; warnings about 22; wrong clothes for 55–56

Welch's Grape Juice 37, 37n4

Wellington, Duke of 106n9

Westgard, A.L. 20n23, 164n1, 181n8, 184n11

Wharton, Edith 2

Wheaton, Illinois 68, 68n4

Wilder, Laura Ingalls, and Samoan Village 237n23

Winslow, Arizona 8, 176, 177, 184, 184n12; shipping car from 185, 185n14, 190, 243, 254, 255

wives, attitudes to husbands 134–135

woman mind reader, Emily Post impressed by 236, 236n21

woman suffrage 160, 160n7

Woman's Rest Room, Iowa City 89–90

women: and camping 222; changes wrought by California 7, 221n5, 222–223, 229–231; and "chauffeurs" 25n2; and clothes 49, 82, 106, 107, 159, 230, 248; and dieting 72; married, expected behavior of 134–135; as motorists 3, 4, 13n1, 96; Native American 166, 166n5, 167, 173, 179; old, respect for 223–224; playing polo 228, 228n22; society 17, 67, 228; traveling alone 162–163; as waitresses 146n6

Woolworth's 71–72, 72n1, 75

Wooten, Richens Lacy, "Uncle Dick" 148, 148n11

World War I 7, 15n8, 91n4; and American tourism, 3, 162n4

X., Mrs. *see* Palmer, Bertha Honoré (Mrs. Potter)

York Harbor, Maine 134, 134n14

Zhu Yuanzhang 225n